Science and Religion in a Post-
World: Interfaith Perspectives

edited by Zainal Abidin Bagir

The Science and Theology Series is a publication of ATF Press. Each volume is a collection of essays by one or a number of authors in the area of science and theology. The Series addresses particular themes in the nexus between the two disciplines, and draws upon the expertise of both scientists and theologians.

ATF Press
Adelaide

ATF Science and Theology Series
Series Editor:
Mark Wm Worthing

Science and Religion in a Post Colonial World: Interfaith Perspectives

Edited by

Zainal Abidin Bagir

ATF Press
Adelaide

First published September 2005

Published by
ATF Press
An imprint of the Australian Theological Forum
P O Box 504
Hindmarsh
SA 5007, Australia
ABN 68 314 074 034
www.atf.org.au

Cover design, Openbook Print, Adelaide, Australia. Printed by Kanisius Press, Indonesia

Contents

Introduction

Zainal Abidin Bagir

All chapters in this book come from a conference organised by the Center for Religious and Cross-cultural Studies of Gadjah Mada University, Yogyakarta, Indonesia in January 2003. The university is among the largest and oldest in Indonesia, but the Center was only two and half years old at the time of the conference. It was unique in Indonesia in the sense of being the only graduate program in a non-religiously affiliated university offering a degree in religious studies. One of the issues we faced since the beginning concerns the appropriate format of a religious studies program for the specific context of Indonesia, which is the most populous country in the Muslim world and at the same time has strong presence of the world religions which it has hosted since its earliest history.

We faced similar problems when we started planning the conference in 2001. Beside the fact that discussion concerning science and religion has taken place in Indonesia for quite some time, it has not developed into a systematic discourse—the kind we see in the United States and Europe in recent decades—nor has it been conceived as an inter-religious enterprise. These were our goals: to start developing a systematic discussion on religion and science and do it as an inter-religious enterprise, as all our programs have tried to do. When we started conceiving the conference, there were issues about the representation of religions (Should all religions in Indonesia be represented? Who are the legitimate representatives of those religions?); what topics among many options should we take up (should we concentrate on certain scientific disciplines? should we put more emphasis on theological, or ethical issues?), and a few other crucial questions. We may not have answered them satisfactorily. But with all those limitations, we are happy to say that, as participants and speakers at the conference testified, it was a success.

The conference was the Center's first major activity. Since then we have conducted several workshops, seminars, and other events—all on the topics of religion and science and all with a view toward achieving the two goals above—and have gotten responses from our audience.

Zainal Abidin Bagir

As a result we now have better understanding as to how best to conceive the agenda of the discourse, considering the limitations we have as well as the opportunities and the resources.

The conference was titled 'Religion and Science in the Post-colonial World'. With this we have tried to address selected issues in the emerging field of science and religion and at the same time acknowledge the situation of Indonesia (or, more generally, a 'Third World' country) as the locus of the conference. In general, the agenda of the conference was set as religions respond to shared challenges posed by science, as new theories in cosmology, physics, and the life sciences have brought challenges to many traditional religious ideas. There are also more generally epistemological challenges which reflect the recent success of natural science as a mode of inquiry. These are felt as problems in both the Western and non-Western worlds, but with an important difference. While the Western world is considered the 'legitimate owner' of modern science, some in the Muslim world, and the Third World more generally, see modern science as a cultural alien imposed on them, due to its initial introduction in the colonial period.

The first part of the book consists of three articles which address these issues. Steve Fuller starts with his critical assessment of recent science-and-religion discussions. For him the main issue is not to decide whether science and religion are in a perennial conflict or whether all scientific and religious doctrines are mutually compatible or complementary. But the decision that has to be taken is between *anthropic* and *karmic* orientations toward the science-and-religion duplex; the anthropic-karmic is more fundamental than the science-religion distinction. The anthropic orientation is represented by monotheistic religions, which put humanity at the centre; while the karmic by Hinduism, Buddhism, Confucianism, Taoism, which regard humans simply as one among other forms of life. In this shift, secularisation, a process taking place in Christianity which has spurred the growth of science, has turned into customisation. He mentions two forms of 'customised science': the evangelical ('Islamic science' or 'creation science') and the capitalistic (as in bioprospecting), and contends that the second is more dangerous. The next two articles take up two different forms of what Fuller calls 'customised science'. Meera Nanda discusses the idea and the dangers of Vedic science which develops among Hindu fundamentalists, and how the postmodernist arguments have been essential in legitimising it. She ends her piece with a warning about the dangers of an over-hasty reconciliation between science and religion in general. Zainal Abidin Bagir examines the notion of Islamic science, which has been a popular position in Islam-and-science discourse. He distinguishes between versions of Islamic science and, using some historical arguments, finds that 'secularisation' (or 'deideologisation') of science may be a form that 'Islamisation' takes.

Three articles in the next part ('Science and the Sacred') take us to a different, more theological, facet of science-and-religion discourse. Mehdi Golshani argues for a 'sacred science', as distinguished from 'secular science'. Sacred science is about framing knowledge in a theistic worldview. By 'framing', he refers to the work of interpretation of facts, and shows that at this level the scientist's metaphysical framework plays its role. Philip Clayton takes as the centre of his discussion the notion of law. For the three Abrahamic religions, to believe in God is to believe in both natural law, which is the object of the study of science, *and* revealed law. The challenge for those religions is to think together those two very different types of law. After presenting several options to present the two in a unified framework, he concludes that though the two are conceptually different, they need not be at war. An important message Clayton tries to convey repeatedly is that Jewish, Christian, and Muslim theists can work together in answering this challenge. Responding to Golshani and Clayton, Osman Bakar believes that it is desirable and possible for science to become sacred again. This can be done through two ideas that Golshani and Clayton speak about: sacred knowledge and sacred law.

The third part of this book focuses on the notion of creation. The two scientific disciplines dealt with here are cosmology and evolution, which have been at the centre of the science-and-religion debate. Three articles deal with cosmology, the other three with the theory of evolution. Both Karlina Supelli and Bruno Guiderdoni start with an observation that developments in cosmology have created difficulties for those who try to find (evidence of) a Divine Being in the 'creation' of the universe. As Supelli shows, in some cosmological models the moment of 'creation' can be avoided; in Guiderdoni's terms, the general trend in science is that the efficient causes push the final causes backwards and eventually eliminate them. Among genuine ways religious believers could face this issue, the two authors, Supelli and

Guiderdoni, as well as J Sudarminta, who responds to them, agree that efforts to find lower level accordance between scientific theses and holy Scriptures is not one of them. Guiderdoni suggests Islamic metaphysics as the background for Muslim scientists' contemplation to find the meaning of the universe. Sudarminta, on the other hand, reminds us to understand the scriptural doctrine of 'creation' in its distinctive context, not as something that can be directly compared with scientific theories about the origin of the universe. Yet the two are not wholly irrelevant to each other. He then goes further by specifying some points in scientific cosmology that may help theological reflections.

Reactions to the theory of evolution have become the most contentious issue in the discussion of science and religion, at least in the Western Christian context. In his article, William Grassie provides a helpful background to understand why this is the case, followed by a survey of a variety of religious responses to the theory. He then discusses more specifically some constructive theologies among prominent Christian thinkers today. In the Islamic (more specifically, Arab) context, Mahmoud Ayoub traces in great detail the responses to the theory since late nineteenth century until today. One of his conclusions is that this theory did not create a religious crisis in the Muslim world as it did in the West, despite the fact that the debate still continues. Contemporary Muslim opposition to Darwinism, he contends, is a form of political opposition to the West in general, and one which is inspired by contemporary Western scientific and religious critiques of Darwinism. In his brief and systematic piece, Teuku Jacob focuses on the religious attacks on the theory and delineates the main disagreements between creationism and the synthetic theory of evolution.

It is only fitting that this books ends with Larry Rasmussen's discussion of the care for the earth. It is here that the interest of people coming from different religious traditions as well as disciplines converge. The biggest challenge to both religion and science today is ultimately about the creation of a sustainable global community. More concretely, Rasmussen points to the Earth Charter as a document that provides a common basis for an alliance of science and religion (and of religions) in this direction. It is an alliance that focuses not on differences of our scientific or theological orientations but on the real problem that we all, whatever cultural backgrounds we come from, share, and that lies right in front of us. In the beginning of this introduction I mentioned how the conference as well as our other activities have enabled us to best conceive the agenda of the discourse and issues in the field of science and religion we need to deal with. One of them is precisely this issue of forming alliance between people of different religions to contribute, in however small a way, to the creation of a sustainable global community. Both religion and science will have the most important roles here.

We hope this book will be the first of a series of volumes that CRCS will produce in the future in the field of science and religion as well as interreligious dialogue and cooperation. Our programs in science and religion are supported by a generous grant from the Templeton Foundation, and we sincerely thank them, not only with regard to the financial contribution, but also the freedom it has given this very young Center of ours to explore this new and exciting enterprise.

Zainal Abidin Bagir
Center for Religious and Cross-cultural Studies,
Gadjah Mada University,
Yogyakarta, Indonesia

Part One

Religion and Science in a Post-colonial World

1

Humanity as an Endangered Species in Science and Religion

Steve Fuller

1. Introduction

In the twenty-first century, a decision of world-historic proportions will need to be taken between coalitions of sciences and religions. The choice is roughly captured by the difference between monotheistic religions (Judaism, Christianity, Islam), which place humanity (as created 'in the image and likeness of God') at the centre of science and politics, and non-monotheistic religions (Hinduism, Buddhism, Confucianism, Taoism), which regard humans as constituting only one among many forms of life that deserve equal scientific and political treatment: In short, *anthropic* versus *karmic* perspectives. Several factors throughout the world currently conspire to shift the balance of power toward the karmic perspective. At stake are the distinctive features of the anthropic perspective that have spurred the growth of scientific inquiry. I discuss some of these features, especially the unique role of heresy in Christianity that has enabled the West to excel in both high levels of innovation and resistance to innovation.

Secularisation can be considered a normal part of this process. However, as nation-states have loosened their monopolies on science, secularisation has turned into customisation, which may either go the route of evangelism (as in 'Islamic science' or 'Creation science') or capitalism (as in bioprospecting). Contrary to much *bien pensant* Western thinking, I believe that the latter form of customisation threatens the universality and humanity of science much more than the former. I further argue that aspects of monotheistic religious funda-mentalism may serve as a useful antidote to the excesses of the increasing capitalisation of science, indeed as a worthy successor to Trotskyism. Here I adapt the recent coinage 'Occidentalism'—the mirror image of 'Orientalism'—to capture the dehumanisation that unwittingly results from the maximally tolerant attitude associated with today's neo-liberal environment for science and technology.

In the final two sections of the chapter, I explore how the karmic perspective has infiltrated Western philosophy and sociology science, as well as science-based policy. Specifically, I refer to a greater acceptance of providence and fate as operating and limiting human capacities for change. This extends to a scaling down of the ambitions for international development policy, a tendency that ironically travels in the guise of greater concern for the global environment.

2. The new world-historic challenge to science and religion

The twentieth century was full of international conferences in which leaders from many religious faiths and scientific disciplines pasted over doctrinal differences in a diplomatic discourse of 'interfaith dialogue' full of vague abstractions and strategic omissions. This is neither surprising nor entirely blameworthy. An ecumenical attitude toward the relationship between science and religion emerged in the late stages of European imperialism and peaked in the Cold War. Throughout this period, science and technology clearly contributed to exploitation and militarisation, not least because they were so unevenly distributed across the globe. Under the circumstances, it was easy to reach agreement that we all share the same ultimate ends but are divided by the means at our disposal. Ecumenism thus became a religious strategy to reorient science from its more destructive and divisive uses. Unfortunately, this admirable goal has been under-written by an exclusive and unified association of, on the one hand, 'ends' with religion and, on the other, 'means' with science. This distinction is both historically and philosophically suspect. Moreover, as the balance of global economic and political power is slowly but surely redressed, the course of scientific inquiry becomes increasingly open to competing religious sensibilities.

Just as it is nonsensical to speak of a perennial battle between science and religion, as if they were locked in some timeless Manichaean struggle of good versus evil, it is equally foolish—though undoubtedly more pleasant—to assert that all scientific and religious doctrines are mutually compatible or even complementary. I shall address both errors, though I believe that the latter error poses the greater threat to any genuine integration of scientific and religious interests. In the twenty-first century, a decision of world-historic proportions will need to be taken between coalitions of sciences and religions. The choice is roughly captured by the difference between monotheistic religions (Judaism, Christianity, Islam), which place humanity (as created 'in the image and likeness of God') at the centre of science and politics, and non-monotheistic religions (Hinduism, Buddhism, Confucianism, Taoism), which regard humans as constituting only one among many forms of life that deserve equal scientific and political treatment. It is a decision between what I have called *anthropic* and *karmic* orientations toward the science-and-religion duplex (Fuller 2002b).

The dominant tendency of biological research done under the neo-Darwinian paradigm has been to discredit claims to a unique human nature that have traditionally provided an empirical underpinning to the anthropic orientation. Instead, the overwhelming genetic overlap between us and other life forms point to a karma-friendly pannaturalism that sees humanity as continuous with the rest of nature. I say 'karma' because that word captures a generic 'life force' in many of the great Eastern religions, especially Hinduism and Buddhism. It is a broad-gauged term whose function is comparable to 'genes' in modern evolutionary theory. Four claims are common to karmic and genetic discourse:

(a) that one's own actions are somehow constrained by past lives, be it as a potential or a necessary determinant;
(b) that actions can be taken in one's own lifetime (often related to lifestyle) to mitigate, but not completely eliminate, the worst aspects of one's legacy;
(c) that there is no intergenerational or interspecies sense of progress, unless the goal is defined as physical extinction;
(d) that the life force is common to all life forms, regardless of surface differences in appearance and emotional attachment.

The closest ancient Western tradition to the karmic sensibility is atomism and the associated ethical doctrine of Epicureanism, which espoused the minimisation of suffering in the face of the irreducible contingency of things. A sign of karma's recent theological ascendancy is that the minimisation of suffering has been proposed as the foundation for an 'ecumenical anthropology' (Charry 1987). From an anthropic standpoint, this is to set the standard of religious observance much too low.

My argument, simply put, is that modern science imperils much less the existence of *God* than the existence of *humanity*. At the very least, this is because nations traditionally dominated by karmic religious cultures are producing an increasing proportion of the world's scientific knowledge. This is a by-product of a growing middle class in places like India and China, who have aspirations to be players on the world's scientific stage. The significance of this fact should not be underestimated. Perhaps the most resilient vestige of Eurocentrism is the presumption that one must reproduce European cultural history—especially its modern science-religion conflicts—to become truly scientific. This is to commit the genetic fallacy, which consists of confusing what philosophers of science call the context of discovery with the context of justification. Thus, that Europe was the origin of the theory of evolution by natural selection does not imply that Europe (let alone, America) has provided the most hospitable environment for its reception. Indeed, the Far East much more quickly accepted evolution than socialism, as Herbert Spencer predated Karl Marx in Chinese and Japanese translation by several years. (See Fuller 1997, chapter 6, on Japan's 'defensive modernisation.')

However, Westerners sometimes mistakenly interpret the relatively easy acceptance of Darwinism in the Far East as evidence for the universal truth of evolution. This is to look at matters the wrong way round. It is far more likely that the monotheistic privileging of humans over other life forms has impeded the acceptance of Darwinism at home, since religions upholding the unity of nature and the fundamental equality of life forms should find—and have found—Darwinism metaphysically quite congenial. There is a general lesson here: claims to epistemic universalism are often little more than a superstitious response to a tortuous tale of legitimation. Specifically, someone whose work is at first dishonoured at home manages to be honoured somewhere else, which then enables the work to be reabsorbed at home, but now in the guise of having been independently vindicated. The superstition here lies in the mystified notion of 'independence,' which masks the fact that the work is subject to each reception-culture's normal evaluative procedure, the overall import of which is to lend a transcendent air of 'universality' to the work, simply because the evaluative standards vary across cultures (Fuller 1996).

Moreover, the future existence of humanity is threatened by two other sources that will be the focus of this paper. The first is that scientists from nations traditionally dominated by anthropic religious cultures are becoming sceptical of their own ability to improve the human condition. This largely Western tendency has crept into orthodox scientific thinking much more than the catchall term 'postmodernism' would suggest. It is marked by subtle turns toward a more karmic sensibility, including an acceptance of 'fate' as an irreducible feature of reality and a belief that the sheer abundance of humans—also known as 'overpopulation'—poses a serious threat to the global ecology. The second and insidiously overarching tendency is the increasing susceptibility of the direction and application of scientific research to market forces. This serves to dissolve any unified sense of human welfare into a set of discrete exchanges between knowledge 'producers' and 'consumers'. This tendency represents the negative side of what I have called the *secularisation of science* (Fuller 1997, chap. 4; Fuller 2000a, chap. 5).

3. The state of contemporary science: secularisation in overdrive

Any discussion of secularisation should always recall the historical specificity of European Christianity. Here secularisation consisted of the formal separation of church and state. Because the churches could no longer count on the state to bolster their authority (or finances, for that matter), they had to engage in recruitment campaigns. This period is usually said to have begun with the Treaty of Westphalia in 1648, which ended the Thirty Years War between German Catholics and Protestants. It led to a form of proselytism known as 'evangelism,' in which the representatives of many Christian denominations realised that they were competing against each other. This newly created market environment influenced the evangelists' arguments, which led them to stress the direct relevance of universal doctrines to their potential converts' lives in a way that had been unnecessary when religions enjoyed state monopolies. In section 4, I shall delve into this much misunderstood respecification of universalism.

The post-Cold War devolution of state support for science worldwide, most of all in the West, should be understood as an intensification of just this process of secularisation. The idea of science as the state church of the modern world has received much rhetorical, philosophical, and institutional support, ever since the emergence of

German Idealism and French Positivism in the early nineteenth century. Both aspired to replace the popular narrative of Christian salvation with that of scientific progress, be it redeemed by philosophy or physics. For the rest of the century, the European nation-states assumed and consolidated the educational responsibilities previously in the hands of the Christian clergy and delivered them to those secular surrogates for the old monks and priests: that is, researchers and experts, respectively. However, as these secular surrogates have become entangled in the forces of social and economic reproduction in the twentieth century, their own authority has been met with charges of both compromised judgment and doctrinal error. Martin Luther would knowingly smile—were it not that this latest round of secularisation has opened science to a decision-making environment in which choice of epistemic authority is significantly constrained by market forces, the metaphorical equivalent of jumping out of the frying pan and into the fire. The next two paragraphs provide a religious and an economic elaboration of this point.

The sequence of consolidating, corrupting, and reforming epistemic authority—first in the clergy and now in the scientific community —may be unique to Christianity among the great world religious traditions: a pagan Greek fixation on seasonal cycles married to an internalised persecution complex. In a word: *heresy*. Science has secularised this process as an endless generation of hypotheses and tests. The heresiological roots even extend to the excommunication of unrepentant deviants, who may nevertheless go on to found their own churches (also known as 'disciplines'), all the while claiming allegiance to a conception of truth that covers themselves and their persecutors. While it is common for religions to condemn desecration and blasphemy, and some like Islam are deeply divided over the prospect of living a sacred life in a secular polity, Christianity stands out for its schizoid tendency to *both* encourage the profession of personal witness to God and persecute those whose witness significantly deviates from the community norm, regardless of the sincerity of the witness. Karl Popper's much vaunted 'method of conjectures and refutations', which is meant to epitomise all that is rational about modern science, updates this tendency by attenuating the epistemic status of the scientist's 'profession of faith'. Thus, a conjecture or a hypothesis is no longer to be seen as an unshakeable commitment but an entertaining thought, whose refutation would allow its entertainer a second chance (Fuller 2003: chapters 10–11). All told, Christianity's preoccupation with heresy may help explain the West's unique ability to excel in *both* high levels of intellectual innovation and resistance to innovation, while the East displays simultaneously low levels of both.

From an economic standpoint, the increasing exposure of science to market forces has occurred at a time when all nations with relatively large GDPs—including highly populous ones that still have relatively low GDPs per capita—have developed scientific elites. Much of this is attributable to the capitalist mode of production expanding more rapidly than compensatory regimes of social welfare provision. This situation has made the global future of science more volatile than ever. And as the idea of a unitary path for the development of science loses its material basis in the state, so too does the idea's intuitive grip on the minds of intellectuals. The concept of postmodernism, which Jean-Francois Lyotard (1983) invented in a 1979 'report on the state of knowledge,' was designed to highlight the diverse origins of the twentieth century's key scientific innovations, which include such decidedly non-academic settings as war and commerce. Lyotard himself wanted to undermine the university's claim as the premier site of knowledge production, a goal that indirectly demystified the state's power to direct the overall course of knowledge—especially given Europe's traditionally nationalised university systems. Cynics with the benefit of hindsight might conclude that Lyotard provided financially overburdened states with just the excuse they needed to offload academic research activity to those willing and able to pay for it.

4. The Janus-faced character of customised science

In any case, Lyotard's report unintentionally issued a licence for the *customisation* of knowledge to particular constituencies. In this context, it is important to draw a sharp distinction between two types of customisation. On the one hand, everyone might be invited to convert to one's own religion in order to enjoy the benefits of science. This strategy updates the old evangelical model of competing universalisms. Most recently, it has spawned movements often called 'creation science' and 'Islamic science.' On the other hand, the benefits of science may be restricted to those who meet some financial threshold, regardless of how the money was made and why the science is wanted. This new and profoundly relativistic reduction of knowledge to exchange relations appears in the emerging intellectual property regimes. Both versions of customised knowledge retain elements of universalism, but only the former remains faithful to the classic Enlightenment idea that knowledge is not truly universal until it is within everyone's reach, and hence functions as an instrument for diffusing, rather than concentrating, power. Given the religious basis for creation science and Islamic science, their latter-day alignment with Enlightenment goals is ironic—to say the least—but not unfounded.

The frequently heard charge that creation science or Islamic science is 'relativistic' should be dismissed as resting on a confusion of medium and message: the message remains as universalistic as ever, but the medium requires a personalised appeal. When religion is protected by the state, there is no need to appeal to personal justifications for belief. Religious instruction is simply mandated by the state educational authority. However, once state backing is removed, then 'the product cannot sell itself', as the marketing people say. This does not necessarily make the product any less worth buying (ie it does not diminish the universal status of a religion's knowledge claims), but it does increase the need to make explicit the reasons why particular people should make a purchase (ie how the religion's universal knowledge claims are to be realised in one's life). Western defenders of the scientific orthodoxy have become so accustomed to state monopolies on knowledge production that they often turn hostile to the audiences whose sympathies they now explicitly need to cultivate. The repeated rhetorical failures of evolutionary biologists in US public school forums provide a striking case in point (Fuller 2002c).

Nevertheless, to those used to science policies based on state monopolies, there is something vaguely suspect about the evangelism associated with the promotion of creation science or Islamic science. However, for purposes of comparison, it is worth noting the form that science evangelism has taken in the West since the end of the Cold War, as the locus of funding has shifted from physics to biology. Physics had reigned supreme as the state church of science by purporting to benefit everyone at once, say, in terms of military defence or renewable energy, both of which economists reasonably dub 'public goods' (Fuller 2002a, chapter 1.4). The benefits flowed from laws of nature so fundamental that it would cost more to exclude 'free riders' than to include everyone. However, with the era of the nuclear holocaust (hopefully) behind us, continued public support for secularised science must be increasingly justified in more instrumentally specific terms. Thus, the latest ten-year plan of the UK's Biotechnology and Biological Sciences Research Council is entitled

'Towards a More Predictive Biology'. The theme of this report is that basic research in biology has reached a critical mass, and now it is time to focus the field in delivering products that will assist in policymaking, healthcare, and environmental protection. To be sure, these products will benefit some more than others, but then that is suited to a science whose knowledge claims are grounded in probabilities that cannot guarantee returns on investment.

Moreover, by loosening their state science monopolies, Westerners have intensified secularisation to a point that threatens to undermine any robust sense of the universality of scientific knowledge. This turn is epitomised in new regimes of intellectual property. As the race to map the human genome first brought to light, knowledge producers are being forced to compete against not only other public-spirited producers but also profit-oriented ones who promise consumer-friendly knowledge products in return for private ownership of the means of knowledge production. This disturbing situation was most clearly driven home in the recent settlement by transnational pharmaceutical companies to supply South Africa with drugs for the treatment of AIDS at discount prices, in exchange for South Africa not developing its own biomedical industries (Fuller 2002a, chapter 2.1). Widely reported as a victory for South Africa (home to fifteen per cent of the world's AIDS sufferers), nevertheless the settlement marked a blow to the idea of knowledge that is both applicable *and* available to everyone. The transnational companies have effectively driven a wedge between the ability to produce and consume knowledge, thereby converting universalism from a doctrine of emancipation to subordination.

This conversion pattern is all too familiar from economic history. The world-systems theorist Samir Amin (1991) has distinguished ancient from modern forms of imperialism in terms of the dominant power's impact on the local political economy. In the ancient empires of Rome and China, the dominant power taxed its subject-nations but left their local modes of production and social relations largely intact. In contrast, the modern empires emanating from Western Europe radically restructured, or 'rationalised,' local economies to make them efficient producers of surplus value for continually shifting and expanding markets, resulting in what both the liberal John Hobson and the socialist Lenin recognised as the emerging global division of labour. The analogous movement in the global knowledge economy is from a situation in which Western science, technology, and medicine coexisted—be it in harmony or tension—with local knowledges to one in which the Western forms either pre-empt or absorb local knowledges by the imposition of intellectual property regimes. The South African case exemplifies pre-emption, the epistemic equivalent of mercan-tilism. Perhaps the most serious form of absorption, the epistemic equivalent of capitalism, is *bioprospecting*, or the alienation of genetic information for commercial purposes (Fuller 2002a, chapter 2.7). Knowledge that a eugenicist can use to control the means of biological reproduction coincides with the knowledge a capitalist can use to control the means of economic production. Thus, bioprospecting forges an unholy alliance of the most exploitative tendencies of planned and unplanned economies.

5. Religious fundamentalism as a reasoned response to capitalised science

In the wake of the destruction of New York's World Trade Center on 11 September 2001, intellectual and political leaders are perhaps more sceptical than ever that religious fundamentalism could be a reasoned response to anything. Nevertheless, a strand of *monotheistic* fundamentalist thought constitutes a worthy counterbalance to the specific deformation of secularised science described in the previous two sections (cf Armstrong 2000). Given that specifically Islamic fundamentalists have taken responsibility for the acts of terror against the secular world since 11 September, the focus on monotheistic religions adds relevance to my argument. (In contrast, I take so-called Hindu fundamentalism to be a specific political project based on a certain purist image of Indian national identity: cf Nanda 2003) My main point here is that the distinction between what might be called 'fundamentalist' and 'liberal' responses to the contemporary scientific world order roughly corresponds to what I originally called 'anthropic' and 'karmic' orientations to the science-and-religion duplex.

Without further elaboration of the analogy, the reader may be surprised that I associate fundamentalism with the anthropic perspective and liberalism with the karmic one. After all, do not fundamentalists resort to suicide bombing, while liberals have been, all things considered, exceptionally cautious about risking human life in retaliation? More generally, have not fundamentalists opposed the extension of civil rights to women, persecuted people for pursuing deviant lifestyles, and arrested the development of science and technology—all of which have been championed in liberal societies? The answer to these questions is, for the most part, yes. Nevertheless, I urge that the resurgence of fundamentalism be interpreted as a reminder to liberals of the long-term dangers of doing the right things for the wrong reasons, or perhaps simply forgetting the right reasons for doing the right things (Fuller 2001b, 2002d, which initiated the British sociological response to 11 September 2001).

In post-colonial studies, 'Orientalism' is typically used to signify the West's pejorative construction of Islam (and the East more generally) in the modern period. In this sense, a popular latter-day 'Orientalist' is Bernard Lewis, the bane of Edward Said's existence. However, Said, himself a Palestinian Christian schooled in the UK and US, originally meant something more ambivalent, insofar as the targets of Orientalism often unwittingly lived up to the Western stereotype (Said 1978). Something similar might be said of the career of the recently coined 'Occidentalism' (Margalit & Buruma 2002), which is meant to be the mirror image of Said's Orientalism. Both terms capture a demonised stereotype of 'the other' by a party anxious to justify and extend its own sense of virtue.

For a variety of European scholars and writers over the last 200 years, Orientalism served as a reminder of the decadence into which their own cultures could easily fall if they did not follow the righteous path—in this case, of secular progress. After all, Islam and Christianity share the same roots, and indeed Muslims were largely responsible for preserving and consolidating the Greco-Roman intellectual heritage that enabled the Christian revival of learning in the High Middle Ages. However, whereas the Christian world carried forward this heritage into modernity, the Islamic world remained locked in a medieval dogmatism, squandering their initial material advantage over the West. To Europeans with ambivalent views about the changes undergone by their own societies through industrialisation and secularisation, the contemporaneous state of the Islamic world stood as a living reminder of what might have been their own fate, had they rejected modernity. Thus, the spectre of Orientalism bolstered Western resolve to push ahead with modernisation.

In the case of Occidentalism, here too we begin with the common ancestry of Islam and Christianity, but now focusing on their shared conception of the unique relationship between the human and the divine. From that standpoint, the secularisation of Christianity has been marked by an increasing indifference to the material differences between people. The West has thus lost sight of the anthropic vision it originally shared with Islam. For example, the very idea of progress presupposes the existence of more advanced humans who show the way so that the rest of humanity might catch up. However, the progressive promise has often turned out to be empty because the maintenance of differences between people itself became the standard against which some people were judged to have succeeded, or are better than others.

Behind this relativisation of standards is the idea that the advancement of humanity can be judged on *distributive* rather than *collective* terms: that is, the relative status of humans with respect to each other rather than the overall state of humanity with respect to common matters that threaten their survival. In short, the doctrine of progress destroys the sense of a universal human community. Consequently, Western societies—as epitomised in the isolationist foreign policy normally pursued by the United States—are characterised by a profoundly asymmetrical perspective to humanity at the extremes: On the one hand, they are acutely sensitive to risking the lives of their own citizens in principled conflict; but on the other, they blithely ignore the regular yet non-violent termination of life that poverty produces elsewhere in the world. They would much rather minimise the suffering than maximise the welfare of humanity. As the Occidentalist sees it, this is empiricism and Epicureanism run amok: 'Out of sight (or touch), out of mind.'

Occidentalism may be understood as a moralised version of classical scepticism's singular lesson to philosophy, namely, that the relentless pursuit of the means of reason can easily undermine the ends of reason, if the ends are not themselves regularly recalled as a second-order check on the means. Put more bluntly, mindless attempts at improving the efficiency of a practice can destroy the point of engaging in the practice. Thus, one must periodically return to 'fundamentals'. A very interesting analysis of this situation has been recently provided by a US psychiatrist who argues that classic Western religious conceptions of *sin* amount to self-defeating behaviour that arises from either an ignorance or an unwillingness to engage in what economists call 'inter-temporal comparisons'—that is, the impact of short-term on long-term satisfaction. It was in the hope of remediating this deficiency that the concept of *will* was invented (Ainslie 2001).

Contemporary fundamentalists may thus be seen as chastising liberals for a failure of will. From a more scholarly standpoint, an Occidentalist could cite two features of Europe in the seventeenth and eighteenth centuries that are relevant to this point, which Marx had already recognised as a perverse application of Hegel's 'cunning of reason' in history (Adorno & Horkheimer 1972). The first is the severing of feudal ties between lords and serfs, which produced a putatively free labour market. The second is the creation of academies whose independence of church control enabled free scientific inquiry. Both measures officially aimed to realise the full potential of humanity, but their unchecked pursuit turned out to be dehumanising, indeed perhaps raising the West's tolerance for inhumanity.

Thus, capitalism dissolved the concept of humanity into an ethic of individual responsibility, while scientism dissipated it into a species-indifferent respect for life. At the level of political economy, human value has been reduced to sheer labour-power, a material factor replaceable by technology. At the level of philosophy, humanity's unique species being has been reduced to marginal differences in genetic composition that encourage trade-offs between the maintenance of particular humans and non-humans, depending on their capacity to live full lives of their own kind. Little surprise, then, that our own latter-day Herbert Spencer, Peter Singer (1999), has recently synthesised both strands of this Enlightenment heritage in an explicitly post-Marxist call for a 'Darwinian Left' (Fuller 2001a).

The preceding discussion of Occidentalism may be summarised in the following paradox: *Fundamentalists are intolerant of the indefinitely tolerant, while liberals are notoriously tolerant of the intolerant—and perhaps even the intolerable.* From that standpoint, the terrorists intellectually aligned with fundamentalism are best understood as having taken advantage of the liberal's 'value neutral' attitude toward education in science and technology to promote a specific normative agenda. After all, if one passes the relevant examinations and can pay the relevant fees, which Western institution of higher learning—barring state interference—is nowadays likely to decline such a person admission on grounds of political motives?

Westerners who find the Islamic fundamentalist response to the current world order objectionable tend to misread its anti-establishmentarian posture as 'other-worldly', perhaps because fundamentalists often appropriate practices from a bygone, putatively purer era. That this view is mistaken became clear from the reaction of Christian fundamentalists in the US in the hours immediately following the destruction of the World Trade Center. Several preachers who would otherwise not be associated with radical domestic politics, including Jerry Falwell, interpreted the disaster as a sign of divine disapproval for secular America's self-absorption. But more to the point, my reading of Muhammad Iqbal (1964) and Sayyid Qutb (1990)—the Pakistani and Egyptian heroes of the modern pan-Islamic movement —inclines me to regard Islamic fundamentalists as the natural successors of Trotskyites, still eager to have the secularised mono-theistic promise of the Enlightenment fully redeemed, but reaching back beyond Karl Marx to the Qur'an. A kindred Christian spirit is to found in the 'liberation theology' of Roman Catholic Latin America, which converts biblical talk of a 'salvation' passively bestowed by God into a active political campaign of universal human entitlement to the means of production (Guttierez 1990).

Fundamentalists set a society's moral benchmark by its treatment of the weak, poor, and infirm. It is here that humanity's connection to God is most sorely tested, as the divine is manifested in its least outwardly attractive and most socially burdensome human form. To be sure, in this respect, fundamentalists are quite close to the intentions of the original liberal reformers who as children of the Enlightenment called for the political and economic enfranchisement of traditionally disadvantaged social groups. In principle at least, fundamentalists and liberals are agreed in condemning the wastage of human life in the name of sectarian self-advancement. However, liberal societies have usually ended up enhancing the political and economic wellbeing of their members for reasons unrelated to these original noble sentiments of greater inclusiveness. For every violent overthrow of an *ancien regime* in the name of democracy, there have been ten cases in which the dominant class simply came to realise that it was in their interest to admit these 'humanistic' reforms—perhaps because they would open up the labour market, expand the consumer market, replenish the pool of future leaders, or simply keep the peace. This strategic concession then set the stage for what by the dawn of the twentieth century Georges Sorel had already recognized as the 'fallacy of optimism', which via Robert Michels has come to be seen as the 'co-optation' of the vanguard into the new establishment—long before the project of humanity had reached completion.

6. Fatalism secularised: providence as the West's philosophy of science

Contemporary Western defences of science have a disturbing tendency of dialectically pre-empting the idea that things could be other than they are. It is not that philosophers and sociologists deny that things may improve, but improvement comes only at science's own natural pace, not from a recognition that, say, recent scientific developments have been for the worse. The result is that a superstitious 'trickle-down' science policy governs the relationship between basic and applied research (Fuller 2000c: chapter 5). For example, the past quarter-century has been given to fashionable, self-avowed 'realist' philosophical arguments, which follow Hilary Putnam (1975) in claiming that the 'success' of science would be a miracle, were it not getting closer to the truth. We might marvel at the enormous questions begged here: What success? What science? What truth? Nevertheless, sociologists have similarly followed Robert Merton (1977) in holding that a principle of 'cumulative advantage' governs scientific achievement, whereby graduates of the best universities tend to make the most substantial contributions, which in turn vindicates their having received the best training. Both Putnam and Merton suggest that access to ultimate reality is tracked by the accumulation of capital, be it defined in strictly economic or more broadly cultural terms.

Thus, we witness a massive shift in the burden of proof to potential critics, as epitomised in the following rhetorical question: Why *would* such a large amount of human and material resources be bound up in the conduct of, say, molecular biology, and why *would* the results of its research have such considerable impact, were it not that molecular biology provides reliable knowledge of the nature of life? Of course, there may be a more direct, and less mystified, connection between massive investment and massive impact than the question suggests—and that the appeal to 'reliable knowledge' as a mediating explanation functions as a self-serving 'god of the gaps'. That is, *any* research program with a large enough share of the available resources at its disposal might display the same features, left to its own devices in a relatively friendly sociopolitical environment. In that case, the special epistemic (or spiritual) status retrospectively attributed to research programs lucky enough to have been given such treatment is mere superstition. Unfortunately, the burden of proof is loaded so that one is made to feel like an ignoramus for even entertaining such contrary thoughts.

From a theological standpoint, the philosophical and sociological defences of science outlined above look like secularised versions of Providence. According to the neo-orthodox Christian theologian, John Milbank (1990), this is no accident. Milbank regards the emergence of a 'scientific' approach to human affairs as not only the secular displacement of Christian theology, but also the vindication of a particular theological perspective. (Milbank complains only about the former not the latter development.) In most general terms, it marks a decisive shift in Western culture from a focus on humanity's self-formation to the historical formation of humanity. In the former state, humanity appeases and perhaps even realises God through good works. Original sin is reduced to humanity's mirroring of the Creator's own fundamental incompleteness, both of whom are then jointly realised in creation. In the latter state, humanity is born radically alienated from God, whose perfection contrasts sharply with the radical imperfection that is original sin. The extent of our reconciliation to God can only be assessed indirectly, as we act in ways that may eventually be seen as having met with divine approval.

In the annals of heresiology, this transition marks the ultimate triumph of Augustine over Pelagius (Passmore 1970: chapter 5). Thus, Augustinian doctrines of grace, providence, and the elect metamorphosed into such explanatory staples of the social sciences as the invisible hand, the cunning of reason, and natural selection (Fuller 1999). Presupposed in each case is significant slippage between intention and consequence, in the midst of which, in more religious times, God had moved in characteristically mysterious (or, in Reinhold Niebuhr's sense, 'ironic') ways. However, common to the religious and secular versions of Augustinianism is the view that individuals should be interpreted as instruments of larger forces—be they theological or sociological—beyond their own or anyone else's control. In that case, divine reconciliation may imply coming to understand one's own fate in the larger scheme of things, that is, to cope with what is ultimately irreversible. Thus, intervention is replaced by contemplation: political action by a depoliticised conception of social science that increasingly verges on subsuming humanity under a karmic pan-naturalism. Nowhere is this trajectory more evident than in the modern history of international development policy.

7. Conclusion: The karmic turn in development policy

Policymakers first became preoccupied with population 200 years ago, as birth rates started to outpace mortality rates in the West. The trend testified to improved living conditions, but in the absence of any clear plans about what to do with the extra people. At the time this was seen as much an opportunity as a problem. For optimists like the French Catholic aristocrat Marquis de Condorcet, the demographic upturn meant that humanity could finally exercise dominion over the earth. But for pessimists like the English Protestant parson Thomas Malthus, the excess population was a perturbation that would be redressed by what Darwin later called 'natural selection' (Rothschild 2001). Until the late 1960s, Condorcet's optimism inspired international development policy. The idea was to grow societies and redistribute their fruits. Malthus-inspired worries about overpopulation were associated with eugenics because usually it was claimed that one type of people was proliferating at the expense of a more favoured type. The invidious politics behind such judgments were transparent.

However, by the late 1970s, socialism was in retreat, welfare states faced fiscal crises, while developing countries remained politically unstable and economically backward. The gap between the rich and the poor nations—and the rich and the poor inside nations—was starting to widen again. Policymakers thus became increasingly pessimistic about the prospects for global development. Biologists replaced economists as the gurus of choice, and the field of development was widened to cover ecological stewardship. It became increasingly fashionable to speak of *all* of humanity as a blight on the planet. Now both our productive and reproductive capacities had to be curtailed.

Perhaps the most influential biologist in this context has been EO Wilson (1992). His doctrine of 'biodiversity' warns of an impending 'era of solitude' in which human beings will be the only species left, unless we change our ways. To be sure, from a strictly Darwinian viewpoint, biodiversity is a strange doctrine, since the regular extinction of species provided Darwin himself with the evidence he needed for natural selection at work. Is Wilson then trying to reverse the course of nature? On the contrary, Wilson wants to introduce a sense of justice into natural selection, which would provide each species an equal opportunity for survival. This is motivated by 'biophilia', an ethics based on the ninety per cent + of genetic overlap among all life forms. The logical conclusion to Wilson's argument is that any anthropocentric development policy is bound to be short-sighted.

As a basis for development policy, biodiversity is remarkably presumptuous. Only some of the available ecological models claim that there has been a recent rise in species extinction rates, let alone demonstrate that human activity has been responsible for such a rise (Lomborg 2001: Parts II and V). Wilson's most important assumption turns out to be that species will be eliminated as more people come to adopt the lifestyles of the wealthiest nations. Yet, given the past failure of development policy to narrow the gap between the rich and the poor, it is very unlikely that this will happen in the foreseeable future. In that case, Wilson may be seen as providing a kind of 'sour grapes' explanation for why development policy should not have been so ambitious in the first place. This conclusion has been explicitly drawn by the British political theorist, John Gray (2002), who is also drawn to the scaled-down expectations of the Eastern religions as an antidote to the anthropic hubris of the West's secularised monotheism. Thus, science succeeds by offering solace for failure.

That the world includes much more than mere *homo sapiens* need not add to the burden of policymakers. Ironically, taking on the entire planet may lighten their load. Ecological outcomes are defined in terms like carbon dioxide emissions (ie the Kyoto Protocols) that are removed from politically sensitive zones of engagement, such as income per capita or life expectancy. A market that trades in pollution shares is politically more palatable than a super-state that redistributes national incomes. Policymakers may believe that ecological and human indicators are somehow connected, but the scientific ambiguities surrounding the connection offer much scope for 'creative implementation' that may end up trading off the interests of humans against those of other creatures or the environment more generally. The rise of 'corporate environmentalism' shows only too clearly that clean industries can exploit people at least as efficiently as dirty ones, even as they help to maintain the ecosystem (Hoffman 1997). A good example comes from the 2002 Johannesburg Earth Summit, where agreement was reached on the need to provide the world's poor with clean water but not with water as such. This seemingly strange result is comprehensible from a ruthless 'logic of capital': If the poor already have access to water, then cleaning it up is an efficient step toward enabling them to participate as workers and consumers. However, for drought-stricken regions, the provision of water would require substantial capital investment, the returns to which would take years to materialise.

What is striking about the recent history of international development policy is not the belief that all species are created equal or that humanity is an expendable feature of the cosmos. These ideas have ancient pedigrees, notably in the great karmic religions. But never before have they been so enthusiastically embraced by self-described political progressives in the West. Peter Singer has eloquently written of the need to 'expand the circle' of concern from humanity to the rest of nature. But as the endless succession of failed 'earth summits' demonstrates, we have never properly closed the moral circle around humanity. Prophets of overpopulation who follow in Malthus's footsteps believe that we never will and that our best strategy is to diminish humanity's overall presence on the planet. This strategy of cutting losses simply uses science to mask a loss of political will, thereby turning Occidentalism from a myth to a reality that is rightly contested by both religious and secular peoples everywhere.

7. Postscript

A necessarily shortened version of this paper was presented in Yogyakarta as part of the fourth plenary session, 'Science, Post-colonialism, and Religion,' alongside presentations by Meera Nanda and Zainal Abidin Bagir. Some questions raised by the audience about the compatibility of a scientific worldview and various forms of Christian and Islamic fundamentalism are addressed in the full text. In sum, I would have Westerners, and those sympathetic with Western liberalism, come to appreciate how their beliefs and actions look to an 'Occidentalist,' a label that I believe more precisely captures the relevant 'clash of civilisations' than older terms like 'fundamentalist' or 'evangelist.' In particular, the elimination of species differences and the assimilation of development policy to environmental policy are easily, and perhaps even justifiably, seen by Occidentalists as a retreat from a standpoint that privileges human beings above the rest of nature—a position common to the great monotheistic religions and the European Enlightenment, which in turn has motivated the major legal and medical innovations of the past 250 years.

However, most of the questions concerned the role of the social sciences—conspicuously absent from the conference proceedings—in forging the bridge between science and religion, especially with the aim of renovating the concept of humanity. Since I believe that the fate of the social sciences in the twenty-first century hinges on their recovery of this very concept, I have devoted an entire book to the topic (Fuller 2004). I make a few basic points on this matter below.

First, there is nothing inherently antagonistic about the relationship between science and religion that requires 'bridging.' Indeed, modern science is an outgrowth of the secularisation of Christendom, with clear roots in the medieval Islamic quest for a unified understanding of reality. The relevant antagonism is purely institutional, namely, the displacement of theology by the natural sciences for the intellectual and spiritual leadership of European and American universities. The rise of Darwinism in the late nineteenth century sparked this conflict, which was then projected backward by ideologically inspired historians to cover, say, Galileo's persecution, which in its day was understood as a dispute amongst fellow Christians. As for the quite obvious skirmishes between science and religion in the twentieth century, these are best interpreted—as I do in this paper—in terms of 'religion' reminding 'science' of their common aims, namely, the ennobling of humanity. To be sure, these reminders have often fallen on deaf ears, and not simply because scientists were not listening. However, it is important to distinguish between competing strategies for ennobling humanity and a much more fundamental opposition, namely, between those who believe that science should ennoble humanity ('anthropic') and those who believe it should not ('karmic'). It is those adhering to the latter perspective who have been responsible for the increasing incidence of laboratory vandalism on behalf of 'animal liberation.'

The anthropic-karmic distinction cuts across—and is more fundamental than—the science-religion distinction. For example, one could practice technically advanced natural science as a Buddhist, arguing that these sciences aim to provide a harmonious understanding of nature in which our anthropocentric urges are first sublimated in the species indifference of genetics and then ultimately dissolved in a probabilistic distribution of subatomic particles. Indeed, I am surprised that a neo-Darwinian biologist no longer in the grip of the anthropic vision has not explicitly argued that all species are worth understanding in their own right, and that the continued fascination

—nowadays, by evolutionary psychologists—with looking to animals for clues to the human condition is tantamount to using modern astronomy as a source of astrological insight: in both cases, the non-human is subsumed to the human in a thoroughly superstitious fashion. (Here it is worth recalling that astrology, like evolutionary psychology, is predicated on the assumption that both humans and non-humans are effectively alternative arrangements of common matter.)

However, the social scientific understanding of religion has often obscured the depth of the anthropic-karmic distinction. To be sure, many of the distinctive methods (eg 'interpretation') and objects ('consciousness') of the social sciences are secular descendants of Christian concepts that originally demarcated humanity's unique spiritual existence from the rest of the animal and material world. In this respect, the anthropic roots of social science are very clear. But at the same time, the conception of 'society' on which the founders of social science fixated was the secular nation-state, whose general *modus operandi* was to supplant the traditional seats of religion—the church and the family—as the primary locus of authority and allegiance. At best, 'religion' in this sense referred to a functionally differentiated ('private') part of society; at worst, it represented an atavistic form of social life altogether. Thus, common to the practices we continue to call 'religions' today—a motley array of monotheisms, polytheisms, pan-theisms, and atheisms that range across the anthropic-karmic divide—is simply their capacity to organise social life into complex, long-lasting, and far-flung patterns of behaviour without requiring the agency of the nation-state. Of course, states and religions have often enjoyed symbiotic relationships, but typically the religions have predated and sometimes even helped to create the states.

I end on these historical observations because at a time when some scientists, including social scientists (eg Atran 2002), believe that the brain houses a distinct 'module' for religion, we need to remind ourselves that the science-religion distinction is ultimately an artefact of late nineteenth century European cultural conflicts and that a rather different distinction—between anthropic and karmic worldviews—may more profoundly divide devotees of *both* science and religion.

Bibliography

Adorno, Theodor and Max Horkheimer. *The Dialectic of Enlightenment* (New York: Continuum, 1972). (Orig. 1943)

Ainslie, George. *Breakdown of Will* (Cambridge, UK: Cambridge University Press, 2001).

Amin, Samir. 'The Ancient World-System versus the Modern Capitalist World-System, *Review* 14, 1991: 349–386.

Armstrong, Karen. *The Battle for God: Fundamentalism in Judaism, Christianity and Islam* (London: Harpercollins, 2000).

Atran, Scott. *In Gods We Trust* (Oxford: Oxford University Press, 2002).

Charry, Ellen Zubrack. 'A Step toward Ecumenical Esperanto', in L Swidler, editor, *Toward a Universal Theology of Religion* (Maryknoll NY: Orbis, 1987).

Fuller, Steve. 'Recent Work in Social Epistemology', in *American Philosophical Quarterly* 33 1996: 149–166.

Fuller, Steve. *Science* (Milton Keynes UK and Minneapolis: Open University Press and University of Minnesota Press, 1997).

Fuller, Steve. *The Governance of Science: Ideology and the Future of the Open Society* (Milton Keynes, UK: Open University Press, 2000).

Fuller, Steve. 'The Reenchantment of Science: A Fit End to the Science Wars?', in K Ashman and P Baringer, editors, *After the Science Wars* (London: Routledge, 2000), 183–208.

Fuller, Steve. *Thomas Kuhn: A Philosophical History for Our Times* (Chicago: University of Chicago Press, 2000).

Fuller, Steve. 'The Darwinian Left: A Rhetoric of Realism or Reaction?' POROI 1:1 http://inpress.lib.uiowa.edu-/poroi/vol2001/fuller2001.html, 2001

Fuller, Steve. 'Looking for Sociology after 11 September'. *Sociological Research On-Line*. 6, 3, http://www.-socresonline.org.uk/6/3/fuller.html, 2001.

Fuller, Steve. *Knowledge Management Foundations* (Boston: Butterworth-Heinemann, 2002).

Fuller, Steve. 'Karmic Darwinism: The Emerging Alliance between Science and Religion', in *Tijdschrift voor Filosofie* (Belgium) 64, 2002: 697–722

Fuller, Steve. 'Demystifying Gnostic Scientism', in *Rhetoric and Public Affairs* 5 2002: 718–729.

Fuller, Steve. 'Will Sociology Find Some New Concepts before the US Finds Osama bin Laden?', *Sociological Research On-Line* 6, 4, http://www.socresonline.org.uk/6/4/fuller.html 2002d.

Fuller, Steve. *Kuhn vs Popper: The Struggle for the Soul of Science* (Cambridge, UK: Icon, 2003).

Fuller, Steve. *Re-Imagining Sociology* (London: Sage, 2004).

Gray, John. *Straw Dogs: Thoughts on Humans and Other Animals* (London: Granta, 2002).

Gutierrez, Gustavo. *The Truth Shall Make You Free* (Maryknoll NY: Orbis, 1990).

Hoffman, Andrew. *From Heresy to Dogma: An Institutional History of Corporate Environmentalism* (San Francisco: Lexington Books, 1997).

Iqbal, Muhammad. *Thoughts and Reflections of Iqbal*, editor S Vahid (Lahore, Pakistan: Ashraf, 1964).

Lomborg, Bjorn. *The Sceptical Environmentalist* (Cambridge UK: Cambridge University Press, 2001).

Lyotard, Jean-Francois. *The Postmodern Condition.* (Orig. 1979). (Minneapolis: University of Minnesota Press, 1983).

Margalit, Avishai and Ian Buruma. 'Occidentalism', in *The New York Review of Books*, 17 January 2002.

Merton, Robert. *The Sociology of Science* (Chicago: University of Chicago Press, 1997).

Milbank, John. *Theology and Social Theory: Beyond Secular Reason* (Oxford: Blackwell, 1990).

Nanda, Meera. *Prophets Facing Backward: Critiques of Science and the Making of Hindu Nationalism in India* (New Brunswick NJ: Rutgers University Press, 2003).

Passmore, John. *The Perfectibility of Man* (London: Duckworth, 1970).

Putnam, Hilary. *Mind, Language and Reality* (Cambridge UK: Cambridge University Press, 1975).

Qutb, Sayyid. 'That Hidden Schizophrenia', in P Griffiths, editor, *Christianity through Non-Christian Eyes* (Maryknoll NY: Orbis, 1990).

Rothschild, Emma. *Economic Sentiments: Adam Smith, Condorcet, and the Enlightenment* (Cambridge MA: Harvard University Press, 2001).

Said Edward. *Orientalism.* (New York: Random House, 1978).

Singer, Peter. *A Darwinian Left: Politics, Evolution, and Cooperation*
(London: Weidenfeld and Nicolson, 1999).
Wilson, EO. *The Diversity of Life* (Cambridge MA: Harvard University
Press, 1999).

2

Vedic Science and Hindu Nationalism: Arguments against a Premature Synthesis of Religion and Science

Meera Nanda

In India today, religion and nationalism—two of the most potent motivators of mass mobilisations—have become fused, leading to a monstrous movement for Hindutva, or Hindu-ness. For the last decade, India has been ruled by BJP, a party committed to the ideology of Hindutva. The idea behind Hindutva is to declare India a Hindu nation, and force the Indian State to reinterpret the Constitution in ways that are in keeping with Hindu values.

The dark side of this Hindu nationalism is that anyone who is not a Hindu is not considered fully Indian. India's 120 million Muslims and about 30 million Christians are being turned into aliens in their own homeland. Worse, they are being targeted as the enemies of the Hindu nation. The recent killings of Muslims in Gujarat and the low-intensity warfare against Christian missionaries and churches are examples.

These facts about the rise of Hindutva are well known, evident to anyone who pays attention to the foreign-affairs pages of daily newspapers. What is less well known is the fact that the Hindutva movement is obsessed with modern science. Something called 'Vedic science' lies at the heart of its ideology. Vedic science is not very different in spirit from creation science or Islamic science, in that it attempts to create a science of nature that does not contradict the sacred teachings of the Vedas.

Hinduism is not a religion of the book. It is not known by any one sacred book. Therefore, some of you may not be familiar with what the Vedas are. Vedas are the sacred books of orthodox Hindus that were composed over many centuries starting around 1500 BCE. There are four Vedas, followed by nearly 200 Upanishads which were composed during the axial age of Hinduism between 800 and 400 BCE. The Upanishads, also known as Vedanta, contain the philosophical core of

Vedic teachings. The Vedanta teaches an idealistic spiritual pantheism. God is not separate from nature and humankind, but the whole world and all that it contains is God, called Atman or Brahman. This Brahman is not a personal God, but has the form of spirit, or consciousness, without matter. This Absolute Spirit constitutes the very substance of all that exists. The strictly monistic form of Vedanta, Advaita Vedanta, holds that there is only one ultimate reality, that of Brahman, and the visible world is an illusion.

The project of Vedic science has two main goals. The first is deeply scientistic—namely, to declare Vedic teachings, which go back 1500 years before the CE, to contain all the advances of modern science from the Newtonian to Einsteinian physics, from human physiology to molecular biology. The second is deeply relativistic—namely, to declare the Vedic ways of knowing to be as rational and empirical within the monistic metaphysics of Vedanta as the methods of modern science are within the dualistic metaphysics of the Abrahamic religions.

Now, the dialogue between faith and reason, idealism and naturalism is not new to Hinduism. Indeed, the more mystical, world-denying teachings of the Vedas and the Upanishads have *always* been in a tension with the more empirical and materialistic strains of un-orthodox, non-Vedic philosophies which are *also* a part of Hindu heritage. Nearly all phases of Indian intellectual history, from the birth of the Buddha in the sixth century BCE, to the coming of Islam in the eleventh century, and then the British and Christianity in the seventeenth century, are marked by debates and attempts at synthesis between the Vedantic pantheism and other dualist and materialist worldviews. The Indian nationalist movement in the nineteenth and twentieth century was affected by this conflict and produced the first attempts at absorbing modern science into the Vedas. The contemporary Hindutva picks up where the earlier generation of Hindu nationalists left off and are now aggressively pursuing the Vedic science project.

Because this conference is about science and religion in the *post-colonial world*, I will concentrate only on the contemporary Vedic science movement.

In this paper I want to underline two aspects of the post-colonial world that make the talk of Vedic science extremely dangerous. First, theories of Vedic science are being produced and used by the Hindu chauvinist political movement and the intellectuals affiliated with them. Second, the post-colonial world is intellectually dominated by a postmodernist suspicion of modern science. Western philosophers of science, feminist intellectuals, and other cultural critics have themselves become suspicious of the universal claims of modern science and the culture of modernity in general. The Vedic science proponents are making free use of the West's internal critics of the Western experience of modernity and extending it to deny the importance of modern science for an Enlightenment and reformation of their own religions. In other words, postmodern critiques of the Enlightenment in post-Enlightenment societies are being used to deny the need for the enlightenment in pre-modern cultural contexts, where religion continues to exert an enormous and often socially oppressive influence on the life of the people.

In the rest of the paper I will look at three aspects of the Vedic Science paradigm.

First: how the conflation between modern science and Vedic myths is aiding the ideology of Hindutva, and why we should worry about it.

Second: how the proponents of Vedic science use the social constructivist and postmodernist logic to defend the most mystical, world-denying idealistic traditions of the Vedanta as scientific.

Third: why India needs secularisation and a disenchantment of nature.

1. Political uses of Vedic science

I am going to give you three very brief examples to show how science is being equated with Hindu mythology and how this Hindu science is being put to work in politics.

India test-fired a nuclear bomb in May 1998. The explosion of the bomb was celebrated in India with a frenzy matching that of a religious enthusiasm. The desert in Pokharan where the explosion took place was declared to be a sacred ground, VHP promised to build a temple at the spot of the explosion to the goddesses of Shakti (power) and Vigyan (science). There were plans to take the sand from Pokharan for public worship ceremonies around the country. There were religious processions in which the idols of gods were made with nuclear halos around their heads.

In Bhagwat Gita, a sacred book of Hindus, God Krishna reveals himself to Arjuna in the battlefield with these words: 'I am the radiance of the thousand Suns, the splendor of the Mighty one. I am become death.'

If you recall, Robert Oppenheimer, the physicist who helped create the first atomic bomb, cited these words of Krishna when he realised that human beings had unleashed the destructive power that used to be reserved for the gods alone. Whereas Oppensheimer spoke these words with great sorrow, in India this verse from the Gita was made into a prophecy. It was said that the bomb was foretold in the Gita and it was India's destiny to become great. What is more, the ages-old myth that the Gita contains all the physics needed to make a nuclear bomb, and that the West had stolen nuclear physics from the Gita, was repeated many times. Not just the explosion of the bomb, but even the science behind it was supposed to be prophesied right there in the Gita.

Thus an ugly and dangerous development was turned into a celebration of Hindu greatness. India's nuclearisation of the entire subcontinent was turned into a mythic war between good and evil, with the promise of God Krishna to come to the aid of the righteous India.

My second example comes from space. India is the one and only country in the world that simultaneously launches satellites to explore the space *and* teaches astrology as a Vedic science in its colleges and universities.

In April 2001, India for the first time successfully launched a geostationary communication satellite using a home-made launching pad and a home-made satellite. In July 2001, the education ministry of the Indian government announced that three-year colleges and universities would start teaching astrology as a science subject. There will be labs and libraries and postgraduate studies in the universities engaged in 'further research' in astrology. Astrology is only one of the Vedic sciences that will be offered. The Indian government is funding all traditional sciences, some of them of extremely dubious scientific value, such as *vastu shastra* (like Chinese *Feng Shui*), cow-urine therapy, Vedic mathematics, parapsychology and faith-healing.

The equal status for traditional sciences derived from the Vedas with modern science in schools and universities is not just rhetoric any more. With the blessings of the supreme court, a massive Hinduisation of education in government-funded state-run schools and colleges has already begun. Over and above public education, India has a vast and growing network of schools run by radical Hindu nationalist groups, especially RSS and VHP. To cite figures reported by the New York Times, there are some 20,000 privates schools, teaching 2.5 million students, with 1000 schools being added every month. In these private Hindutva schools which receive government subsidies, education has become thoroughly saturated with Hindu nationalism. These schools are the Hindu equivalents of madarsas in Pakistan. The only difference is that Hindu schools do not reject modern science outright, but teach it as just another version of the Vedas and the Vedanta.

What we are witnessing in India is a reactionary form of modernity in which advances in modern technology are being actively used to promote traditional values and traditional sciences.

The third example comes from declaring the Vedas and even the pre-Vedic Indus-Valley civilization to be the creation of the Aryans. India is being declared to be original homeland of the Aryans. Finding all the science in the Vedas has this subtext: to declare India, and not Greece, as the mother of all science. The appalling Eurocentric version of history is being replaced by an equally appalling Indocentric version of history. What is worse, all the myths about the superiority of the polytheistic, pantheisitic Aryans against the monotheistic Semitic religions are being revived. Again, this Araynisation is no longer a matter of intellectual debate. The *New York Times* on 30 December reported that new school books clearly refer to the Indus Valley civilisation as Saraswati-Indus civilisation, claiming the entire pre-Vedic history of this region for the Aryan Hindus.

2. Legitimation of Vedic science

I now turn to the arguments that are offered to defend Vedic science. These arguments fall into two main categories, political and epistemological. Ironically, both of these arguments borrow heavily from the social constructivist, feminist and post-colonial critiques of science that are popular among the mostly left-wing academic critics of science in Western universities. These postmodernist, anti-Enlightenment arguments, unfortunately, have been very popular among Indian intellectuals and social activists as well. In fact, intellectuals of Indian origin have been most prominent in the debates over the universalism of science. In the creation of Vedic science, we see that the left-wing academics have unintentionally given aid and comfort to a religious right-wing movement for which they have no sympathy.

Let us look at the political justification first. The proponents of
Vedic sciences see themselves as part of the post-colonial project, no
different from the left-wing secular intellectuals who have long argued
for the 'decolonisation of the mind'. Using the ideas of Thomas Kuhn,
Paul Feyerabend and more recent Western critics like Richard Rorty,
Sandra Harding, Vandana Shiva and Ashis Nandy, Vedic science
proponents argue that modern science is only a Western, Christian
understanding of nature. Modern science is not universally valid, but
valid only within the metaphysical assumptions of a dualist ontology
of Christiantiy in which god is separate from and transcends nature.
India must take only those elements of modern science which are in
agreement with Hindu metaphysical values of unity between nature
and god (eg quantum mechanics, ecology). For the rest, Indians must
use Hindu categories of thought, derived from the Vedas, to construct
their own science of nature.

The underlying idea that each culture and religion will have its
own science of nature which uses and affirms the religious metaphysics of that culture is, in my view, fundamentally mistaken. It
mistakes the *origins* of modern science in the Christian theism of a
Kepler or a Newton or indeed of the entire Royal Society with the
essence of scientific method and scientific worldview. I believe that
Christian theistic science was necessary only for getting the process of
scientific experimentation started. Gradually, science became autonomous from religion and developed the standards for legitimate
questions and answers from within its own accumulated tradition.
That accumulated tradition is by no means bound by Judeo-Christian
metaphysics and is available to all cultures. What is more, other
cultures have an obligation to see that their own religious cosmologies
do not contradict what we know about the world through this
accumulated tradition of science. I stand with Abdol Karim Soroush
who has argued that religious consciousness must become cotem-
porary, that is, theology should not contradict modern scientific
findings. Vedic science is an attempt to evade this challenge.

Let us look now at the more interesting epistemological defence of
Vedic science, and here too falls the shadow of postmodernist relativist
conceptions of science favored by secular academics in science studies.

So far I have argued that the Hindutva ideologues claim that it is
their patriotic duty to decolonise knowledge and to cultivate an
alternative science that is an organic outgrowth of the core, or the
essence, of Hinduism. The natural question is, what do they see as the

essence of Hinduism? Is that essence compatible with the naturalism and empiricism of modern science?

According to Vedic science proponents, the essence of Hinduism is spirituality, the Vedantic belief in the presence of the spirit, the Absolute Consciousness or the Brahman in all things. Most of us think of spirituality as an opposite of empirical and logical analysis of evidence required by natural science. But Vedic science theorists claim that *Hindu spirituality is scientific,* that it is a rational and empirically adequate way of making sense of the *natural* world as well as the world of the spirit. Hinduism is spiritual but in a scientific way. The conflict between the two is a Semitic problem. Indeed, the very idea of a contradiction is a Semitic idea, for Hindus only connect and harmonise opposites.

In fact, they claim that Hinduism is the only religion whose conception of god is affirmed by the findings of modern science. The external god who stands apart from nature and lays down nature's laws has been disproved by science, but quantum physics has affirmed the presence of Brahman or consciousness in nature. This, needless to say, is a very biased interpretation of quantum physics. Perfectly realist explanations of the paradoxes at the subatomic level that quantum physics pose are available and are routinely used by most working physicists.

But the claims of scientificity of spiritualism go deeper than merely drawing parallels between quantum physics and the so-called Eastern wisdom. A newer generation of Vedic physicists has claimed that the method of spirituality—going inward through yoga and meditation—is an adequate method for acquiring objective knowledge of the material world. Unfortunately, if you look at the history of science in India, this kind of introspective spirituality practiced by the Brahmins has actually served to *block* advances in science. Traditional spiritual practices have led to magical thinking based upon correspondences and associative logic. Vedic science proponents are claiming that not only was this spiritual method scientific in the time of the Vedas, but is scientific even *today.*

I want to give you a quick example of how spirituality is redefined as the method of Vedic science. (There is a recent crop of books on Vedic physics by Subhash Kak, Ram Mohan Roy and David Frawley. The names may be unfamiliar to you, but they are becoming prominent in India.). Kak has written many books claiming that the

Vedic verses are actually a record of astronomical findings: those
verses in the Yajurveda which instruct the priests how to build fire-
altars are actually coded formulae for such cosmological findings as
the length of the tropical year, the distance between the sun and the
earth, and even the speed of light, all of which turn out to be exactly
what modern physics has found, down to the last decimal point!
Clearly Kak is reading back the modern findings into the Vedic verses.
Kak's work has inspired other, even wilder interpretations which find
even fermions, bosons and quarks already described in the venerable
old scriptures.

The question these Vedic physics always face is: how did the Vedic
sages know all this physics? What was their method? Why don't we
find any remains of their observatories, or records of their experiments?

Invariably, the answer one gets is that the Vedic sages 'intuited',
'directly perceived in a flash' or 'experientally realised' the laws of
nature by altering their consciousness through yogic meditation. By
getting in touch with the Brhaman, the consciousness inside, they came
to know the Brahman or the consciousness that is in the world of
nature. Through deep introspection, they could see the likenesses,
homologies or equivalences between the cosmic, the terrestrial and the
spiritual.

This 'method' of finding homologies between the microcosm of
human life and the macrocosm of the entire cosmos is precisely the
method of astrology, palmistry and other occult sciences which
understand and try to control the natural world to fit human meanings
and purposes. The method of correspondence is the method that
natural science as we know it broke away from.

But according to Kak and associates, to think of associative logic as
magical is a Western prejudice. In the Veadantic metaphysics, in which
there is no dividing line between god and nature, spirit and matter,
knowledge of the spirit is a legitimate method of knowing the material
world. What is magical in the West is scientific in India. (Not just in the
past, but today. This is how they justify the scientificity of vedic
astrology!) Ultimately, what is scientific is to be decided not by
empirical adequacy, but by the metaphysical framework. Different
metaphysical starting-points justify different methods as scientific.
There is no reason to hold science as we know it to challenge magical
thinking in Hinduism.

3. The dangers of Vedic science

I want to end this talk with a few remarks about the dangers of Vedic science in particular and the dangers of an over-hasty reconciliation between science and religion in general.

Under the guise of Vedic sciences, there is a veritable counter-Enlightenment and counter-reformation going on in India today. This counter-Enlightenment is fuelling a Hindu chauvinism that not only spells disaster for religious minorities, but is also extremely harmful for the majority of Hindus themselves. For under the guise of cultural authenticity, magical thinking and superstitions are being promoted as scientific. As long as this kind of thinking prevails in Indian society, Indian people will remain captives of false prophets.

In the postmodern, post-Enlightenment world, many have become disillusioned by secular ways of thinking and living. But whatever be the flaws of the Enlightenment, the fact is that it did help disenchant the mind, it did help human beings break out of the fear of cosmic consequences of their actions in the here and now. The Enlightenment did lead to a house-cleaning in organised religions so that room could be created for the right of individuals to think for themselves, to ask questions, to challenge authority.

By denying the progress and universality of modern science, the project of Vedic sciences and indeed, the project of 'alternative sciences' more generally, is disarming the forces of secularisation and the Enlightenment in India.

At a more general level, regarding the synthesis of science and religion, I strongly believe that we have got to be honest to science. It will not do to fit the findings of physics and biology into the metaphysics, even when the two are clearly at odds. Theology must become contemporary, if it is to continue to engage the whole of human beings, both their minds and their hearts.

I do not for a moment discount the importance of the sacred and the holy in human life. A completely secular and rational life would be emotionally thin. It is not a mode of life worth fighting for.

But the sacred need not be tied to the supernatural. What humans seek in religion is a sense of transcendence of the here and now. For the kind of thinking beings humans are, this sense of transcendence can survive the death of God.

3
Islam, Science and 'Islamic Science': How to 'Integrate' Science and Religion

Zainal Abidin Bagir

In today's science-and-religion discourse the term 'integration' seems to capture the sentiment of religious believers very well, that somehow science and religion should not be separated. 'Separation' (if we take it as the opposite of integration) does have some negative tone, and opens the space for either indifference between the two or even possible conflicts, while 'integration', in one way or another, joins them in harmony. That notion has been developed both in the Western Christian world and in the Muslim world. In the former, where conflict seems to be the main, and sometimes the guiding, theme in science-and-religion discourse,[1] it has been developed most prominently by Ian Barbour and a few other leading figures that may be grouped into his 'Integration' position. (Barbour 2000) In the Muslim world, the notion of integration—formulated in different ways, including the one close to Barbour's—has also been popular. Here 'integration' (or 're-integration') seems to be one of the main themes, taking as the norm for the relation between science and religion numerous Qur'anic verses that praise faithful seekers of knowledge, or the development of science in the Golden Age of Islamic Civilisation. On the other hand, separation of the two is usually perceived in terms of the secularistic trend of separating the religious/sacred and the worldly. And many Muslims have been quite suspicious of secularism.[2]

---

1. We can see this in so many works on science and religion which open with a description of the conflict followed by attempts to say that it does not have to be necessarily so and a proposal for more constructive engangement of science and religion. For example, in the typology of four positions in Ian Barbour as well as John Haught, this is a very important position which in some ways motivates the formulation of other positions.

2. Note Ernest Gellner's remark: 'In the last hundred years the hold of Islam over Muslims has not diminished but has rather increased. It is one striking counter-example to the secularisation thesis' (Gellner 1993, 36).

We can see this trend in most Muslim scholars, scientists and writers who write on the subject. In the more specific context of Indonesia, the most populous Muslim country in the world, we can see very strong indications for this,[3] and the most important source that informs this idea has been the literature on Islam and science available in the Muslim world in the past four decades. The Barbourian notion of 'integration' has added a certain degree of authoritativeness to that notion despite widely different meanings attached to it. And that precisely is the main issue here: what is meant by 'integration'?

In this paper I shall start with a brief survey of Muslim responses to modern science, which introduced during the colonial times, and proceed to discuss one strand which I see as most influential, that is, the idea of 'Islamic science'. By using philosophical and historical arguments I will show parts of the idea which are acceptable and parts which I object to. I conclude this paper with some reflection about a methodologically responsible way to 'integrate' modern science with Islam. In some places I shall draw parallels between what happens in Islam and in other religions, which, I hope, may indirectly show some indications how religion and science can be discussed fruitfully as an inter-faith issue.

---

3.   In Indonesia, we can find not only the trend, but even the word '(re-) integration' is liberally used in official documents. For instance, 'integration' (*integrasi*) is mentioned explicitly in the syllabus (in a specific unit on science and religion) for the compulsory religion course at the university level which is issued by the Ministry of Religious Affairs. This applies to each of the five religions which are regulated administratively by the Ministry: Islam, Protestantism, Catholicism, Hinduism, and Buddhism.

'Integration' has reverberated more strongly recently when the State Institutes of Islamic Studies, which are available in many parts of Indonesia, begun the transformation to become full-fledged universities. This means they will now offer not only religious sciences (Qur'anic exegesis, Islamic philosophy, jurisprudence, literature, etc) but also the 'non-religious', modern sciences (physics, medicine, sociology, anthropology, psychology, etc). One question here is: should these non-religious sciences be offered in some different way from the way they are taught and developed in the secular (non-religiously affiliated) universities? What seems to be the 'religiously correct' thing to do in this regard is to 'integrate' the teaching of those sciences with Islamic values. Indeed, one of the idealistic arguments for this transformation is that the sciences (the 'religious' and 'non-religious') have to be 're-integrated'.

1. The colonial encounter with modern science and post-colonial reactions

To put the issue in the wider context, we can note that, normatively, Islam has never been ambivalent about the pursuit of knowledge. Many Qur'anic verses can be readily cited to show how Islam highly regards men of knowledge above others, and how God repeatedly commands believers to observe and reflect 'Our signs in the horizons and in themselves'. Nevertheless, despite those normative sources, since the beginning of the Islamic intellectual tradition certain tensions between knowledge derived from revelation and that gained through rational means have been kept alive. These tensions were carried on well into the time when modern science was introduced to Islamic lands. The modern tensions are best understood in the broader context of Muslim responses to modernity, of which modern science is its essential component.

Historically, modern science was introduced to Muslims mainly through Western colonisation of Muslim lands. This brought about many complexes that are still alive until today. For early modern Muslim intellectuals—such as Sir Sayyid Ahmad Khan, Jamaluddin al-Afghani, and Muhammad Abduh—the challenge was real: Muslims needed to gain scientific knowledge in a level advanced enough to counterbalance their colonial rulers. What was superior in the West that they could conquer the Muslim lands? The answer was not hard to find: they had better knowledge, ie the science that could tame the natural world, absorb its power, and made it subservient to man's will. The Ottoman, the last bastion of the millennium age-old Islamic caliphate, in the early eighteenth century adopted a policy that would send hundreds of Muslim students to Europe to study the knowledge that had given it the power. Knowledge *was* power.

However, while Muslims were never ambivalent about the practical use of the new science, there were already some questions regarding the suitability of certain parts of this science to Islamic beliefs. The main issue concerned Darwin's theory of evolution. The ideological debate about the theory was very heated (and documented well in Adel A Ziadat, *Western Science in the Arab World: The Impact of Darwinism, 1860–1930,* 1986). Take Jamaluddin al-Afghani, for example, who was a staunch pro-modern science advocate. He went to the extent of saying that modern science is simply a continuation of Islamic science that once flourished amazingly in the 'Golden Age of

Islamic civilisation'. Pursuing modern science means putting in practice the Qur'anic injunctions to reflect on the natural world as God's creation. Yet he kept serious reservations about what he perceived as the materialistic elements in the theory of evolution. In general, there have always been some reservations regarding the values that are perceived to be inherent in modern, Western science.

This ambivalent attitude is reflected very well in today's various Muslim responses to modern science. I shall mention four of the most important of them.

(1) A group of Muslim scholars and scientists take science as a completely neutral enterprise, and focus on Muslims' need to catch up their scientific backwardness. If there is any issue with science at all, it has to do mostly with its application. The two can be strictly separated. The remedy for this is Islamic ethics. A popular metaphor pictures science as a knife—in itself it is neutral, but it may be employed for good or bad ends. The only way to guarantee that it is put to good ends is by employing ethical criteria. This *first* group may be loosely termed instrumentalist. Science is simply an instrument to be used by anyone who wants and can use it. Science does not oppose nor support religion. It would not be surprising to find proponents of this relatively safe position (theologically) in all religions.

(2) The second group wants to establish the superiority of Islam with its Qur'an compared to other religions, by trying—and always finding—Qur'anic verses for each new scientific discovery. These 'scientific miracles' supposedly prove the truth of the Qur'an. In terms of its aim, the *second* group is quite close to the idea of 'Vedic/Hindu science', of which Meera Nanda has severe and sustained criticisms in the last few years.[4]

(3) Another group criticises strongly the other groups, for both accept the legitimacy of modern science. For this group, science is not value-free; modern science is coloured by Western secular values; thus Muslim needs their own science loaded by Islamic values—it is sometimes called 'Islamic science'; in another formulation, some would say that there is a need to do 'the islamisation of knowledge'. As I shall note later, the ideas of Muslim scholars who belong to this category are quite different from each other. But in general this *third* group's idea is similar in some senses with the idea of 'theistic science' which has been

---

4.   See Nanda's contribution in this volume.

intensively discussed among certain American Christian groups, most prominently by the analytic philosopher Alvin Plantinga.

(4) Recently, there is another group, led mainly by Harun Yahya, which is on the rise. Its focus is criticism of the theory of evolution. Harun Yahya would vehemently reject the charge that they are anti-science. They are only against materialistic, secularistic science, the chief paradigm of which is Darwinian theory of evolution. On the other hand, they accept big bang cosmology since in general it can be easily interpreted as supporting the traditional idea about God. This group is almost identical—in terms of their arguments, aims, and strategy—with the American Intelligent Design movement.[5]

It is instructive to note here that it is difficult to find something like a conflict view in Barbour's typology. Even the Muslim creationists like Harun Yahya, who would certainly qualify as a proponent of Barbour's Conflict view, as their American counterpart does, would vehemently reject the idea of conflict between Islam and science. Instead, they may as well argue that what they do is 'integrating' modern science with Islamic beliefs, by sieving out the godless values, and accepting those which support (or are acceptable to) the faith. Similarly, the most radical of the proponents of Islamic science, though trying to delegitimise science by rejecting what they regard as the epistemological and metaphysical foundations of modern science, could hardly be called anti-science. What they want to do is in some sense, again, 'integrate' science with Islamic values. In short, all those attempts to relate science and Islam may as well be called attempts to integrate science with Islam.

With this I want to emphasise the fact that Muslims tend to reject outright the idea of conflict between our rational understanding of the natural world and their religious beliefs. They might be in certain tension (not conflict), but it is only 'religiously correct' to say that the two are and should be in harmony. Further, based on the above

---

5. Before proceeding further, I would like to note an important point. It is interesting to see that, as I already indicated, we can find Christian responses similar to the four above-mentioned Muslim responses in other religions. This indicates an important fact that modern science has posed challenges which are shared by a few other religions. As such this can be a basis for doing comparative study of the religious responses to modern science, and also indicates that there is an important avenue for dialogue between religions in facing the challenges posed by science.

considerations, it is not surprising that the idea of integrating science and religion is quite popular, despite (or probably precisely because of) the fact that it could mean a number of very different things. As such, being clear about how science could be 'integrated' with Islam is therefore of paramount importance and has far-reaching implications in the education of sciences (see footnote 3).

In this regard, the third group mentioned earlier (those who advocate 'Islamic science') deserves special attention as it seems to be the most attractive option for Muslims involved in the effort to conceive the teaching of sciences in a context which takes Islamic values into account.[6] Part of its attractiveness lies in its dealing not only with certain branches of science, but with the very foundation of science. Besides, among the others, this group does have the most sophisticated philosophical arguments, and as such is more effective in delegitimising modern science.[7]

The objectionable part of modern science is sometimes couched in terms of its metaphysical foundations which are seen to be at variance with Islamic metaphysics, sometimes in epistemological (or political) terms of the coloniality of knowledge. We may remark in passing that the issue of the coloniality of knowledge has not failed to bring about not less interesting reactions in other religions of the colonised lands. Sometimes we see appropriation of knowledge in specific cultural terms, other times there is rejection. For example, whereas in the Muslim world of nineteenth century the Muslim reformer al-Afghani

6.   In terms of the educational implication, the fourth group, the creationist, at present is probably the most 'threatening', since some of its proponents have strongly indicated their intention to repeat the career of creationism in the US in trying to introduce their 'theory of creation' as the rival to the theory of evolution in the schools in some Muslim countries. But I shall leave discussion of this issue to chapters on evolution in this book.

7.   Some proponents of Islamic science, like Ziauddin Sardar, make use of the arguments developed in post-positivistic philosophy of science (eg Thomas Kuhn and Paul Feyerabend). Similar arguments are, interestingly, but not surprisingly, also used by proponents Vedic science, Philip Johnson's science, as well as feminist science. It is not surprising since this post-positivistic (or 'post-modernist') view of science is taken by some as opening ways for the insertion of one's specific cultural values into the epistemology of science. Meera Nanda's contribution in this volume as well as her article (Nanda 1998) show how the postmodernist arguments are used to argue for these new kinds of science.

tried to trace the root of modern science to earlier Islamic civilisation, in nineteenth century India, during the British colonisation, Dayananda Sarasvati reminded the Hindus that much of modern science was actually already contained in the Vedas. This was part of the modern Hindu reform movement he advocated, whose main idea is Hindu renewal by returning to the Vedas. With regard to Buddhism, colonialism deeply affected the Buddhists' attitude toward modern science, such that in Cabezon's typology of the relation between Buddhism and science, the position of 'conflict', which in Barbour characterises theological opposition to certain scientific theories, is here 'enmeshed with . . . Asian Buddhist opposition to European colonialism' (Cabezon 2003, 41).

Below I shall not discuss this aspect (rejection of the coloniality of knowledge) in the idea of 'Islamic science', but focus instead on its philosophical and historical arguments.

2. 'Islamic science', 'sacred science', and 'islamisation of knowledge'

How to understand the idea of 'Islamic science'? A popular understanding of this idea, as represented by its critic, the Pakistani physicist Pervez Hoodbhoy, takes it as a new kind of science founded on an epistemology radically different from modern science, with objects of study that are far wider than those of modern science to include supernatural realm. If Islamic science is that, can there be an Islamic science? (Hoodbhoy 1992, 77). Though one can criticise the too simplistic historical and philosophical account of science he presents in his arguments, Hoodbhoy rightly concludes that there has not been and can't be such an Islamic science. Indeed, after decades of discussions, proponents of Islamic science have wildly different understandings of what it exactly is, and it is still impossible to point to theories produced by a 'contemporary Islamic science'. It is true, as Hoodbhoy said, specifying a set of moral and theological principles does not enable one to build a new science from scratch. Science, as understood today, indeed does not come into existence that way.

But these criticisms, coming from a physicist who is gravely, and rightfully, concerned about the fate of science in his society, have failed to address the main issue and motivation behind the idea. Although he is to be applauded for launching criticisms of preposterous ideas about 'Islamic science'—mainly those affiliated with the scientific miracles of the Qur'an project—he clouded the criticisms by indiscriminately grouping different ideas under one notion called 'Islamic science'. The idea of 'Islamic science', and its variants under different names such as 'Islamisation of knowledge', has been in circulation in the last four decades. It is important to pay attention to differences in the variants of this notion, since many different ideas go with this expression, and in terms of its attitude toward modern science it ranges from one which accepts current modern science entirely to those which seem to want to replace the system totally and build a distinct new system of science founded on ·and imbued entirely with Islamic values, and many positions in between the spectrum. Hoodbhoy's severe criticisms hit right at the target if 'Islamic science' is understood in a particular way.

But as a matter of fact, most prominent proponents of Islamic science, like Seyyed Hossein Nasr and M Naquib al-Attas, would rule out 'creating a new science from scratch' as what they mean when they speak about Islamic science, though it might include objection to certain parts of the so-called 'philosophical implications' of science. They would say that what they propose is not discarding particular scientific theories like Newton's mathematical formula of force or Einstein's theory of general relativity, or the periodic table of the elements. Their idea of science is certainly much broader than Hoodbhoy, as a scientist involved in the actual practice of science, understands. Their main attention is directed toward questions about certain values or worldviews which somehow are associated with modern science in one way or another. At its heart is the issue of the philosophical implications of certain scientific theories or the metaphysical presuppositions of science.

Nevertheless, even here there are indeed questions about what precisely is meant by 'philosophical implications' or 'metaphysical presuppositions'. Here I will take as an example Nasr's ideas. Despite his many strong criticisms of modern science, he categorically accepts the legitimacy of modern science in the following way:

> In contrast to what many have said about our being opposed to the cultivation of Western science, we have never advocated [that opposition.] Rather, our proposal has been to master in the best manner modern science *while* criticizing its theoretical and philosophical bases and then through the mastery of

these sciences, to seek to Islamicize science by taking
future steps within the Islamic world-view and
distinguishing what is based upon scientific 'facts'
from how that is interpreted philosophically . . . (Nasr
1995, 82).

The distinction between 'what is based upon scientific facts' from
its philosophical interpretation is very crucial here and will be
important for my argument later. When he says that science is not
value-free, but 'based on the particular value system and a specific
world-view rooted in specific assumptions concerning the nature of
physical reality, the subject who knows this external reality, and the
relation between the two' (Nasr 1995, 75), we can understand the
value-system and the worldview as the basis of philosophical
interpretation. From this Nasr's next step is to propose 'Islamicisation
of science'. I shall offer a different lesson one can learn from this
distinction and some criticisms of Nasr later.

But it needs to be pointed out that this distinction can be justified
by using some popular views in recent literature on philosophy of
science, and also one employed by a number of philosophers in similar
attempts to build 'religious sciences' (as well as a proposal like
'feminist science'). A case in point is the Christian analytic philosopher
Alvin Plantinga who has recently argued for a 'theistic science' on a
similar basis to Nasr's. He develops a similar distinction and spells out
a differentiation between the part of science that is supported by
evidence and what one may call 'the metaphysics of science' in his
discussion of two alternative conceptions of science.

He calls the two conceptions Augustinian and Duhemian science,
after Pierre Duhem, the nineteenth century scientist, and historian and
philosopher of science. The first is a kind of science 'in the service of a
broadly religious vision of the world', (1996, 370) while in the second
scientific activity is conceived more narrowly, such that it is
metaphysically neutral. Formulated in this way, most scientists would
probably say that the more popular conception is the second one. But
the issue is not that straightforward. Pieere Duhem himself notes that
in the history of science there are two competing understandings of the
aim of science—one takes science to the task of the explanation of
phenomena, the other is content with saving them. For Duhem himself
the aim of science should not be to give (metaphysical) explanations,

which he understands as an attempt 'to strip reality of the appearances covering it like a veil, in order to see the bare reality itself' (Duhem 1914, 7). The reason is that to answer the questions about the nature of things, the empirical evidence is not sufficient by itself. So the theory needs additional elements which can only be supplied by a metaphysics. 'Therefore, *if the aim of physical theories is to explain experimental laws, theoretical physics is not an autonomous science; it is subordinate to metaphysics'* (Duhem 1914, 10).

In advocating this position, is he, like the twentieth century positivists, being hostile to metaphysics? He is not. In one place he suggests that metaphysics should be informed by scientific theories; but it is a discipline totally different from science. What he tries to do is protect science from the unending disputes which have plagued metaphysics since its earliest history. The division of physics and metaphysics is motivated mainly by the need to make science a common endeavour. Duhem's first philosophical statements on the character of scientific theory (1892) already mention what he sees as a disturbing trend in physics. That is, physicists (represented most prominently by Descartes) attempted to give metaphysical explanation of their theories, and as such their physics leads to 'the incessant upheavals that theoretical physics has suffered, and, consequently, the discredit into which this science has fallen in the mind of many physicists' (Duhem 1892, 11). '[Such physicists] believe they are contemplating the very structure of the world but will have before their eyes only a fragile construction soon to be destroyed to make room for another' (Duhem 1892, 15). Instead of being an autonomous discipline, here physics becomes dependent on metaphysics. 'In that way, far from giving it a form to which the greatest number of minds can give their assent, we limit its acceptance to those who acknowledge the philosophy it insists on' (Duhem 1914, 19).

Plantinga rightly sees that what Duhem objects to is not so much metaphysics per se, but divisive metaphysics, which hinders cooperation between scientists. In this case, atheistic or anti-religious beliefs could stand in the way of universal consent just as certain religious beliefs could as well. Thus, for Plantinga, a strictly Duhemian science 'will not employ hypotheses about God, but it also won't employ any hypotheses whose cogency involves or presupposes metaphysical naturalism' (Plantinga 1996, 382).

Beside Duhemian science, there is, for believers, an option to do a kind of Augustinian science which he calls 'theistic science'. Similar to Nasr as quoted earlier, Plantinga stresses that his proposal does not imply that theistic science is a fully exclusive enterprise or that practitioners of theistic science cannot cooperate with other scientists—they can, but only insofar as the science pursued is Duhemian, ie that which can claim universality.

> [W]e would all work together on Duhemian science; but each of the groups involved—naturalists and theists, for example, but perhaps others as well—could then go on to incorporate Duhemian science into a fuller context that includes the metaphysical or religious principles specific to that group (Plantinga 1996, 383).

At this point we note another similarity with Nasr. 'Incorporation of science into a fuller context that includes metaphysical or religious principles' sounds quite close to Nasr's 'integration of science into higher levels of knowledge'. By making distinction between what is based upon scientific facts from how that is interpreted philosophically, there is a way for believers to incorporate solid scientific knowledge into 'a higher level of knowledge' (Nasr 1982, 180). However, a crucial problem here concerns which part of science can be taken as Duhemian.

Do all modern scientific theories need to and can they be so integrated? Plantinga stresses that theistic science applies only to areas 'where it looks as if thinking about the matter at hand from that point of view might lead to conclusions or emphases different from those ordinarily to be found' (Plantinga 1996, 370). For example, for him chemistry and physics are 'overwhelmingly Duhemian', or metaphysically neutral, so doing theistic science in this area is not urgent at all, while in evolution and psychology the situation is different. Nasr, however, does not seem to draw that kind of distinction between scientific disciplines or theories. In Nasr's case, an example that might give us a clue comes from the physicist Wolfgang Smith, who, in a volume dedicated to Nasr, tries to do what Nasr calls 'integration of [modern science] into higher orders of knowledge'.

Specifically, Smith tries to integrate quantum mechanics to the perennial philosophy of which Nasr is one of the strongest defenders today.[8] In Smith's own account, the first thing he does here is free modern physics from what he regards as the flawed Cartesian, epistemological premise of bifurcation (of *res extensa* and *res cogitans*); next, he proposes an ontological model derived from perennial philosophy in place of the Cartesian, and in this way he tries to integrate quantum mechanics into the higher orders of knowledge (Smith, 2001, 472–476).

If such integration can be done to quantum mechanics, can it be done to any other scientific theories, say, the theory of evolution? Nasr has serious objections here, since he sees that there is a huge difference between the two theories. Unlike quantum mechanics, he regards the theory of evolution as lacking empirical evidence, such that it may not even be called a scientific hypothesis, but a dogma (Nasr 1996, 144; 1968, 124).

But it is clear that Nasr's more weighty reason to oppose the theory of evolution has more to do with metaphysics. For Nasr, the theory is 'metaphysically and logically absurd' (Nasr 1996, 144). In one place, he succinctly describes his position toward evolution:

> I reject Darwinian evolution and the idea of transformation of one species into another by merely natural causes as described by Darwin. Biologically speaking, I oppose macroevolution, not the adaptation of a species to new conditions which occurs all the time. But more than that, I oppose the whole ideology based on evolution which would derive the greater from the lesser and force us to believe in the most illogical and improbable scenarios in order to be certain

---

8.   Nasr himself endorses Smith's attempt enthusiastically. In his very lengthy review (Nasr 1997) of Smith's *Quantum Enigma: Finding the Hidden Key*, he calls the book 'one of the most remarkable works written in recent decades on the metaphysical interpretation of modern physics', while the author is 'the first physicist to our knowledge who is also deeply rooted in traditional metaphysics in general as well as traditional Catholic theology in particular and his work is the first to interpret quantum mechanics in such a way as to be able to integrate it into the scheme and hierarchy of the traditional sciences.' He repeats this praise in his reply to Smith's writing above (2001, 486).

to cut off the Hands of God from His Creation (Nasr 2001, 273).

The very idea of the evolution of species from the lower to the higher destroys the traditional idea of hierarchy of beings. 'A species could not evolve into another because each species is an independent reality qualitatively different from another' (Nasr 1968, 124).

We can see here the tension between Nasr's commitment to evidence and his traditional metaphysics. Suppose at one point the evidence has accumulated for the evolution—and it, as a matter of fact, has—would his metaphysical critique fail? If that fails, would it mean something for the doctrines of perennial philosophy? That's quite unlikely to happen, since the metaphysics is independent of empirical evidence. Indeed, no amount of evidence might force him to revise his metaphysics; instead, the metaphysics is to judge the results of sciences, as Nasr illustrates in the last chapter of his early work (1968).

On the other hand, when he launches scientific criticisms of evolution, he says that his purpose 'is not to open a biological debate but to distinguish between scientific facts and the philosophical assumptions that underlie them' (Nasr 1968, 127). Nevertheless, his rejection of even the *fact* of evolution due to its metaphysical absurdity shows that his strong commitment to perennial philosophy has clouded this process of making distinction, because facts (even those that may be discovered in the future) can be rejected in principal in the name of a metaphysics.

There are two problems here. First, an important part of the difficulty in judging scientific theories by using a certain metaphysics (eg 'Islamic worldview') as criteria is that it is not something agreed upon by all Muslims except in very general terms. Specifically in Nasr's case, Muslims may question whether his perennial metaphysics is *the* Islamic worldview. Agreement may be reached with regard to general issues like the existence of God; the oneness of God; or God's creation of the universe. But further than that, the history of Islamic philosophy has shown that quite different elaborations of those tenets are possible.

Second, Nasr, it seems to me, is too quick to derive the 'metaphysical implications' of a scientific theory like evolution. As I shall show shortly, just like other scientific theories this theory is to a great extent *metaphysically ambiguous*. It may have 'metaphysical implications', but, they do not directly, necessarily, and logically imply claims of the non-existence of God, or even abolition of hierarchy. This is the problem I also found in Plantinga earlier. His suggestion that scientists can all work together in the Duhemian science, but that it is also legitimate for those who want to go further to pursue Augustinian science, is not difficult to accept. But the determination of what counts as Duhemian hinges on what counts as 'divisive metaphysics', which, in turn, really depends on Plantinga's reading of the theory. Many people would see that the theory of evolution, for example, does not contain divisive metaphysics; but Plantinga does. Just like the objection to Nasr's notion of metaphysical implication above, Plantinga seems to assume that the implications or presuppositions of a theory can be read off directly from the theory.

3. Metaphysical/theological ambiguity of science: some historical and philosophical considerations

While for scientific realists it is difficult to say that scientific theories are fully metaphysically neutral, if there is anything called metaphysical implications, they are ultimately ambiguous. For example, it has been widely suggested that Newtonian cosmology implies determinism. But is it true? Until quite late in the twentieth century, Newton's theory was regarded as the hallmark of determinism. Acceptance of this theory seemed to imply acceptance of the deterministic world picture it suggests. Newtonian science is regarded as, in the words of van Fraassen, a closed text which admits no interpretation (van Fraassen 1991, 8–11). Newton, in his *Scholia*, dictates comprehensively how his work should be interpreted. The classical world picture thus was thought as demanded by classical mechanics. But, as shown in history, it was just not clear whether subsequent scientists subscribed to Newton's own interpretation when they completed the so-called 'Newtonian world picture'. This concerns technical issues such as what counts as force function, but also metaphysical issues such as determinism. In his *A Primer on Determinism*, for example, John Earman has shown that the Newtonian mechanics did not have the allegedly intrinsic deterministic character. Not only is determinism is not implied by classical physics, but there is a possibility that the two might not even be compatible! Similar ambiguity can be found in other supposedly characteristics, or 'essence', of modern science such as materialism.[9]

In his essay in the *Science* journal (2001), Brooke argues persuasively against drawing metaphysical/theological implications too quickly: 'A lesson that history emphatically teaches is that scientific theories are not born with implications but have implications thrust upon them'. This essay is quite rich with historical examples of how metaphysical/theological implications of theories are never a straightforward issue.[10] For example, the displacement of the Earth from the centre of the cosmos did not necessarily imply the displacement of the divine privilege for human beings. One can see it instead as the elevation of the imperfect earth to the realm of the incorruptible heavens, as contemporaries of Copernicus and Galileo did. To take another example: Newtonian mechanics may imply an autonomous universe (as understood by French Enlightenment philosophers), but for Robert Boyle and Newton himself, clockwork images implied fine engineering and a degree of cosmic maintenance (Brooke 2001). Looking at current scientific theories, we can multiply Brooke's examples. Two most prominent examples would be the theory of evolution and quantum mechanics. An impressive bulk of recent literatures on science and religion has shown how both have been given metaphysical/theological meanings which vary across a wide spectrum.[11]

---

9.   See for example, van Fraassen's discussion of materialism as false consciousness in his *The Empirical Stance* (2001).

10.   His two books of course show this more convincingly: *Science and Religion: Some Historical Perspectives* (Cambridge, UK: Cambridge University Press, 1991; and, with Geoffrey Cantor, *Reconstructing Nature: The Engagement of Science and Religion* (Edinburgh: T&T Clark, 1998).

11.   Space would not allow discussion of a sample of theological interpretations of scientific theories to show this point. But to give just one good example with regard to quantum mechanics, one may look at the excellent volume published by the CTNS and Vatican Observatory, *Quantum Mechanics, Scientific Perspectives on Divine Action* (2002). With evolution, the literature is richer; some of the obvious names one can cite are Arthur Peacocke and John Haught who try to reconstruct Christian theology into an 'evolution-friendly' one. Of course criticisms may be launched of those efforts, but the point is that many theological interpretations of one or a set of theories are methodologically possible.

That theories have been understood to 'imply' quite different metaphysical views by different scholars should not come as a surprise. If there is an underdetermination of theory by empirical evidence, as has been argued very persuasively in recent philosophy of science, we can expect there would be more radical underdetermination of metaphysics by scientific theories. This certainly does not mean that *any* metaphysical implications can be read into theories. Certain metaphysical readings are ruled out by the theories, and that seems to be, at least partly, the reason for rejection of theory of evolution by theologians who see that their traditional conception of God and creation are ruled out by the theory. Ambiguity, indeed, does not mean neutrality.

Furthermore, besides implications of certain scientific theories, it is difficult to deny that the scientific revolution of the seventeenth century had presented a new view of the world, a phenomenon that Max Weber aptly called *the disenchantment of nature*, which has become a very important source of discontent with modern science. But this should simply remind us of the limitation of science: that it is methodologically incapable of functioning as a worldview, inadequate if expected to replace the all-encompassing worldview provided by traditional metaphysics or religions, and also that we have to be really careful when speaking about 'scientific worldview', by not imagining it as derived directly from scientific theories (which Bas van Fraassen calls 'reification of the *content* of science').

Interpretation is what bridges the gap between scientific theories and the supposedly implied metaphysics, worldview, or theology. And interpretation is never unique. This suggests a move further than distinction between theories and their philosophical interpretations as suggested earlier. That is, an awareness that there is no one single, necessary interpretation of theories.

One of the lessons Brooke draws from the history of science is that 'the original implications of a scientific conclusion could be very different from later (and sometimes uncritical) reconstructions' (Brooke 2001). It reminds us that the so-called 'metaphysics of science' is not some kind of uniform doctrines accepted by all scientists, and it is not a logical, direct implication of scientific theories. As such, criticising modern science by way of its metaphysics, as is done by many proponents of Islamic science, is not always appropriate. Most of the time, the critics criticise the simplified, grand form of modern science (eg that it sees nature in a mechanistic, dualistic, secular way) as a basis for asserting the need for an Islamic science. Such reconstruction of the history of science also happens with regard to science as developed in the past Islamic civilisation.

An important part of the arguments for Islamic science comes from a reading of the history of science—both modern science and the science which developed in the past Islamic civilisation. Academically speaking, the state of the history of Islamic science today would not allow for a full reconstruction of the story, simply because the material needed for such a reconstruction is not available. The very texts that would become the most important source for such a reconstruction are still scattered around the world (Sabra 1987). Any attempt to draw such a grand story would be premature.

Yet, stories of what took place in the history of science have been constructed to justify a variety of modern Muslim responses to modern science. Among early modern Muslim reformers, whose interest was to master the instruments that made their colonial master succeed, modern science was advocated as simply a continuation of Islamic science in its glorious past, and thus there should be no problem at all in absorbing—or regaining—it. On the other hand, Nasr, for example, believes that there was a radical metaphysical rupture between Islamic science, which later was transferred to late medieval Europe, and modern science, which was born partly due to this transfer. For him, Islamic science was all designed consciously by its practitioners to reflect the most important traditional Islamic values, as seen in the epistemology and metaphysics of science. The most important value is *tawhid*, the Unity of the Divine Principle, which is reflected in the unicity of nature (Nasr 1964, 5). Thus, in Islamic cosmology, it is a logical necessity that it reflects faithfully that value. Nasr acknowledges that the development of science in Islamic civilisation started with substantial borrowing of material from Greek and other civilisations. However, not all things are transferred, but there were rejections as well. The result was a distinctive Islamic science. This is what he wants to do as well with regard to modern science.

However, other historians of Islamic science present a different picture. One of the most authoritative voices in the history of Islamic science, Al Sabra, for example, indeed strongly criticizes the attempt to present the whole history of Islamic science as passive processes of 'reception', 'preservation', and 'transmission'. Sabra's seminal article

(1987) urges historians of science to be really careful when trying to characterise or reconstruct what really happened in the period. Put in the right context, those terms are hardly adequate. Instead, Sabra proposes 'appropriation' and 'naturalisation' as the more accurate terms. In any case, this process is far from what the recent term 'Islamisation' tries to describe.

I would here take just one example of a recent writing by F Jamil Ragep (2001) on astronomy and its relation to religion in the golden age of Islamic science. Focusing on medieval Islamic astronomy, which is the most exact science of the time, Ragep notes that one of the two ways in which Islamic influence manifested itself was in the attempt to make astronomy as metaphysically neutral as possible. This is reflected, for example, in Avicenna's categorisation of astrology, which previously was grouped together with astronomy, as a part of natural philosophy, whereas astronomy was categorised as a strictly mathematical discipline. With this, astronomy was freed from its metaphysical baggage, and considered a religiously neutral mathematical discipline—an attempt to secure the acceptance of 'foreign sciences' among Muslims. A similar move was made by al-Ghazali, when he differentiated which parts of that science were acceptable to Muslims. Abu Rayhan Al-Biruni and Nasiruddin al-Tusi, too, insisted on a clear separation of astronomy from natural philosophy, which would have premises or first principles that might be objectionable from religious point of view.

> Furthermore, Tusi himself made clear . . . that an astronomer should prove most cosmological matters using 'proofs of the fact' rather than 'proofs of reasoned fact' (that 'convey the necessity of that existence' using physical and/or metaphysical principles); the latter kind of proofs are given by Aristotle in *De Caelo*. In other words, the astronomer should avoid dealing with ultimate causes and instead establish the foundations of his discipline by employing the apodeictic tools of mathematics (Ragep 2001, 59).

For al-Tusi, the regular motion of the heavenly bodies is explained in such a way that the source of that motion becomes irrelevant to astronomy, 'thus sidestepping the problem of ultimate causation'. The Islamic influence that we see here is not in the 'Islamisation of science', in the sense of imbuing the science with certain values—which, it should be noted, might not be agreed by all Muslims—but instead freeing it from the taint of metaphysics. In this way a broader basis for agreement can be attained. This is quite a different picture than the one we get from Nasr's history of Islamic science, in which all sciences are based directly on Islamic metaphysics—a picture that he uses as an argument to revive 'Islamic science'.[12] A caveat needs to be immediately added here: that this is only one of several ways in which astronomy interacted with religion. Ragep also notes another kind of interaction, ie attempts to give religious value to astronomy ('astronomy in the service of Islam'). For example, astronomy is the instrument used to help Muslims determine the direction of Mecca or determine prayer times. In addition astronomy could be the way to reveal the glory of God's creation. Two points I want to emphasise here. The first is Ragep's perceptive note about 'a remarkable diversity of opinion in Islam regarding various aspects of the relationship between science and religion, which makes attempts to generalize an "Islamic" attitude toward science foolhardy' (Ragep 2001, 50). The second point is that one such relationship, which is very significant philosophically, takes the form of freeing astronomy from the taint of metaphysics.

A similar conclusion is also reached by Ahmad Dallal after his study of the traditions of astronomical research in Islamic civilisation. There was the Western Islamic tradition, which, following the Greek, subscribed to Greek metaphysics. On the other hand, the Eastern Islamic tradition separated out the metaphysical, which is a potential source of conflict with Islamic teachings. Astronomy here becomes a more or less neutral enterprise; it's much more mathematical than metaphysical. 'It is thus legitimate to think of this [Eastern] tradition of astronomical reform as a specific Islamic development, and of the

---

12.   Ragep very strongly criticises Nasr, and some other recent authors of works on the history science in Islamic civilisation (such as Pervez Hoodbhoy, and Toby Huff), due to their, at best, careless use of the history of Islamic science to support their grand theory about the relation of Islam to science. He calls the genre to which these works belong as being characterised by 'reductionism, essentialism, apologetics, and barely masked agendas' (Ragep 2001, 49–50).

views espoused in the formulations of members of this tradition as indications of what is "Islamic" about Islamic science' (Dallal 2002, 216). His conclusion is very instructive:

> Thus conceived, the areas in which science and religion overlap are reduced, and scientific knowledge is separated from religious knowledge. In other words, one of the consequences of the separation of science and philosophy was the separation of religion and science. To a certain extent, therefore, the Islamization of science in the practice of medieval Muslim astronomers actually meant its secularization.

4. How to 'integrate' modern science and Islam: some concluding remarks

Those historical considerations echo Duhem's warning about divisive metaphysics. What one can gather from contemporary historians of Islamic science discussed above is that getting rid of divisive metaphysics was precisely what took place in the past. In other words, even if the science was not neutral, what needs to be done is to neutralise it as much as possible, not imbue it with values of one's choice.[13] This means, among other things, launching a critique of, in John Haught's term, conflation of science with beliefs—be they atheistic or theistic.

Scientism, which is an attempt to bypass the ambiguities of science by presenting it as the final word in all matters, including the non-empirical ones, is indeed a bad ideology. What religious believers object to is the atheistic ideology which is pronounced by some prominent scientists as the 'implication' of their science. The answer to this challenge is not to replace it with another (religious) ideology, but,

---

13. This is a criticism that has been launched against the proponents of 'feminist science'. For example, Sandra Harding, a prominent proponent of feminist science, sees that science has masculinist biases; the remedy she proposes is a standpoint epistemology, an epistemology which deliberately sides with the female standpoint, which, she hopes, results in a stronger objectivity. With a similar line of arguments as above, I contend that what needs to be done is instead neutralise science such that it becomes as gender-neutral as possible, where men and women can work together.

rather the 'deideologisation' of science from atheistic as well as theistic ideology, so that it can be a common endeavour for people of all persuasions—in the way that early Muslim scientists freed their science from metaphysics.

The distinction between that which is supported by scientific facts and their metaphysical interpretation, as Nasr and Plantinga have pointed out, needs to be sharpened, to strengthen the methodological autonomy of both science and metaphysics or theology. This is a work of clearing the ground to make it ready for a possible next step, which is giving interpretation to the scientific theories, noting that they probably are not metaphysically neutral, but ambiguous. This second step is certainly outside the scope or beyond the level of science proper, and may be undertaken by believers who may feel the need to integrate the knowledge they get from science with that coming from their religious sources.

At this point there may be a question: does not speaking about being 'outside the scope or beyond the level of science proper' simply assume a semantic convention of what science is? But why should we insist on one definition of science rather than another? Why couldn't one go on including science and its metaphysical interpretation all under the heading of 'science'? There are several reasons for not doing this. First of all, non-metaphysical science is the science as practised and understood today, at least that's the ideal. So, using 'science' in a different way may very well mislead people into thinking that there needs to be a distinctive contemporary Islamic science which, at its worst, would do away with centuries of modern scientific achievements; as a matter of fact, it has misled many people. As a consequence, though it's probably of minor significance, I would as well suggest that in speaking about the need to separate science from its philosophical interpretations, and the suggestions for religious believers to further pursue some kind of 'Augustinian science', we don't use terms like Islamic or theistic science, simply for the pragmatic reason of avoiding misunderstanding.

After all, putting aside Nasr's rejection of the theory of evolution, what he does, *methodologically* speaking, is not much different from what Ian Barbour, for example, does with his theology of nature; or Arthur Peacocke or John Haught with their theologies of evolution. Yet, to my knowledge, no one has accused them of wanting to create a totally different science based on a particular set of values of a religion.

What they do can be seen as giving a metaphysical/theological interpretation of science. But of course, acceptance of this as a work of interpretation carries an important consequence: that is, interpretation is never unique, always hypothetical, and will never reach the status of certainty (as traditional metaphysicians tend to speak of their enterprise). This is based on the premise that scientific theories do not dictate their definite metaphysical implications. In many places in his writing Nasr has made the distinction but, it seems to me, when speaking about the implications of science he has failed to admit the metaphysical ambiguity involved.

As a comparison, Mehdi Golshani who also speaks about 'Islamic science' and 'sacred science' urges the making of this distinction in many of his articles but takes a different position. In his article 'How to Make Sense of Islamic Science' (2000) he makes clear what is acceptable and unacceptable in the idea of Islamic science. It is not a discussion of the so-called scientific miracles of the Qur'an; not about possible ways of *proving* God; and not about doing scientific activity in a new fashion. Instead, Islamic science moves in the levels of the metaphysical presuppositions of science (and ethical issues in the applications of science). Further, it is interesting to note that, regarding the first, he speaks about *rooting* the metaphysical presuppositions of science in religious worldviews, which is quite similar to what the Christian theologian John Haught says about his Confirmation approach.[14] So Islamic science is not directly about science as practised by contemporary scientists, but its metaphysical presuppositions and applications. More specifically, speaking about cosmology and creation, his recommendation is to 'explore our universe through science as much as we can, but avoid making claims about the absolute origination of the universe on physical grounds' (2003, 245). This caution with regard to cosmology points to another important issue.

That is, the level of ambiguity, thus the kind of interpretation that can be given, is different across different scientific theories. The theory of evolution, for example, can be interpreted more readily, since what

---

14.   In his *Science and Religion* (1995), Haught speaks about science's 'rooting itself in religion's fundamental vision of reality as an intelligible whole grounded in the ultimate trustworthy Being that followers of Moses, Jesus, and Muhammad call by the name "God"' (22). In the next page he speaks about the epistemological *roots* of science which are ntimately connected to religion.

it says about the world is relatively clear. On the other hand, the greatest caution should be given when dealing with quantum mechanics, the most striking case of a theory which is really unclear in what it says about the world, despite the fact that it is among the most accurate. (It is ironic, therefore, that quantum mechanics is also the theory which is at the centre of works that compare science with Eastern mysticism, or with the New Tantra).

Finally, speaking about the 'integration' of science and religion, what we have discussed so far is limited to the metaphysical and epistemological aspects. In a broader context, there are two other more specific areas where religion, particularly Islam, may be integrated with science. First, the issues related to the ethical dimension of scientific activities as well as their technological application. Second, religion and ecology. Despite a number of criticisms of Nasr I raised earlier, Nasr has done more than any other contemporary Muslim scholars with regard to ecological discussion since the 1960s. It should be noted also that this is the area where inter-faith explorations have been most developed.[15]

Bibliography

Barbour, Ian G. *When Science Meets Religion* (San Francisco: HarperSanFransisco, 2000).

Brooke, John Hedley. 'Science and Religion: Lessons From History?', *Science* (accessed through the Internet on 24 October 2002; http: www.sciencemag.org/cgi/content/full/282/5396/1985).

Brooke, John Hedley, Margaret J Osler, and Jitse M van der Meer, editors. *Science in Theistic Contexts, Cognitive Dimension* (*Osiris*, 2001 v. 16).

Cabezon, Jose Ignacio. 'Buddhism and Science: On the Nature of the Dialogue', in B Allan Wallace, editor, *Buddhism and Science* (New York: Columbia University Press, 2003).

---

15. To cite just one example, Harvard's Center for the Study of World Religions has very recently published a series of nine big volumes on ecology and religion (Buddhism, Hinduism, Confucianism, Daoism, Jainisim, Judaism, Christianity, Islam, indigenous religions).

60   *Zainal Abidin Bagir*

Dallal, Ahmad. 'Islamic Paradigms for the Relationship between Science and Religion', in Peters, Iqbal, Haq, editors (Ashgate, 2002), 197–222.

Duhem, Pierre. 'Physics and Metaphysics', in Duhem, *Essays in the History and Philosophy of Science* (translator and editors, Roger Ariew and Peter Barker, 1983), (Indianapolis and Cambridge: Hackett Publishing Company, 1996).

Duhem, Pierre. *The Aim and Structure of Physical Theory* (Princeton: Princeton University Press, 1914).

Gellner, Ernest. 'Marxism and Islam: Failure and Success', in A Tamimi, editor, *Power-Sharing Islam?* (London: Liberty for Muslim World Publications, 1993).

Golshani, Mehdi. 'How to Make Sense of "Islamic Science"', *American Journal of Islamic Social Sciences*, vol 17, no 3 2000.

Golshani, Mehdi. 'Creation in the Islamic Outlook and in Modern Cosmology', in Peters, Iqbal, and Haq, editors (Ashgate, 2002), 223–248.

Hahn, Lewis Edwin, Randall E Auxier, and Lucian W Stone J, editors. *The Philosophy of Seyyed Hossein Nasr* (The Library of Living Philosophers, vol 28) (Chicago and La Salle, Illinois: Open Court Publishing Company, 2001).

Hoodbhoy, Pervez. *Islam and Science—Religious Orthodoxy and the Battle for Rationality*, republished in Malaysia by S Abdul Majeed & Co in association with Zed Books, 1992.

Nanda, Meera. 'The Epistemic Charity of the Social Constructivist Critics of Science and Why the Third World Should Refuse the Offer,' in Noretta Koertge, editor, *A House Built on Sand: Exposing Postmodernist Myths about Science* (Oxford: Oxford University Press, 1988).

Nasr, Seyyed Hossein. *Man and Nature* (George Allen & Unwin Ltd [Mandala edition, 1976], 1968).

Nasr, Seyyed Hossein. 'Islam and Modern Science', in S Azzam, editor, *Islam and Contemporary Society* (Longman, 1982), 177–190.

Nasr, Seyyed Hossein. 'The Islamic World-View and Modern Science', *Islamic Quarterly*, vol 39, no 2, 1995: 73–89.

Nasr, Seyyed Hossein. 'Perennial Ontology and Quantum Mechanics: A Review Essay of *The Quantum Enigma* by Wolfgang Smith', *Sophia: A Journal of Traditional Studies*, vol 3, no 1 (Summer 1997): 135–159.

Nasr, Seyyed Hossein. 'Reply to Shu-Hsien Liu', in LE Hahn, RE Auxier, and LW Stone, Jr, editor (2001), 270–276.

Plantinga, Alvin. 'Science: Augustinian or Duhemian?', *Faith and Philosophy*, vol 13, 1996.

Peters, Ted, Muzaffar Iqbal, and Syed Nomanul Haq, editors. *God, Life, and the Cosmos: Christian and Islamic Perspectives* (Ashgate, 2002).

Ragep, F Jamil. 'Freeing Astronomy from Philosophy: An Aspect of Islamic Influence on Science', in Brooke, Osler, and van der Meer (*Osiris*, 2001), 49–71.

Ragep, F Jamil and Sally P Ragep. *Tradition, Transmission, Transformation* (Leiden-New York-Koln: EJ Brill, 1996).

Sabra, AI. 'The Appropriation and Subsequent Naturalization of Greek Science in Medieval Islam: A Preliminary Statement', *History of Science*, 1987: 223–243.

Smith, Wolfgang. '*Sophia Perennis* and Modern Science', in LE Hahn, RE Auxier, and LW Stone, Jr, editors (2001), 469–485.

Van Fraassen, Bas C *Quantum Mechanics: An Empiricist View* (New York: Oxford University Press, 1991).

Part Two

Science and the Sacred

4

Perceiving God in the Lawfulness of Nature: Scientific and Religious Reflections

Philip Clayton

Physical science, it might appear, leaves no place for divine action. For modern science presupposes that the universe is a closed physical system, that interactions are regular and lawlike, that all causal histories can be traced, and that anomalies will ultimately have physical explanations. But the traditional belief that God acts in the world conflicts with all four of these conditions: it presupposes that the universe is open, that God acts from time to time according to his purposes, that the ultimate source and explanation of these actions is the divine will, and that no earthly account would ever suffice to explain God's actions.

The theistic traditions rely on an important resource: the notion of *law*. We do not need to assume that *either* the universe functions solely under the rule of natural law *or* that it suffers under the rule of a capricious deity. Instead, to believe in God is to assert that the laws of physics, chemistry and biology are supplemented by further laws: the laws of human nature, the moral law, the revealed law, and the never-changing, essential characteristics of the divine nature, or what we might call the law of the divine nature. Muslims, Jews and Christians believe in natural law *and* revealed law.

But is it possible to use the one word *law* to cover such diverse topics? Or do we equivocate when we use the term in both senses? After all, the meaning of the word *law* is vastly different when it describes the regular acceleration of a falling object than when it describes fundamental guidelines for human living. Perhaps the same notion should *not* be used to express both claims. Only if we can find some broader account of what features are shared in common between the natural realm and the supernatural real—only then, perhaps, can we explain what it means to *perceive* God in the lawfulness of nature.

1. Science and the challenge of determinism

Physical determinism is fundamentally a claim about causal *laws*—the claim, namely, that all that happens is a necessary and lawlike effect of antecedent causes. It entails that the causal chain is all of a piece; no one cause stands out from the others as more fundamental. For example, neither genes in the biological sphere nor intentions in the realm of psychological can be taken as the Areal determining factors without reference to *their* causal antecedents. At the same time, determinism claims that all physical occurrences are lawful: the universe is such that a given set of physical events can give rise to only one successor set.

Debates about determinism often turn into debates about what is physically possible. In a broad sense of the term, it is physically possible that a supernatural law exists—a set of ideals for how humans should live and, for each law, specific consequences that follow from observing or denying this law. But how, the scientist asks, could this law be known? Surely not by the methods of the sciences. If not by science, how could this other law be known at all? What other ways *are* there of knowing? If there are other ways of knowing—say, knowledge through revelation from God—how are they compatible with the work of science? Do they not negate all science whatsoever? If there are indeed multiple ways of knowing, are they consistent: do they lead to compatible results? And if so, is there any overarching perspective from which the laws of science and the laws of revelation can be thought—a single, unified, systematic perspective that might embrace them all?

2. Five types of law

Enough has been said about the first type of law (natural law) to underscore the difficulty that theists face today. After analyzing this difficulty I shall turn to the other four types of law in order to see whether they are sufficient to overcome it.

The way that scientists speak of natural law may sound strange to the ears of Muslim, Jewish and Christian theists. After all, all three traditions maintain that the laws and regularities in the natural world exist only because of the One who designed them all. The laws of nature reflect something of the character of nature's Creator. For believers, *natural law is part of revealed law*. This belief in creation by

God has several implications: First, studying the laws of nature provides a window, however dusty it may be, into the mind and creative intent of its source. Second, those laws cannot in the end be comprehended fully without reference to the One whose nature they reflect.

Yet this perspective is foreign to most scientists today. How then can we reconnect the realm of natural law and the realm of divine action? To many they seem to express the tensions of a dualism, even a contradiction: the creation *versus* God, the natural *versus* the supernatural. Although the word *law* is used in both senses, any apparent connections may be dwarfed by the enormous gap between the two meanings today. Unless we can find some sort of a mediation, one worries that the tensions will outweigh the similarities.

I suggest that our religious traditions *do* offer a mediation, in the form of an intermediate point, which helps to make the conceptual transition between the natural and the supernatural. The Muslim, Jewish and Christian traditions speak not only of physical nature, but also of *human* nature. If there is a human nature, there are presumably also underlying laws that characterize the beings that we are. The laws of human nature thus represent the second type of law. To understand what I mean by the *law* of human being, it is helpful to think of *the form of man*, a concept first developed by Aristotle and then adapted for the context of monotheism by Ibn Rushd (Averrroes). These laws of human nature, however we may finally formulate them, express our connection with the other animals and with the biological evolution of life forms on earth; they thus tie us with the entire natural order. At the same time, they include distinctively human features—features such as rationality, self-consciousness, and the awareness of moral obligations —that point toward the third and fourth types of law.

The third type of law is the *moral* law. If you accept that this type of law exists, then you accept that some laws express not only descriptive regularities—regularities of fact, if you will—but also *normative* regularities, regularities as *ideals* for our behavior. Moral law describes a regularity toward which all humans should strive, whereas natural law describes a regularity from which natural objects cannot diverge. Introducing the idea of moral law thus marks a crucial transition, however: rather than connoting actions that *must* occur, moral laws now focus on actions that *ought to* occur. Indeed, this *ought* implies that not all actions in fact correspond to the moral law. To speak of moral law is to admit that much falls short of the ideal: our actions, our characters, our institutions, our religious practice.

For theists, moral laws exist as a reflection of the nature of God. As Thomas Aquinas argued, if God is Goodness itself (*bonum ipse*), then every good action participates in some way in the divine nature. (Must we not then say that in every good action God Himself also act—that the good part of the action reflects a partnership between the human agent and the One who is the source of all Goodness?) At any rate, our religious traditions have spoken of this goodness as an inherent, necessary feature of the being of God. With this recognition we encounter the fourth sense of law. Goodness is, if you will, a *law* of the divine nature. Indeed, for the theologian this fourth sense of law actually has priority over all the rest. Think of it as a generalization of the argument I just sketched: not only Goodness, but *all law*, all regularity, exists only as an extension or reflection of the divine nature. For example, nature is lawlike only insofar as it participates in the divine nature. There is natural law only because God's nature is to be regular, reliable, enduring, loving and trustworthy—in short, because it is the nature of God to be lawlike. And the laws of morality and of human nature likewise exist for the same (theological) reason.

Finally, there is a fifth type of law that plays a crucial role for Muslims, Jews and Christians: *Revealed Law*. Revealed law shares three features with the other types of law: it encompasses both the natural world and human beings; it describes regularities that God has established in the created world and in human nature; and it presents ideals which all humans are called to follow. In this paper my goal is to think together revealed Law and the laws that we discover through the study of the natural world, rather than treating them as opposed to one another.

3. The search for analogies

The key question is: What are the analogies between natural law and revealed Law? Can we discover a unified framework that leaves place for both—one that describes the similarities between them from a single overarching perspective? Since theists believe that both types of law issue forth from a single God, it should be possible to express a theological vision that recognizes and formulates this unity. Given the challenge raised by the sciences today, it is extremely important that

Muslims, Jews and Christians become partners in responding to this challenge.

Of course, I must admit that this project is not popular in today's world. Nor, during much of the modern period, did one find significant portions of Muslim, Jewish and Christian thought devoted to expressing the synthesis of natural and revealed law. As a result, naturalists grew bolder in asserting that there *is* no unified vision of the cosmos, except perhaps at the level of matter and natural law.

The silence of theists on this topic is not only unfortunate but also surprising given the great tradition of reflection on the topic that exists in all three of our traditions, especially in the classical or medieval period. At that time it seemed that the best of scientific thought (then called natural philosophy), the best of metaphysics, and the best of revealed truth could be synthesized into a single system. One thinks of the synthesis of Hebrew thought and Plato in the work of Philo, of the integration of Islam and Aristotle in Ibn Rushd, and of the Christian Aristotelian system of Thomas Aquinas. Recently, there are signs that Muslims, Jews and Christians are returning to this great theological project and are finding important new resources for speaking to the contemporary world. In what follows I consider four of the most promising options that our traditions have bequeathed to us.

4. Four options for thinking together natural and revealed law

(1) *God as Being Itself.* All else exists only insofar as it participates in its Divine Source. This view was first developed in the context of monotheism by Al-Farabi, although its most famous exponent is Ibn Sina (Avicenna). Similar positions, strongly influenced by Neo-platonism, dominated Muslim thought in the tenth century. There is natural law, these theologians argue, only because all that is flows from God, whose nature it is to be regular, reliable, enduring and trustworthy—in short, because it is the nature of God to be lawlike. The laws of reason, morality and human nature likewise have their source in God.

The philosophy of Ibn Sina gives powerful expression to the absolute dependence of all things on God. Also, it is able to give a reason for the existence of the world (as that which emanates from God), in contrast to those views that make the world a brute fact, that is, a random outcome of an unexplained decision of God (voluntarism).

(Of course, some have charged that certain of the teachings of Ibn Sina, such as the necessary emanation of the world from God and the minimal degree to which God could have knowledge of the world, are incompatible with orthodox Muslim teaching. This is not a controversy that I am competent to resolve. It is worth pointing out, however, how powerfully (and how beautifully) the great ninth and tenth century Muslim theologians were able to combine their philosophical quest for a grand intellectual synthesis with their religious and mystical quest for connection with God. Clearly, any reappropriation of classical Islamic philosophy today will have to retain the same deep pursuit of the inner experience of God that tempered Ibn Sina's thought and transformed it into an expression of faith.[1])

(2) *God as the form of all things.* Ibn Rushd (Averroes, 1126–1198), the greatest advocate of Muslim Aristotelianism, forged the strongest alliance between the Greek philosophical tradition and belief in one God. His system not only *completed* Greek thought in the eyes of theists; it also set the stage for the Scholastic period in Christian theology, which produced the greatest systematic works of philosophical theology in my own tradition. Ibn Rushd's teachings on creation (eg, the direct creation of the higher intelligences by God) show how God could be the direct Cause of the world and hence its Maker; they thus come closer to the Biblical and Koranic picture of creation than had his Neoplatonic predecessors. Because Ibn Rushd makes *essence* more fundamental than being (in his thought, being supervenes on essence), he is able to draw a sharper distinction between God and what God creates. God is essentially good, eternal, all-powerful and all-knowing, whereas created things are essentially dependent on God while lacking God's essential characteristics.

For Ibn Rushd, created things participate in the forms supplied by God, who is the *Giver of Forms*. These patterns or forms are the deeper foundations for what we today call laws. Since they are not primarily physical in nature, there is no reason to limit the realm of law to the physical world: as long as there is a form (formal essence) for humanity, there must also be laws of human nature. And since forms represent the ideals for all created things, it is natural to speak of moral law and revealed law as ideal patterns for behavior. We become like

---

1.   RC Zaehner, *Hindu and Muslim Mysticism* (London, 1960), eg pages 162ff.

God insofar as we participate in His formal nature. But because of the essential differences between God and world, our participation in God via the forms does not lead to the confusion of natural being and divine being that (Ibn Rushd believed) appeared in the work of the earlier philosophers.

(3) *The Idealist tradition.* The eighteenth and nineteenth centuries brought new resources for thinking a being who exists primarily as subject. Based on these developments it has become possible to specify the differences in the mode of being between *things* and *subjects* in a way that was not possible using only the Greek concept of substance. As a result, Muslim, Jewish and Christian thinkers can now draw distinctions in speaking of the God-world relationship that were unavailable to the classical medieval thinkers in our three traditions. Specific problems, such as the tendency toward pantheism in thinkers such as al-Bustami and al-Hallaj, can therefore now be avoided. Moreover, we can now express the crucial differences between the rule of law for an electron or a cell and the rule of law in the life of a human being. Only after we have shown scientists that the notion of law that works in physics is not sufficient for explaining the actions of at least one entity in the natural world—namely, ourselves—can we begin to argue that the notion of revealed law may be indispensable as well.

(4) *Emergence and process thought.* The twentieth century has not been utterly bereft of metaphysical progress. In the last decades major attacks have been made on the atomist and materialist philosophies that once dominated modern thought. The new sciences of emergence, for example, recognizes that events in the natural world are not explained solely by *reducing* them to their smallest components, but also by linking objects and events to the broader and broader contexts of which they are a part.[2] *Law* takes on ever new meanings as one moves up the ladder of emergence to the level of beings with free will such as ourselves.

Working together with emergence theorists, process philosophers have managed to conceive the ebb and flow of history—and the God who interacts with this world-in-process'—without losing sight of the eternal and unchanging side of God, which they call God's *antecedent*

---

2.   Philip Clayton, *The Emergence of Spirit* (Oxford: Oxford University Press, 2004).

nature.[3] They have also described what it means for God to be *law-giver* in a way that is consistent with God's nature as the highest personal being who aims to draw all other persons to himself. The divine law must not function in a deterministic fashion, like the laws of Newton; instead, it must lure us toward God, lifting us by example, by understanding and by love.

Like the Idealist philosophies of the human and divine subject, emergence theory and process thought offer a means for us today to extend the work of the great religious philosophers of the classical age, to overcome their inadequacies, and to show in new ways how science, philosophy and theology can relate to each other in a harmonious fashion.

In the end, however, we will not possess an adequate theistic meta-physics until we have modified the earlier options in light of the insights of Idealist thought, process philosophy, and emergence. There will be no reconciliation of natural law and revealed law until we theists have learned in this way to incorporate the newer results of science and their metaphysical implications. We may differ on the details of the resulting position. But we can perhaps agree on a more basic point: that faith and science, natural law and revealed law, will remain opposed to one another until we learn to engage again in the *type* of reflection that Ibn Sina and Ibn Rushd have modeled for us so brilliantly.

5. Conclusion

It is time to summarize the thesis of my argument: natural law and revealed law are conceptually different, but they need not be at war with one another; one can research and respect both. One way to overcome the widespread sense that they are opposed to one another is to follow the conceptual progression through the five types of law: natural law, the laws of human nature, moral law, the *laws* of the nature of the divine, and revealed law. When we recognize the metaphysical similarities and differences between the five types of law—or better: when we formulate a metaphysical system broad enough to encompass all five—we have the chance to leave behind the

---

3.   David Ray Griffin, *Reenchantment without Supernaturalism: A Process Philosophy of Religion* (Ithaca, NY: Cornell University Press, 2001).

expensive, damaging, and unnecessary oppositions between science and theology.

In recent years we have entered a period in which metaphysics, the systematic project of thought, has again become possible. Of course, one must not be naïve: there are many forces today that make such a mediating project difficult and, in the eyes of some, impossible. At the same time, there are also grounds for optimism. Consider some of the recent changes:

- Muslims, Jews and Christians are coming together to consider what we share in common as believers in the one God. Meetings like the one from which these volume arose are now taking place around the world. Consider what it means that Indonesia, the most populous Muslim nation in the world, has invited Jewish and Christian scholars to join with Muslim scholars in reflecting on the one world known by science and on the one God in whom we all believe. Meetings of this sort demonstrate that there need be no tension between the belief in God and the best results of natural science. Indeed, the common task that we share is to show that belief in God actually *supplements* those results; it answers the very questions that the sciences raise but leave unanswered.

- The science of our day is increasingly open to such a synthesis. There was a time when Newton's laws seemed to reign supreme, when it was believed that all could be reduced to *particles in motion*, when the universe seemed to lack beginning or end, and when the laws of nature, strictly interpreted, seemed to rule all interactions from electrons through simple organisms and even to human action itself. But those days are past. The science of our day has accepted limitations on prediction (quantum theory), on axiomatisation (Gödel's Theorem), on determinism (the Copenhagen interpretation of quantum physics), on atomism (Bell's inequalities and non-locality experiments), and on the law-based understanding of human behavior (Davidson's anomalous monism). Emergence theory now suggests that nature is *upwardly open*. For example, the upwardly-open nature of human consciousness, infused as it is with intimations of immortality, offers a powerful model of the integration of mind and spirit—exactly the sort of picture that theists have long sought to place at the center of the God-world relation. Just as the neurophysiological structure of the higher primates is upwardly open to the emergence and causal power of the mental, so the mental or cultural world is upwardly open to the influence of the Creator Spirit.

• The *philosophy* of science has also began to change its tone. Early in the twentieth century it was broadly held that materialism, atomism, determinism, and reductionism were the only valid philosophical positions in light of science. Far fewer voices are making that claim today. In fact, each of these four *isms* has come under attack of late, and strong arguments have been given *from within the philosophy of science* to reject each one of them. Such changes signal a new openness to holism in the philosophy of science.

• The West, which was dominated by secularism during the middle of the twentieth century, has recently become the location of a renewed interest in what is called *spirituality*. More and more people in the West today look for a sense of the spiritual nature of reality in many places: in nature, in human relations, and in the psyche itself. The spirituality movement is not yet religion, perhaps, nor is it equivalent with theism. But it is overturning the secular emphasis which was dominant in the West for so many decades, if not centuries. It should not be disregarded, since it offers an opportunity for demonstrating anew the explanatory power of the mono-theistic traditions.

• Finally, we are beginning to see a renaissance of metaphysics, that is, of systematic reflection on the nature and activity of God. Logical positivism may have declared metaphysics dead; yet it seems to have been logical positivism that has met its demise. Of particular interest, Muslim, Jewish and Christian theists are now engaged again in exploring the broad explanatory power of the notion of God.

In light of these developments, it is especially significant that all three of our traditions have shared roots in the great intellectual tradition of the Middle Ages. Of course, one cannot simply bring Ibn Sina or Ibn Rushd without commentary into the contemporary world;

they must be updated and made consistent with science as it has developed since their time. But their fundamental metaphysical insights offer powerful invitations for systematic thinkers today.

Thus I close with this call: Let us draw on the best of recent science, the best of our philosophical traditions, and the best of our scriptural sources in order to restate a theistic vision for the twenty-first century. Let us learn from each other as we return to our theological traditions in order to find a powerful voice for the coming decades. Let us meet together, in Indonesia and elsewhere, in order to renew the constructive encounter between theology and science as it was so powerfully pursued by the great thinkers of the past. After all, the integration of religion and science does not mean the elimination of the uniqueness of either pole. Both are essential. Only the methods of natural science can unveil the natural laws that undergird the cosmos. And only theology can lead to an understanding of what theists call revealed law—the nature of God and of God's plans for humanity as they are known through revelation.

There are of course differences between our three traditions in the understanding of revelation. Differences are good; they reflect the richness, and add to the diversity, of these three great *religions of the Book*. But there are also fundamental similarities—we share much more in common than divides us. None of us has to compromise on the core beliefs of our particular religions in order to acknowledge all that also binds us together as theists.

Let this text, then, be a call to renewal. Theists have much to say to a secular world. We offer a vision that extends beyond natural law to include the dimensions of moral law and revealed law as well. May the meeting of minds between the three traditions help us to find our voice again: both individually—as Muslim, Jewish and Christian believers —and collectively, as theists who believe in the One God and Creator, may His name be glorified.

5

Sacred Science vs Secular Science

Mehdi Golshani

I. Introduction

The *Encyclopedia Britanica* defines 'sacred' in the following way: 'The power, being or realm understood by religious persons to be at the core of existence and to have a transformative effect on their lives and destinies'. In the Islamic outlook everything is centered around God. Thus, the word sacred (*muqaddas*) is principally applied to God, but by extension it could be applied to other things, in proportion to their role in bringing proximity to God. This includes knowledge in its generic sense. Here we shall elaborate on the characteristics of sacred knowledge.

2. Islam and knowledge

The word *'ilm'* and its derivatives are frequently used in the Qur'an. It means 'knowledge' in its generic sense, including the sciences of nature and humanities:

> And we taught him the making of coats of mail for you, that they might protect you in your wars . . . (21: 80)

> ·And we have not taught him poetry, nor is it meet for him . . . (36: 69)

It also includes both revealed and acquired knowledge:

> Then they found one from among Our servants whom We had granted mercy from Us and whom We had taught knowledge from Ourselves.(18: 65)

. . . and they learn what harms them and does not
benefit them . . . (2: 102)

The Holy Qur'an has a high praise for the learned:

. . . God raises the ranks of those among you who
believe and those who were granted the knowledge . .
(58: 11).

The Islamic tradition too is full of praise for knowledge and the
learned. Thus, eg, we have from the Holy Prophet Muhammad
(SAWS) that 'The acquisition of knowledge is incumbent on every
Muslim',[1] and that 'Seek knowledge even if it is in China'.[2]

Thus, seeking knowledge is a religious quest in the Islamic
outlook.

The aforementioned verses and prophetic sayings indicate clearly
that the acquisition of knowledge, in the Islamic view, is not to be
confined to the specifically religious sciences, as, eg China was not a
proper place to learn Islamic teachings. There is, however, a constraint
on the type of knowledge recommended by Islam. The holy Qur'an
rebukes those who seek the kind of knowledge which does not benefit
its owner:

. . . they learn what is harmful and does not benefit
them . . . (2: 102).

The same point is narrated from the Holy Prophet (SAWS):

Ask God for useful knowledge, and seek refuge in
God from that kind of knowledge which does not
benefit.[3]

---

1.   Ibn Majah, *Sunan* (Damascus: Dar al-Fikr,?) Introduction, Sec. 17, No
      224; Kulayni, *al-Usul min al-Kafi* (Beirut: Dar Sa`b Dar al-Ta`aruf,
      1401 H.).

2.   AM al- Ghazzali, *Ihya Ulum al-Din* (Beirut: Dar al-Ma`rifah,?), vol 1,
      14; Majlisi, MB, *Bihar al-Anwar* (Beirut: Dar Ihya al-Turath al- Arabi,
      1403 H.), vol 1, 180.

3.   Ibn Majah, *op cit*, vol 2, Sec 1263, no 3843.

The word 'useful' is not used here in a utilitarian sense. To clarify this point, we have to refer to the Islamic idea of human life.

According the Holy Qur'an, human beings were created to worship God: And I have not created the Jinn and the men except that they should serve Me (51: 56).

The term 'worship' is an all inclusive concept in the Islamic outlook. It applies to any action that pleases God. It is not confined, as some people have misunderstood, only to rituals such as prayer or fasting. For example, any contribution to the welfare of one's fellow human beings is a sort of God's worship.

Worship has two dimensions: believing in God and what God has revealed through His messengers (prophets), and doing good deeds: And as for him who believes and does good, he shall have goodly reward . . . (18: 88).

Now, in order to enable human beings to accomplish what they have been asked to do, God has endowed humankind with senses and all other essential faculties of learning:

> And Allah brought you forth from the wombs of your
> mothers—you did not know anything—and He gave
> you the hearing and the sight and the hearts that you
> may give thanks (16: 78).

Furthermore, God has provided many provisions for human beings in order to take full advantage of their role as Allah's trustees on earth.

> And He it is Who has made the sea subservient that
> you may eat fresh flesh from it and bring out from it
> ornaments which you wear, and you see the ships
> cleaving through it, and that you might seek of His
> bounty and that you may give thanks (16: 14).

They are also advised to make proper use of what God has provided for them and avoid making any kind of corruption on the earth:

> . . . and do good [to others] as Allah done good to you
> and do not seek to make mischief in the land; surely
> Allah does not love the mischief-makers (28: 77).

In fact, human beings are invited to take advantage of Allah's
blessings and compete in doing good deeds:

> Surely We have made whatever is on the earth an
> embellishment for it, so that We may try them [as to]
> which of them is best in works (18: 7).

Thus, useful knowledge is the kind of knowledge that gives a God-
centered orientation to human beings in both theoretical and practical
ways. This can be guaranteed if knowledge is framed within a proper
theistic worldview. In the Islamic context, the Islamic worldview
provides such a framework. In this paper we define sacred knowledge
(science) as the kind of knowledge (science) which is framed within
the context of the theistic Islamic worldview. Sacred knowledge
differs from the secular knowledge in its philosophical
presuppositions, inspirations and goals. It is centered around God and
is supposed to lead to him.

3. Islam and the sciences of nature

The Holy Qur'an refers to natural phenomena as the signs of God and
recommends the study of various phenomena of nature as a path
towards knowing and serving God. To quote the Qur'an:

> And among His signs is the creation of the heavens
> and the earth and the diversity of your languages and
> colours; surely there are signs in this for the learned
> (30: 22).

> Say, behold what is it that is in the heavens and the
> earth . . . (10: 101).

> Say, travel in the earth and see how He originated the
> creation . . . (29: 20).

The Islamic tradition considers the reflection on God's Handiwork as one of the best types of God's worship. For example, it is narrated from Imam Ali (AS) that: There is no worship like reflection on God's creation.[4]

In the Qur'anic outlook, the study of nature is not for its own sake, but it is supposed to serve as a means of bringing one closer to God. The Muslim scientists of the past believed that God's wisdom is reflected in His creation. In the words of al-Biruni, one of the most distinguished Muslim scientists of the eleventh century:

> When a person decides to discriminate between truth and falsehood, he has to study the universe and find out whether it is eternal or created. If somebody thinks that he does not need this kind of knowledge, he is, however, in need of thinking about the laws that govern our world, in part or in its entirety. This leads him to know the truth about them, and paves the way for knowing the Designer of the universe, and His attributes . . .
>
> This is, in fact, the kind of truth that God enjoined His knowledgeable servants to search for, and God spoke the truth when He said:
>
> . . . and reflect upon the creation of the heavens and the earth [saying]: 'Our Lord You have not created this in vain [3: 191].' This verse contains what I explained in detail, and if one works according to it, he/she can have access to all branches of knowledge and cognition.[5]

Similarly, the founders of modern science did not pursue the study of natural phenomena as a means of understanding nature per se or

---

4.　M Rayshahri, *Mizan al-Hikmah* (Tehran: Dar al-Hadith, 1416 H.), vol 3, 2465.

5.　al-Biruni, Abu Rayhan, *Kitab Tahdid Nihayat al-Amakin li-Tashin Masafat al-Masakin*, Persian translated by A Aram (Tehran: Tehran University Press, 1352 HS), 3–4.

for the sake of their own gratification, but as a means of proximity to God. As Robert Boyle put it:

> When with bold telescopes I survey the old and newly discovered stars and planets . . . when with excellent microscopes I discern nature's curious workmanship; when with the help of anatomical knives and the light of chymical furnaces I study the book of nature . . . I find myself exclaiming with the psalmist, How manifold are thy works, O God, in wisdom hast thou made them all.[6]

4. Some important elements of the Islamic worldview

A worldview is a framework within which our minds operate. It includes our metaphysical and epistemological presuppositions about God, the universe and humanity. Our world-view affects our decisions, priorities, values and goals. It brings our thoughts to a unified whole.

Here we mention those elements of the Islamic worldview that affect knowledge in general and the sciences of nature in particular.

(1) The unicity of God (*al-Tawhid*)
The idea of oneness of God is the most basic concept in Islam. It implies the unity of the creation, ie the interrelatedness of all parts of the world. This, in turn, implies the unity of knowledge. Thus, the goal of scientific enterprise has to be the manifestation of the underlying unity of the created world. This means that various scientific disciplines should be synthesised to give a harmonious picture of the world.

According to the holy Qur'an, the unity of nature is a reflection of the unity of the creator:

> If there were [in the heaven and the earth] other gods besides Allah, there would have been confusion in both . . . (21: 22).

---

6. R Boyle, *The Advancement of Learning* (1605), A Johnston editor (Oxford: Clarendo Press, 1974), 42.

Thus, from the contemplation upon the unicity of nature one is supposed to conclude the unity of the Creator. Muslim philosophers have argued from the unicity of nature to the existence of the Creator. In Mulla-Sadra's words:

> The relation of existents to each other . . . is a testimony to the fact that their Creator is absolutely unique. Furthermore, although each part of a human person is intrinsically distinct from other parts, because they are integrated in a natural way and some benefit from others and have a unified order, they indicate that their Designer and Sustainer from dispersion and dissolution is a unique Authority, a unique Principle. Similarly, although world's bodies and forces are separated from each other and are distinct from others by a particular action, because they belong to an orderly system and there is a natural integration between them, they are testimony to the fact that their Creator, Designer and Sustainer, is a real Authority that sustains them.[7]

It was under the influence of Qur'anic teachings that Muslim scientists of classical era emphasized the organic inter-relatedness of various branches of knowledge and tried to embed all imported knowledge within the God-centered matrix of Islamic worldview.

Throughout the human history, there has been a steady effort to find a unity behind the apparent multiplicity of the natural order. Thus, scientists and philosophers of all ages tried to present a unified picture of the world. From the Greek time until our contemporary era the quest for unification has been going on. In our era, we have witnessed the effort of theoretical physicists for the unification of the fundamental forces of nature. But, if for some contemporary physicists the unification of forces and access to a theory of everything is the end of the story, for a believing scientist it is the first step in the quest for the Creator and the sustainer of this harmonious universe:

---

7.   M Mulla-Sadra, *al-Mabda` wa al-Ma`ad* (Qum: Markaz-e Intesharat-e Daftar-e Tablighat-e Islami, 1422 H), 162.

Mehdi Golshani

> In the creation of the heavens and the earth, and the
> alternation between night and day, there are signs for
> the prudent persons. [Those] who remember God
> while standing, sitting and [lying] on their sides, and
> mediate on the creation of the heavens and the earth,
> saying: 'Our Lord, You have not created this in vain!
> Glory be to you! . . . (3: 190-191).

The unitary view about the created order was common among all
celebrated Muslim scientists of the past. Thus, they did not promote
some spheres of knowledge at the expense of others. Today, however,
there is hardly any dialogue between the sciences of nature and the
human sciences. Specialisation has led to the fragmentation of
knowledge and this, in turn, has prevented the learned from getting a
unified picture of the physical world and has narrowed the range of
inquiry. Heisenberg explains this point beautifully:

> Today the scientist's pride is love of detail, the
> discovery and systematizing of the smallest
> revelations of nature within a narrowly circumscribed
> field. This is naturally accompanied by a higher
> esteem for the craftsman in a special subject, the
> virtuoso, at the expense of an appreciation of the value
> of interrelations on a large scale. During this period
> one can hardly speak of a unified scientific view of
> nature, at least not as far as content is concerned. The
> world of the individual scientist is the narrow section
> of nature to which he devotes his life's work.[8]

In our age, there is no choice for scientists but to specialize, and the
specialisation by itself is not a problem. What we have to deplore is
scientist's loss of a unified picture of the universe and specialist's
unwarranted generalisation from his/her proper field of research to
other areas. Attention to interdisciplinary studies, which is becoming
popular these days, attenuates this problem.

---

8.   W Heisenberg, *Philosophical Problems of Quantum Physics*
      (Woodbridge, Conn: Ox Bow Press, 1979), 80.

(2) Faith in supra-natural realities and limitation of human knowledge
According to the Holy Qur'an, our external sources are essential for
understanding nature:

> And God brought you forth from the wombs of your
> mothers—you did not know anything—and He gave
> you the hearing and the sight and the heart, so that
> you may be thankful (16: 78).

But, in the Qur'anic outlook, sense data are not enough for
understanding nature, because all that we get from our senses are
isolated pieces. It is our intellect that relates these pieces together. As
EF Schumacher elegantly put it:

> We 'see' not simply with our eyes but with a great
> part of our mental equipment as well, and since this
> mental equipment varies greatly from person to
> person, there are inevitably many things which some
> people can 'see' while others cannot, or, to put
> differently, for which some people are adequate while
> others are not.[9]

Thus, there are people who have the regular senses, but cannot
correlate their observations and cannot reflect on them:

> . . . they have hearts with which they do not
> understand and they have eyes with which they do
> not see, and they have ears with which they do not
> hear . . . (7: 179).

Furthermore, there are realities in the world about which we
cannot get any information through our external senses:

> Glory be to Him Who created pairs of things, of what
> the earth grows, of their own kind and of what they
> do not know (36: 36).

---

9.   EF Schumacher, *A Guide for the Perplexed* (London: Jonathan Cape
      Ltd, 1977), 52.

And God's is the invisible in the heavens and the
earth . . . (11: 123).

In fact, the Holy Quran mentions two realms: the invisible world
(_lim al-ghayb) and the visible world (_lim al-shah_dah). The knowledge
of the invisible can only be acquired through the revelation (*wahy*):

Say [O! Muhammad]: 'I do not tell you that I possess
the treasures of God, nor do I know the invisible, nor
do I tell you I am an angel. I only follow what is
revealed to me . . . (6: 50).

In short, not all of our information about the world is sense-rooted,
and there are many realities in the world to which we do not have any
access.

The belief in the limitation of human knowledge and the existence
of supra-sensible realities indicates that we should not stop at the level
of sensible realities and we should never claim to have reached a full
understanding of natural phenomena at a certain time.

In the contemporary physics, some theories involve things that are
even in principle unobservable. As an example we cite the case of
extra dimensions introduced by superstring theory or M–theory.

According to the Holy Quran, the prophets were endowed with
special intellectual powers which enabled them to see some truths that
are hidden from normal people. The teachings of the prophets are
essential for guiding human conduct and for enlarging humanity's
vision of the created reality.

(3) Belief in a purposeful universe
In the Qur'anic view, God created everything in measure and decreed
for it a telos: We have not created the heavens and the earth, and
whatsoever is between them, for vanity . . . (38: 27).

The Holy Qur'an talks about a universal notion of purpose and
direction to the created universe: He [Moses] said 'our Lord is He who
gave everything its creation. Then guided it' (20: 50).

This sense of direction is rather evident in the human sphere, but it
is naive to deny it for other categories of existence only on the basis of
our current knowledge of the physical world.

The Qur'anic notion of a *telos* to the created universe is accompanied by the notion of Hereafter, where everything meets its proper destination and the pious feel the presence of God. Without a Hereafter, the whole creation would be in vain:

> Did you think that We created you only for sport and that you would not be returned to Us? (23: 115).

> Do they not reflect within themselves; Allah did not create the heavens and the earth and what is between them but with truth and for an appointed term? And most of the people are deniers of meeting their Lord (30: 8).

(4) Commitments to moral values
The Holy Qur'an considers the commitment to moral values as one of the main objectives of the prophetic mission:

> He is the One Who dispatched a messenger from the unlettered among themselves, to recite His verses to them and to purify them and teach them the Book and wisdom, even though previously they were in obvious error (62: 2).

The Holy Prophet Muhammad (SAWS) said the same thing: Verily, I was sent out to complete high moral standards.[10]

Islam's expectation of Muslims is total commitment to moral values at all stages of their lives.

In the Islamic outlook, one's scientific training should be accompanied by one's ethical education. This is needed to stimulate one's moral concern and responsibility.

5. Some basic points concerning sacred science

The concepts 'sacred science' and 'secular science' are confusing to some people. They say science is an objective value—free enterprise,

---

10. al-Muttaqi, *Kanz al-`Ummal* (Beirut: Moassesah al-Resalah, 1985), vol 3, no 5217, 16; Majlisi, MB, *op cit*, vol 16, 210.

ie it is neutral to all religions and ideologies. Science and religion (or ideology) are two independent spheres of human concern and there is no meaning for talking of Western science or sacred science, etc. Science has a distinctive universal methodology, consisting of experimentation, observation and theoretical work. These are all universal, leaving no room for different kinds of science.

This naive understanding of science and scientific work arises from the neglect of the limitations of science and the roles that philosophies and ideologies have played in science. It is thought that whatever is taught under the banner of science is a scientific fact, rooted in objective reality.

In our view science cannot be divorced from values completely and scientific work is heavily loaded with philosophical and religious presuppositions, and metaphysics plays a very important role at all levels of scientific activity, though this could take place unconsciously. It is too simplistic to think that philosophical or ideological commitments won't enter into the fabric of science.

Here we elaborate on these points in more detail.

(1) The myth of value—free scientific activity

It is normally said that science, as a proper study of nature, and ethics, in the sense of rules of conduct, are two independent spheres of human concern. We admit that one cannot derive 'ought statements' from 'factual statements' straightforwardly. But, we believe that these two categories of statements are related both at the metaphysical level and at the practical level. They meet at the metaphysical level, because one's worldview affects whatever he does. Thus, it provides a bridge between facts and values. They are related at the practical level too, because the whole scientific enterprise involves value-judgments—in the choice of theories and in the applications of science and its technological offspring.

The progress of science in modern era has been effective in marginalising ethical considerations and has led to the spread of moral relativism in modern societies. Furthermore, the wide spread belief among scientists about the absolute separation of facts and values has undermined the role of ethics in the scientific enterprise.

Here, we present some evidences about the myth of value-neutrality of scientific enterprise:

- Scientific activity is a goal—directed enterprise. This means that some values play a guiding role in it. For example, search for truth is a value that has the role of a guiding principle for many scientists.
- All scientific activities involve value-judgments:

1. Some ethical codes like honesty, impartiality and integrity function as a quality control mechanism in the scientific enterprise.

2. Value-judgments can affect scientist's line of research or his/her choice of theories. For example Einstein and Heisenberg had a special emphasis on the simplicity of physical theories. On the other hand, Dirac emphasised on the beauty of physical theories. Pragmatic considerations are some other people's criterion for the choice of theories.

3. Value-judgments affect decision making in the applications of science and technology. The outcome of certain applications of science and its technological offspring could affect a scientist's decision about his/her line of research.

4. Some scholars believe that secular science is ethically neutral, and to make it sacred it is enough to add an ethical dimension to its teachings and applications.

We do not share this view. This relegates religion to the limited domain of private life. Furthermore, as we shall show below the metaphysical basis of these two kinds of science are different as well, and this will have an appreciable effect on their outcomes.

(2) The important role of metaphysics in the scientific activity

Science is the study of nature through experimentation, observation and theoretical reasoning. Thus, on the surface science seems to be free of any non-scientific presuppositions. But, if this is true at the level of descriptions—like melting points—or descriptive laws—like the law of extension of length due to heat—it is not true at the level of explanation. In fact, scientific activity consists of two parts. The first one deals with the collection of facts. The second part deals with the organisation of facts, theoretical reasoning and the interpretation of the data. Now, the collection of facts could take place in a similar fashion in different parts of the globe. But, when we come to the introduction of concepts, theorising and the matter of interpretation, metaphysical presuppositions, religious convictions and psychological and sociological prejudices may intrude. Thus, it is in the choice of theories and the interpretation of empirical data that the difference between various scientists often manifests itself, and this is especially true when we are dealing with universal explanatory theories. Here, a believer looks at the facts and assimilates them within a theistic context, while an atheist interprets them according to his atheistic inclinations. Thus, to jump from the finite sphere of natural to the infinite domain of supernatural one needs a proper metaphysics that accommodates the supernatural.

Ernan McMullin argues that Newton's theistic worldview affected his theoretical work at the levels of inception, construction and development of his theory, and it shaped his theorizing:

> . . . Newton could not have developed his theories without metaphysical principles of some sort.
>
> There had to be decisions about where to make the cuts in Nature, about where to seek causal agency, about what should count as explanation. Such decisions went a long way beyond the inductive warrant afforded by earlier successful science. [11]

Andre Linde, an eminent contemporary Russian cosmologist, concurs that: When scientists start their work, they are subconsciously influenced by their cultural traditions. [12]

I have argued elsewhere[13] that some philosophical schools that prevailed in the early decades of the twentieth century appreciably affected the development of theoretical physics in that era and this sort of influence is still going on. McMullin, commenting on this point, writes:

> One might be tempted to think that regulative principles of a broadly metaphysical kind no longer play a role in the natural sciences. Yet even a moment of reflection about the current debates in elementary-

---

11. E Mc Mullin, *Newton on Matter and Activity* (Notre Dame: University of Notre Dame Press, 1978), 126–127.
12. *New Scientist*, vol 4, October 1997, 31.
13. M Golshani, *From Physics to Metaphysics* (Tehran: Institute for Humanities and Cultural Studies, 1997).

particle theory, in quantum field theory, in cosmology, aught to warn that this is far from the case. True the principles at issue might not be as overtly meta-physical as they often were in Newton's time, but the distinction is one of degree, not kind.[14]

Here we give two examples of the influence of metaphysical commitments on the interpretation of a theory. The first example is the case of the so-called 'anthropic principle'. Recent studies indicate that the emergence of life in the universe is rooted in the fact that the constants of nature, which, eg determine the strength of the fundamental forces of nature, are delicately balanced. A slight change in the strength of one of these forces, in one direction or another, would have eliminated the emergence of life in the universe. This fine tuning of the forces of nature is called the 'anthropic principle'. There are two basic interpretation of this empirical fact. The theist cosmologists have taken it as an indication of a divine plan. Others, especially those with atheistic inclinations, have introduced the idea of infinitely many universes, with all possible combinations of the constants of nature, thereby opening the possibility of the emergence of a universe with proper values of natural constants.

As another example, we cite Darwin's theory of evolution, according to which all living things have evolved by natural processes from preexisting forms and through the mechanism of natural selection. Some evolutionary biologists have taken this as an indication of the rule of chance—leaving no room for Divine action. To quote Richard Dawkin's: 'Chance with natural selection, chance smeared out into innumerable tiny steps over earns of time is powerful enough to manufacture miracles like dinosaurs and ourselves'.[15]

But, some other eminent biologists have interpreted the zoological data theistically. As Arthur Peacocke put it:

> I think the theory of evolution has articulated, unraveled and made clear to us how—to put it

---

14. E McMullin, *op cit*, 127.
15. Quoted from a BBC Program, Jan 1987, and published in M Poole, 'A Critique of Aspects of the Philosophy and Theology of Richard Dawkins', in *Science and Christian Belief*, 6, no 1, 41.

theologically—God has been creating life. The
evolutionary process is one which evolves new forms
of life to come into existence. But it does not answer
the questions why there should be such a process at
all.[16]

These examples, among others, indicate that when we go beyond
the descriptive level and begin to make cosmological inferences from
the available data, commonalities end and the differences between the
theist and the atheist become pronounced. Here decision making on
the basis of science alone is not possible, and the metaphysical
commitments of scientists intrude. Thus, although the observation,
the logic and the theoretical tools of analysis could be the same for
both, the interpretation could be different due to the deeper
metaphysical commitments of the scientists involved.

Furthermore, the extrapolations from limited empirical data to
general laws is always accompanied by explicit or implicit metaphysical assumptions. For example, when we perform some physics
experiments in our laboratory on the earth and extend its results to
other parts of the universe, we are assuming that the local laws of
physics are valid everywhere and for all times. This is not verifiable
empirically. We simply accept it as a matter of faith. Similarly, science
can talk about scientific laws, but it says nothing about the origin of
these laws. As George Ellis said: 'Essentially, investigations of the
foundations of science are beyond the scope of science itself'.[17]

In short, our scientific theories are influenced by our metaphysical
views about the nature of reality, and this, in turn, is often rooted in
our religious or cultural beliefs. Sometimes scientists are aware of
their underlying philosophical beliefs, though they do not admit it.
But very often philosophical biases act like an undercurrent beneath
the surface of the scientific activity. Max Jammes has put the matter
tastefully:

Physicists traditionally refrain from declaring
themselves as subscribing to a particular school of
philosophical thought, even if they are conscious of

---

16.   R Stannard, *Science and Wonders* (London: Farber & Farber, 1996), 54.
17.   GFR Ellis, *Before the Beginning: Cosmology Explained* (London:
      |Boyars/Bowerdean, 1993), 101.

belonging to it. The influence of particular philosophical climate on their scientific work, although
often of decisive importance for the formation of new
conceptions, is generally ignored. It is certainly true
that, philosophical considerations in their effect upon
the physicists' mind act more like an undercurrent
beneath the surface than like a patent well-defined
guiding line.[18]

Sometimes, it is said that science is based on established facts,
whereas religion is based on faith. This view neglects the fact that
even in science we accept certain things as a matter of faith. As Karl
Popper put it:

I am inclined to think that scientific discovery is
impossible without faith in ideas which are of a purely
speculative kind and sometimes crazy; a faith which is
quite unwarranted from the scientific point of view.[19]

and in the words of physicist Harry W Ellis:

If the existence of a benign supreme being is the
fundamental assumption at the heart of religion,
certainly the practice of science is founded on the
unprovable hypothesis that the universe is rational,
that its behavior is subject to human understanding.[20]

The renowned evolutionist Michael Ruse, who had claimed at the
well-known 1981 Arkansas trial that Darwinism required no
philosophical assumptions, reversed his position in his 1993 Address
to the Meeting of AAAS:

---

18. M James, *The Conceptual Development of Quantum Mechanics* (New
    York: Tomash Publishers, 1989), 174.
19. Quoted in John Barrow, *The Universe that Discovered Itself* (Oxford:
    Oxford University Press, 2000), 195.
20. HW Ellis, *Physics Today*, vol 35, Oct. 1982, 11.

> One should be sensitive to what I think history shows,
> namely that . . . evolution, akin to religion, involves
> making certain a priori or metaphysical assumptions,
> which at some level cannot be proved empirically. I
> guess we all knew that, but I think that we're all much
> more sensitive to these facts now.[21]

If we confine ourselves to mere empirical facts and do not seek
inclusive explanatory theories, there is no need to talk about sacred or
secular science. This approach reduces science to a collection of
prescriptions for prediction. But, this is not what the grand masters of
science have been after. Their aim was to understand our world and
this necessarily involves extrapolations that exceed the limits of
science per se. From Einstein, who was one of the most celebrated
physicists of the first-half of the twentieth century, to Witten, who is
one of the most eminent physicists of our time, we hear the same
thing: finding the principles according which the world works. As
Einstein put it:

> I want to know how God created this world. I am not
> interested in this or that phenomenon, in the spectrum
> of this or that element, I want to know His thoughts,
> the rest are details.[22]

and in the words of Witten:

> The purpose of being a physicist isn't just to learn how
> to calculate things. It is to understand the principles
> by which the world works.[23]

---

21. M Ruse, the session 'The New Antirevolutionism', in 1993 Annual
     Meeting of the American Association for the Advancement of Science,
     The Access Research Network web site.
22. A Einstein, *Ideas and Opinions* (New York: Bonanzer Books, nd), 67.
23. E Witten, in *Superstrings: A Theory of Everything*, edited by PCW
     Davies and J Brown (Cambridge: Cambridge University Press, 1988),
     98.

Another important point about the role of metaphysics in science is that some important metaphysical ideas have had a crucial influence on the progress of science. Here we cite two examples:

1. The idea of comprehensibility of nature is shared by all monotheistic religions. This, eg, can be easily inferred from the Holy Qur'an:

    We shall soon show them Our signs in the universe and in their own souls until it becomes clear to them that He is the truth . . . (14: 53).

Einstein admits that this idea is taken from the sphere of religion:

    To this [sphere of religion] there also belongs the faith in the possibility that the regulations for the world of existence are rational, that is comprehensible to reason.[24]

2. The idea of looking for the unification of natural forces is rooted in the monotheistic religions. The Russian born cosmologist Andre Linde, who is considered to be non-religious, admits this fact:

    The whole of modern cosmology has been deeply influenced by Western tradition of monotheism—the idea that it is possible to understand the universe through one ultimate 'theory of everything' is an outgrowth of belief in on God.[25]

Metaphysics can also affect goals and applications of science and its technological offspring. In a theistic framework, the applications of science are to be for securing humanity's felicity and for directing human endeavor towards supreme spiritual goals. Thus, eg, exploitation of natural resources as a source of power and domination or the pollution of environment is not allowed. The science and

---

24. AA Schilpp, Albert Einstein, *Philosopher-Scientist* (La Salle, Il: Open Court, 1970), 285.
25. A Linde, quoted by Jane Lampman, 'In Search of the "One Reality"', in *Christian Science Monitor* (May 9, 1998), B4.

technology of the last two centuries led to the disruption of balance between the spiritual and physical aspects of human life. This, in our view, is a result of the dominance of a secularistic worldview over the mind of scientists, politicians and even some religious institutions. The sacred science of the old times had the goal of discovering the secrets of God's handiwork in nature, where as modern secular science sees nature as a commodity to be exploited.

A scientist working within the matrix of Islamic worldview is careful and cautious in choosing the type of research he/she plans to engage into.

As we mentioned before, some people believe that all harmful products of science are the result of the indifference of modern science towards values and if ethical dimension is added to the scientific research, all misuses of science is going to disappear. While, we admit that many destructive results of the scientific enterprise is due to the neglect of the ethical dimension in science, we believe that part of the problems of the current science lies in its philosophical commitments—the contemporary science has no room for God and the spiritual needs of humankind. Thus, mere addition of ethical codes to the scientific enterprise would not change the secular character of the current science.

Finally, we must emphasize that it is not the methodology of science that marks it as sacred or secular; rather, it is the underlying metaphysical basis that brings in such categorisation.

6. Sacred science vs secular science

As we saw, sacred science is one that is framed within a theistic worldview-a worldview that considers God as the creator and Sustainer of the universe, does not confine the existence to the material realm, believes in a *telos* for the created world and admits a moral order. Secular science, on the other hand, is indifferent with respect to all these points. Sacred science and secular science share the same methodology, ie they both involve experimentation/observation and theoretical work. Their difference is in their underlying worldview which affects their outlook towards God, cosmos and humanity, and affects their practical conesquences. Contrary to what some scholars think, I don't think at all that preoccupation of Muslims with sacred science would dissuade them from being equal partners in the world scientific community.

The worldview underlying science in the classical era of Islamic civilization and in the mediaeval Europe was a theistic one. This outlook changed after the Renaissance. The change, to paraphrase E Schumacher, was from 'science for under-standing' to 'science for manipulation', from discovering the signs of God in nature to the exploitation of nature. In Schumacher's very elegant words:

> The old science—'Wisdom', or 'science for understanding'—was primarily directed 'towards the sovereign good', ie the True, the Good and the Beautiful, the knowledge of which would bring both happiness and salvation. The new science was directed mainly towards material power, a tendency that has meanwhile developed to such lengths that the enhancement of political and economic power is now generally taken as the first purpose of, and main justi-fication for, expenditure on scientific work. The old science looked upon nature as God's handi-work and man's mother; the new science tends to look upon it as an adversary to be conquered or a quarry to be exploited.
>
> The greatest and most influential difference, however, relates to the attitude of science to man. The 'science for understanding' saw man as made in the image of God, the crowning glory of creation, and hence 'in charge' of the world, because noblesse oblige. The 'science for manipulation', inevitably, sees man as nothing but an accidental product of evolution, a higher animal, a social animal, and an object for study by the same methods by which other phenomena of this world were to be studied—'objectively'.[26]

Here we elaborate on the differences between sacred science and secular science:

---

26.   EF Schumacher, *op cit*, 65.

1. Secular science considers the physical world as all there is and sees no room for God in the natural order. Sacred science, in contrast, regards the physical world as created and sustained by an All-knowledgeable All-powerful God. Thus, it is God-centered.
2. Secular science is content with specialization and the ensuing fragmentation of science. Here, different fields of science are separated from each other and are divorced from the sacred. But, sacred science is searching for the underlying unity of the created order. This means that sacred science embraces holistic view of the universe and applies a holistic approach for its comprehension. Thus, the compartmentalisation of knowledge into religious and secular categories is not held to be valid. Any kind of knowledge that fulfils Islamic ideals is to be considered sacred.
3. Secular science confines itself to the sensible realm. Therefore, spiritual realities are considered either as unreal or reducible to the physical. There is no room for supra-sensible realities in secular science, because it reduces reality to sensible experience. This is rooted in the fact that secular science is solely based on an empiristic approach to reality, where only the knowledge rooted in sense-data is considered as reliable. Bertrand Russell puts the matter straight-forwardly: 'Whatever knowledge is attainable, must be attained by scientific methods; and what science cannot discover, mankind cannot know.'[27]

This scientistic approach to reality, often called 'scientism', views empirical science as the only reliable path to truth. Science tells us whatever is to be known about the world. This view, which is really materialism or naturalism in disguised form, is pervasive in most of the contemporary academic circles. Michael Ruse admits:

> And it seems to me very clear that at some level, evolution as a scientific theory makes a commitment to a kind of naturalism, namely, that at some level one is going to exclude miracles and these sorts of things, come what may.[28]

---

27.   B Russell, *Religion and Science* (New York: Oxford University Press, 1970), 243.
28.   M Ruse, *op cit.*

It is really scientism, rather than science per se, that has undermined humanity's quest for the Sacred. By taking sensory perception as the only tool for the perception of reality, it leaves no room for any reality that is not rooted in sensory experience.

Sacred science, however, does not confine the knowledge of reality to the one obtained through experimentation and theoretical reasoning alone, and does not consider the scientific study of the world as exhaustive. By accommodating revelation and intuition, it encompasses spiritual as well as physical aspects of humanity and the cosmos. The claim of sacred science is that there is more to reality than meets human eyes.

Strict empiricism does not admit the introduction of unobservable entities, where as modern theoretical physics makes use of such entities as quarks, etc. Furthermore, the idea of general law cannot be held either, as one always deals with limited observations.

4. Secular science ignores or denies the idea of purpose for nature. This is partly due to the preoccupation of modern scientists with mathematical manipulations and the predictive power of science and partly due to the misconception that teleological considerations hinder the development of science. The success of modern science in certain domains has fortified the idea that present program of science, which lacks teleological considerations, among other things, is all that is needed. The much broader framework of sacred science, however, accommodates *telos* to the universe and sees a positive role for it in the practice of scientists and in enlarging their vision at the theoretical level. Furthermore, we see no inconsistency between a belief in a purposeful world and being a creative scientist.

By emptying the world from any *telos* or spiritual content, secular science has left no meaning for life or the whole existence. Steven Weinberg gives a clear description of this position:

> It is almost irresistible for humans to believe that we have some special relation to the universe, that human life is not just a more—or—less farcical outcome of a chain of accidents reaching back to the first three minutes, but that we were somehow built in from the beginning. As I write this I happen to be in an airplane

at 30,000 feet, flying over Wyoming en rout home
from San Francisco to Boston. Bellow, the earth looks
very soft and comfortable . . . It is very hard to realize
that all this is just a tiny part of an overwhelmingly
hostile universe. It is even harden to realize that this
present universe has evolved from an unspeakable
unfamiliar early condition, and faces future extinction
of endless cold or intolerable heat. The more the
universe seems comprehensible, the more it seems
pointless.[29]

Sacred science, however, holds that our universe has a meaning
which extends beyond us and is connected with the 'purpose of
existence'. Thus, eg, a meaningful life is one that serves the purpose
for which we were created—to serve our Creator.

5. Secular science promotes value-neutrality, but sacred science
   integrates knowledge with values. This is done in such a way that
   leads to accountability and responsibility of the scientist at all stages
   of life, and it takes place at the metaphysical bases of science. In the
   secularist vision, ethics at most plays a utilitarian role. In the Islamic
   worldview, however, the concept of moral values is linked to the
   concept of world's *telos*. In a world free of a *telos*, moral law has no
   intrinsic value. It has only a regulatory role in the society.

   The neglect of moral values in the scientific enterprise is partly
   due to the neglect of teleology in the modern secular science.

6. In a secularistic context, science is sought for the control and
   manipulation of the nature and society. In a theistic context,
   however, science is sought for getting wisdom and for solving
   individual and societal problems—goals which lead to God's
   pleasure. Here, nature is viewed as a trust from God which should
   be handled properly. Thus, all plans for scientific progress and
   technological innovations should be harmonious with the cosmic
   order.

7. Because of the limitations of its scope, secular science can only
   respond to certain questions and cannot present a comprehensive
   picture of the world. It simply leaves unanswered many questions

---

29.   S Weinberg, *The First Three Minutes* (New York: Basic Books, 1993),
      154.

of human concern that arise in science itself. Schrödinger has put the matter elegantly:

> The scientific picture of the real world around me is very deficient. It gives a lot of factual information, puts all our experience in a magnificently consistent order, but it is ghastly silent about all and sundry that is really near to our heart, that really matters to us. It cannot tell us a word about red and blue, bitter and sweet, physical pain and physical delight; it knows nothing of beautiful and ugly, good or bad, God and eternity. Science sometimes pretends to answer questions in these domains, but the answers are very often so silly that we are not inclined to take them seriously.[30]

Eugen Wigner, another eminent physicist of our era, concurs:

> I don't think physics deals with everything. Whether I am happy or unhappy, whether I am afraid or fearless, whether I am noble or I am mean, how does this get represented in science? Even if there are people who would say there is a chemical imbalance, I would like to think that there is something else.[31]

Furthermore, secular science is silent about the meaning and purpose of human life and about morality. Sacred science, however, does not confine reality to the empirical realm and works within a more inclusive metaphysical framework in which higher levels of reality are recognised. Such frame-work can shine light on our meta-scientific questions. George Ellis puts the matter elegantly:

> The underlying order of the universe is broader than described by the understanding of physics alone, and relates to the full depth of human experience, in

---

30. K Wilber, editor, *Quantum Questions* (Shambhala: New Science Library, 1984), 81.
31. Quoted in WM Richardson, RJ Russell, P Clayton and K Wegter-McNelly, editors, *Science and the SpiritualQuest* (London: Routledge, 2002), 244.

particular providing a foundation for morality and meaning.[32]

7. Conclusion

As we mentioned, scientific knowledge can reveal only certain aspects of reality, and it should not be identified with absolute knowledge. To make it more encompassing, one has to assimilate it into a more integrated framework in which higher levels of knowledge are recognized. Then, it can accommodate all aspects of human experience and can answer all questions of human concern. Furthermore, all evils due to the misuse of modern science and its technological offspring can be avoided or minimised.

One such encompassing framework is the Islamic worldview—a God-centered worldview—which is rooted in the Islamic revelation, takes a holistic view of nature, admits a hierarchical structure for reality and has a long range concern for humanity.

During the nineteenth century and much of the twentieth century a prevalent idea was that science per se can solve all problems of humanity and can bring felicity and prosperity for humankind. There is no doubt that science and its techno-logical offspring brought a lot of blessing for humanity, but the promised utopia did not materialised. Instead, science produced means of mass destruction and environmental pollution and disrupted the balance between the spiritual and the materialistic aspects of life, and humanity witnessed world wars, poverty, injustice, moral-void and violence. The industrialised world with all its technological superiority is crying out for meaning—something that advances of science and technology have not provided for humanity.

We believe that all these problems are rooted in the secularistic worldview that has dominated the minds of policy makers, scientists and all other agencies affecting the public. To reverse this trend, there should be a concerted effort by academic institutions and religious scholarship to replace the prevalent secularistic worldview by an inclusive worldview which is centered around God—the sacred. This can give science a proper orientation in its practical aspects and can enlarge scientists' cosmological vision.

---

32. GFR Ellis, *op cit*, 125.

6

Science and the Idea of The Sacred

Osman Bakar

1. Introduction

The title of this essay implies that science once upon a time was sacred in nature and character but it is no longer so today, at least in so far as mainstream science is concerned. Moreover, as the title suggests, it is possible for science today to rediscover its lost identity and to regain its sacred character.[1] But is it really possible? To many people the idea of trying to restore the sacred character of science is simply absurd. After all, they would say, science has fought hard to liberate itself from 'the obscurantism and tyranny of religion' to which, let us be reminded, the idea of the sacred has been inseparably linked. Why should the hard-fought gain of modernity, the pride of science, be sacrificed again in order to return to the supremacy of the sacred? They would further argue that even if philosophically speaking the idea of a sacred science makes sense, science has progressed so far away from religion beyond the point of return and it has become so complex and profane that it would be just practically impossible to change it back to its scared form.

The position I am taking in this essay is that it is both desirable and possible for science to become sacred again. In my view it is a position that Islam as a religion not only encourages but strongly insists on. Islam's commitment to a sacred science may be inferred directly from the pages of its religious scripture and from the pages of its intellectual history. Historically speaking, Islamic culture and civilisation had witnessed the rich cultivation of science that was wholly sacred in

---

1.   Among contemporary Muslim scholars, the most vocal exponent of a sacred science is perhaps the Iranian-American Seyyed Hossein Nasr who is presently a university professor of Islamic studies at George Washington University, Washington, DC. For his views on sacred science see, for example, his *The Need for a Sacred Science* (Albany: State University of New York Press, 1993).

nature and character. For several centuries, from the ninth century to
the fifteenth century, Islamic science had been robust enough to be the
mainstream science despite assuming a sacred character. The
practitioners of the science themselves believed in the idea of the
sacred as, in the case of many of them, both their scientific and non-
scientific works seem to suggest.[2] In faithfulness to that idea they
sought to develop their science, which many Muslims nowadays call
Islamic science. Interestingly, the same science that its practitioners
and other Muslims looked upon as sacred has been described by not a
few Westerners as surprisingly modern in its spirit and orientation. If
despite its sacred character Islamic science with justification has been
observed to have exhibited modern characteristics such as the rational
nature of its language and the scientific nature of its methodological
approach and content, then that observation would be a good enough
a reason to support the argument that the Muslim view and historical
experience of sacred science must have been different from the
Western Christian experience of it.[3] A widely shared view among
Muslims is that a sacred science is not necessarily incompatible with
scientific progress in the real sense of the word.

Theologically and philosophically speaking, the idea of sacred
knowledge of which sacred science is a major branch surfaces
frequently in the Koran, thus deserving to be counted as one of its
major themes. The Koran also talks a lot about other aspects of the
sacred that are all related in some way to sacred knowledge.
Particularly important from the point of view of this essay's topic is the
idea of sacred laws as revealed to various human societies throughout
history as well as to the natural world. In this essay what I propose to
do is to show that two of the several important ways in which we can
make science sacred again are through the ideas of sacred knowledge
and sacred law. I have decided to focus on these two ideas following a
written response I have made to Dr Golshani's and Dr Clayton's

---

2. Ibn Sina (980–1037) and al-Biruni (d. 1051) are two of the greatest
   Muslim scientific minds who have ever lived, but their vast corpus of
   writings include many treatments of non-scientific themes that clearly
   point to intellectual commitments to the idea of the sacred and the
   relations of science to the sacred.
3. See Osman Bakar, *The History and Philosophy of Islamic Science*
   (Cambridge: Islamic Texts Society, 1999), originally published in 1991
   under the title *Tawhid and Science* (Kuala Lumpur: Nurin Enterprise &
   Science University, Penang, 1991).

papers presented at a conference on religion and science in Yogyakarta, Indonesia.[4] Dr Golshani's paper entitled *Science and the Sacred* made many references to sacred knowledge in general and sacred science in particular. As for Dr Clayton's paper, it deals with the important issue of the confrontation between natural law and revealed law, which has been of common interest to Islam and Christianity but to which they have responded quite differently. This essay is based largely on my original critique of the two papers in question.

2. The sacred, its meaning and centrality

The subject of religion and science may be gaining popularity among academics and others these days but unfortunately its sub-domain of science and the sacred has not received as much attention as it deserves. It is important to emphasise that no discussion of religion and science can be considered complete and truly meaningful unless and until the idea of the sacred is brought into the picture and its relations with both are duly clarified. It is in the idea of the sacred that religion and science find their true common basis. For many religious traditions, there is no idea more fundamental than the sacred in shaping human relationships with the ultimate reality and in governing human attitudes toward the natural world. In Islam, the sacred in the ultimate sense is none other than God. The sacred (*al-quddus*) is one of the 99 Divine Names. From the sacred flows everything that is sacred in character, like sacred books, sacred laws, sacred knowledge, sacred art and sacred architecture. Nature itself is of course viewed within the various spiritual traditions as sacred. Since the manifestations of the sacred are many and diverse, we can expect to find its manifold relations with the various domains of human life and thought. Our major concern here is with the relations of the sacred with human knowledge and natural law.

3. When human knowledge is sacred

Some people claim that all the knowledge we humans have and are capable of having is profane in nature. Then there are those who claim that all knowledge is sacred. Yet others claim that some knowledge may be sacred but the rest of knowledge is not and science would be

---

4.   The conference was held on 2–5 January 2003.

an excellent example of it. Why do we have these different views about the ultimate nature of knowledge as to whether it is sacred or not? The answer is that human knowledge can either be sacred or profane depending on how one views it in relation to God as the ultimate reality and God as the ultimate source of all knowledge. It also depends on how one uses and applies knowledge in the light of the values one believes in and upholds. It is only if one believes that God is the knower of all things and also the ultimate source of all knowledge no matter how humans have acquired their knowledge that one could come to accept the sacred nature of every piece of knowledge. And this is precisely what Islam teaches about knowledge: every piece of knowledge is sacred because it may be related conceptually to God.

Let us take as an example the case of science, one of man's greatest and most awe-inspiring creations. As viewed within the Islamic culture and civilisation in the past fourteen centuries it is amazingly rich and complex in its relations with the sacred. From the Islamic point of view, there are many avenues to the sacred and the understanding of its relations with both the natural and human worlds. The subject of knowledge and the sacred, even if we were to restrict it to the domain of science understood in its limited sense, is so vast that it would be impossible for us to discuss all of its aspects within the scope of this essay. However, even as a critique of Dr Golshani's and Dr Clayton's papers this essay does provide a useful discussion of how, conceptually speaking, science can acquire its sacred character again.[5] In trying to highlight the nature and characteristics of sacred science, Dr Golshani has compared and contrasted it with what he calls secular science. In a complementary way to Dr Golshani's, Dr Clayton's approach to the sacred is through the idea of 'the lawfulness of nature', which to my mind necessarily raises the issue of sacred law as understood in Islam and other religious traditions. True enough, in his paper the term *sacred law* never appears, but his proposed idea of a synthesis of natural law and revealed law is what corresponds in traditional Islamic thought to sacred law (*shari'ah* or *namus*).

---

5.   On the more general question of the dimensions of the relations between religion and science from the Islamic perspective within the framework of which the issue of the relations of science to the sacred should be discussed, see my 'Reformulating a Comprehensive Relationship between Religion and Science: An Islamic Perspective', *Islam and Science* vol 1, no 1 (June 2003): 29–44.

4. Response to Dr Golshani's paper

Let me now deal with the essence of each paper as articulated respectively through the ideas of sacred knowledge and sacred law. The idea of sacred knowledge in general and sacred science in particular is central to Islam.[6] We should thank Dr Golshani for taking up this idea as the central theme of his paper. His focus is on the meaning of sacred science and an explanation of its major characteristics and differences from secular knowledge. He has sought to justify and strengthen his arguments for sacred science by appealing to traditional Islamic sources, mainly the Qur'an and the prophetic hadiths, as well as invoking the views of several contemporary philosophers and scientists. I find myself almost in complete agreement with his views. Accordingly, my response to his paper is more by way of complementing it, rather than negating or refuting its standpoints. I will just raise several issues which to my mind are important to be discussed when we are dealing with the subject of science and the sacred.

The first issue is why as a matter of principle does Islam insist on the pursuit of sacred knowledge? We may understand what sacred science means, but we may not fully comprehend why Islam as a religion is so passionate about sacred knowledge in preference to secular knowledge. Dr Golshani has defined sacred knowledge as 'the kind of knowledge which is framed within the context of the theistic Islamic worldview'. He then explains the major integral elements of this worldview. I accept this definition as my own which I sometimes present in another way: 'sacred knowledge is that form of knowledge which is organically or conceptually related to the knowledge of the sacred, the essence of which is *tawhid*'.[7] Islam's basic position on sacred knowledge may be best explained in the following way. Human relationship with the divine is defined primarily in terms of knowledge. The ultimate goal of human existence is to know God and in the light of that knowledge to serve God. If we want to compare Islam with Christianity, we may say that Islam is essentially 'a way of knowledge' rather than 'a way of love' as Christianity claims to be. In

---

6. See Seyyed Hossein Nasr, *Knowledge and the Sacred* (New York: Crossroad, 1981).

7. On the conceptual relationship between *tawhid* and the various branches of science see my previously quoted *Tawhid and Science*.

the Islamic view, knowledge has a saving function. According to Prophet Muhammad, whoever wants success and salvation in this earthly life has to acquire knowledge, and whoever wants success and salvation in the next life likewise has to acquire knowledge. Emphasising further this saving nature and function of knowledge, the Prophet pointed out that it is the sacred duty of every Muslim male and female to seek knowledge.

Islam's vast and open 'way of knowledge' to the divine and the Muslim sacred duty to be steadfast in following the way has two dimensions, one temporal and the other spatial. The spatial dimension is implied by the prophetic hadith 'seek knowledge even if it is in China', quoted by Dr Golshani. If I may add to this, the temporal dimension is implied by another prophetic hadith 'seek knowledge from the cradle to the grave'. But for the purpose of discussion here I am more concerned with the spatial dimension. I have heard before an interpretation of the former hadith along the line suggested by Dr Golshani: the acquisition of knowledge is not confined to the religious sciences, because China was not a place to learn Islamic teachings. Without ruling out the possibility of that interpretation, I am in favour of another interpretation. I think it is not the purpose of the hadith to identify certain kinds of knowledge with certain geographical regions, for example non-religious sciences with China. The hadith is perfectly universal in its spirit and applications.

Sacred knowledge, the kind of knowledge Muslims are encouraged to seek, or the experience of cultivating one or more forms of sacred knowledge, can be found anywhere on the globe. It can be found no less in Taoist and Confucian China or in Malay-Javanese Yogyakarta than in the Middle East, the heartland of Islam. There has always been a universal attempt, especially before modern times, to 'frame science within the context of a theistic worldview'. Let us remember that China at the time of the Prophet and until modern times was not cultivating a profane and secular science but rather a sacred science. The creators of science in traditional China were mainly Taoists in their theological and philosophical persuasions. It was precisely because the sciences Islam had come into contact with or inherited from other civilisations of both the East and the West during the Middle Ages were already framed within the context of the sacred that the Muslims found it relatively easy to integrate those sciences into the framework of *tawhid* and to create a new synthesis of medieval science again within the matrix of the sacred.

Islam's insistence on the human pursuit of sacred knowledge is based on the Koran itself. The first five verses to have been revealed to the Prophet provided the general framework for that pursuit. Believers are commanded not simply to read but to read in the Name of the Lord the Creator. Through this divine command is established the link between human knowledge and the sacred. To read in the divine name does not mean as some would like to think that one piously starts reading with a *bismillah* and finishes with a *Allahu a'lam* but unconcerned with the truth and quality of its content. What it actually means is that human thoughts and human creations of knowledge should be in strict conformity with divine reality. The implication of this meaning is obvious. Science in Islamic culture is necessarily sacred, founded and cultivated as it were with a full awareness and understanding of the divine reality and its all-encompassing relationships with the various sectors of cosmic reality. For several centuries when Islam led the world in science, that was precisely how in practice it cultivated its sciences.

Two questions may be raised here. How did Islamic intellectual culture keep alive that awareness and understanding of the sacred? And why did Jewish and Christian scientific figures who lived and worked in the dominant Islamic culture manage intellectually speaking to go along very well with their Muslim counterparts? These two questions are very pertinent to our contemporary situation. On the first question, the most effective intellectual means of maintaining the sacred character of science was the creation of cosmologies, episte-mologies, and philosophies of science that serve as vital conceptual links between theology and science. The fact that many of the scientists were themselves experts in cosmologies, epistemologies and philo-sophies of science had been a major factor in helping to keep alive the spirit of sacred knowledge within Muslim scientific culture. Today, the quest for a sacred science, be it among Muslims or otherwise, would entail the rediscovery and at the same time the reformulation of traditional cosmologies, epistemologies and philosophies of science in the light of both the sacred and contemporary science. On the second question, we may assert that scholars and thinkers of the three Abrahamic faiths have been able in the past to interact with each other on the intellectual plane with relative ease precisely because they shared many common visions of the sacred. They shared a sacred worldview that transcends faith barriers. In fact, Muslim men of learning in the past shared a vision of the sacred not only with their co-religionists in the Abrahamic family but also with members of other religious families such as with Hindus in India and Taoists and Confucianists in China.

A major issue before us today is this: what is the future of sacred science if indeed we can speak of it as having a future? Many people are saying science has been moving in an opposite direction to the path of sacred science, so much further away and with such speed and confidence of its newfound power, that one can only speak with nostalgia of its past and have a beautiful dream of its future. God knows best! And in the words of Dr Clayton, difficulties aside, 'there are also grounds for optimism'. He is referring to recent developments in science, philosophy of science, metaphysics and Western spirituality that point to the possibility of a new synthesis of religion and science. As ardent believers in that possibility, Muslims everywhere should welcome his optimism and join forces with all those who share that optimism in a global collaborative effort to create this grand new synthesis. There are historical precedents to guide the Muslims in this exciting intellectual venture. These precedents should offer them comfort and confidence. It is an intellectual venture in which they ought to take a proactive stance. For then they would be paying real heed to the call of the Koran to invite the whole of humankind to participate in an affirmation of the sacred. In several of its verses directly addressing humanity, we are all reminded that we live under the same sacred cosmic roof, and although we may live in different religious houses we are spiritual neighbours.

5. Response to Dr Clayton's Paper

We all realise that in contemporary mainstream science, there are troubling and destructive tensions between the realm of natural laws and the realm of divine laws. Many scientists argue that there is no common ground between the two realms. In articulating his thesis on 'perceiving God in the lawfulness of nature', Dr Clayton offers a way out of the tensions. This is through the notion of law as understood in Jewish, Christian and Muslim traditions. I agree with him in identifying the idea of law as one of the most important meeting points of religion and science. But in attempting to lay wide open this common ground between the scientific and religious understanding of law, Dr Clayton has presented a number of ideas which seem to suggest a different notion of law from the one understood in Islamic tradition, at least in some if not all respects he has treated.

His five types of law, particularly the distinction between natural law and revealed law, call for some comments. Let us reproduce here his five types of law. These are the natural law, the laws of human nature, the moral law, the law of the divine nature, and revealed law. I must say that I have difficulty with this classification because it raises certain philosophical and theological issues. There are major overlaps between the types of law that call into question the soundness of that categorisation or classification itself. For example, are the natural law and the laws of human nature two distinct types of law? Not according to classical Muslim philosophers and scientists like Avicenna (Ibn Sina). The laws of human nature are not separate and distinct from the natural law but constitute a subgroup of the latter. This position is made clear by the following evidences. First, in traditional Islamic philosophical, scientific and theological literature, the term *tabi'ah* (nature) is used to refer to both human nature and nature external to humans, such as plant and animal nature. Second, in consequence of the first and as found in many Muslim classifications of the sciences, the term science of nature (*al-'ilm al-tabi'i*) is used to embrace psychology which as a science of the soul deals with human nature. Third, the laws of human nature and the laws of external nature are denoted by a single term, *namus al-khilqah* (law of creation).

Then there is Dr Clayton's attempt to distinguish between natural law and revealed law. Muslim philosophers and scientists did not seek to contrast natural law with revealed law. Their natural law or law of creation (*namus al-khilqah*) was contrasted instead with laws of the prophets (*nawamis al-anbiya'*). The laws of the prophets are not synonymous with revealed law but are only a part of the latter. In the strict sense of the word and as the Koran itself seeks to emphasise, revealed law embraces both the law of creation and the laws of the prophets. In the perspective of the Koran, both the book of nature which is the basis for science and the various sacred books given to the prophets which are the bases for religions are divine revelations. Consequently, both the laws of creation and the laws of the prophets are divinely revealed. In adopting this approach to the notion of law, Islam erases such unnecessary cleavages as between the natural law and the laws of God and between the natural sciences and the humanities.[8] Within the limited time at my disposal, I am not in a position to provide further comments on his ideas of the moral law and the law of divine nature. In any case, my comments thus far on his concepts of law are sufficient to enable me to respond to this crucial question: how can we relate science to the sacred through the notion of law? Briefly stated, science can be related to the sacred through the channels of both branches of sacred law. Through the natural law understood as a sacred law of creation, science can help us to gain a deeper insight into the nature of divine activity and aspects of the sacred, as well as to enhance its own wisdom and sacred character. And through the other branch of the sacred law, namely the law of the prophets of which the moral law is a primary component and the Islamic law (*Shari'ah*) is the last manifestation, science can help to advance the moral cause of religion as well as to enhance the legitimacy of its societal role as an agent of material and human development in the service of humankind.

6. Conclusion

Although I have differences with Dr Clayton in the understanding of sacred law, there are commonalities at a more fundamental level. Certainly our intentions coincide. Dr Clayton has raised such rewarding issues on the future of religion and science and inter-faith dialogue that we all should be thankful to him. He made the following call: Let us draw on the best of recent science, the best of our philosophical traditions, and the best of our scriptural sources in order to restate a theistic vision for the twenty-first century. I answer his call with great enthusiasm and hope. From the point of view of Islam in particular, both the idea of sacred knowledge beautifully expounded by Dr Golshani and the idea of sacred law implicit in Dr Clayton's notion of law he has created are central to any intellectual venture to restore the rightful relations between science and the sacred. Yogyakarta is well known in this part of the world as an intellectual centre that has witnessed several major syntheses of ideas from various civilisations in its history. Let Yogyakarta again be a witness to another major intellectual synthesis, this time in the domain of religion and science.

---

8.   See my *History and Philosophy of Islamic Science*, chapter 4, entitled 'The Unity of Science and Spiritual Knowledge.'

Part Three

Creation in Science and Religion

7

Cosmology and the Quest for Meaning

Karlina Leksono-Supelli

One of the most important discoveries of modern cosmology that appeals for theological studies is a conviction—which has been gaining more acceptance—that the universe has a beginning. Development of ideas in cosmology during the last three decades, however, has made us realize that in some cosmological models the moment that can be interpreted as 'creation' can be avoided. Even the controversial yet widely quoted anthropic principle is not a good candidate for an 'evidence' of any design and purpose of the universe.

This paper attempts to analyse some problems in cosmology, particularly the ones concerning the early stage of the universe, and some methodological constraints in cosmology that triggered the antrophic principle. Then it will show that the relationship between science and religion is not dictated in the first place by lower level accordance between scientific theses and Holy Scriptures.

In 1929, the astronomer Edwin Hubble published the linear relationship between the speed of the galaxies and their distance. It was then known as the velocity-distance law or simply Hubble's law. The law states that the more distant a galaxy, the faster it moves away. A few years before Hubble's discovery, Alexander Friedmann found a solution to Einstein's general relativity equations that suggested an expansion of space. The equation was independently discovered by Georges Lemaître (1927), who noticed the possible connection to Hubble's discovery. The Friedmann papers (1922, 1924) and Lemaître's (1927) were largely ignored by the scientific community working in the field. In October 1931, during a special session at the British Association for the Advancement of Science, Lemaître's work that had lain dormant for more than three years came to be accepted as a generally correct model of the universe

If the space is expanding, we can imagine running the process backward in time to watch the galaxies moving closer to each other. As the shrinking space compresses its contents together, the temperature dramatically increases. At about fifteen billion years from the age of the presently observed universe, the whole universe as we know it is squeezed to an ever smaller size with unimaginable density and temperature. Lemaître called the initial state of maximum concentration the 'primeval atom' in his 1950 book by that title.[1] Although of necessity incomplete, it was the first scientific prediction of the origin of the universe, which led to the presently accepted 'big bang' model.

The essence of the big bang theory is that the universe is expanding and cooling. It is evolutionary in essence, which means that the universe presents a slightly different face each billion years. Parallel to the investigations into the early stage of the universe, the big bang cosmology also presents us with possible patterns of future development of the universe. If the density of the universe is sufficiently high, the expansion may reverse in the future. The universe may begin to re-contract and undergo a process of gravitational collapse. The world as we know it would then end in a hot dense big crunch to match the big bang. In a less dense universe, the deceleration would be so gentle that the universe would continue its present expansion indefinitely, with ever-decreasing density and temperature. It would end in a whimper.

Until the end of the 1920s, scientists avoided the question of the origin of the universe, in part by the belief held at that time that the universe is static or stationary and unchanging, and in larger part, because the question that dealt with the origin of the universe was considered non-scientific. Eddington, who arranged for Lemaître's paper to be translated into English and in so doing endorsed the expanding universe to become a new paradigm in cosmology, found that the notion of a beginning to the order of nature is philosophically displeasing. He was not the only scientist who felt distinctly uncomfortable by the idea.

Hubble's law has not only turned out to be the most important discovery in twentieth century astronomy, but has also opened up the door for religion to re-enter the region that was closed since Galileo's encounter with the Inquisition in the seventeenth century. The origin of the universe, the subject that was once the province of theologians and philosophers, has today become an important chapter of cosmology. The cosmic microwave background radiation (CMBR)

---

1.   Lemaitre, George, *The Primeval Atom*, translated by BH & SA Xorff, (New York: Van Nostrand, 1950).

discovered in 1965 supports the big bang. The radiation was interpreted as the remnant of a very dense and hot stage of the universe. The discussion of the origin of the universe has since completely changed. Once the fossil evidence of the 'primeval fireball' is observed, it is as if astronomers have found the afterglow of 'creation', or as exclaimed by George Smoot at a 1992 press conference reporting the COBE (*Cosmic Background Explorer*) findings that confirmed 1965's detection of the radiation, 'If you're religious, it's like looking at the face of God.'

Over the past three decades, new ideas and extraordinary development in observing techniques have driven cosmology—the attempt to understand the large-scale structure of the universe by the method of natural sciences—forward at a rapidly increasing pace. The empirical testing of cosmological models has been established and many hypotheses have been successfully tested against the evidence of observation.

We now have access to faraway domains of space-time that were even unimaginable during the great methodological debate in the 1930s and 1940s, when the British astrophysicist Herbert Dingle severely criticised some cosmologists for a lack of inductive logic and for being guilty of betraying the true method of science by introducing mentally invented hypotheses. Dingle argued that the study of nature should start from sense observation. He was against the view that certain general principles could be derived rationally without recourse to experience. He pointed to the 'cosmological principle' as an example of such reasoning.[2]

The cosmological principle asserts that the universe is homogeneous and isotropic in the large-scale average (in Einstein's words 'all places in the universe are alike'). The principle is methodologically necessary in cosmology, for without it the range of all possible cosmological models would be too wide. Despite the fact that the cosmological principle functions as an *a priori* rule rather than as an empirical generalisation, the cosmological principle is consistent with the observed expansion of the universe and the properties of the microwave background radiation. The fact that the radiation comes

---

2.   See, Dingle, Herbert, 'Science and the Unobservable', in *Nature* 141 (1938): 21-28, Dingle, Herbert, 'Modern Aristotelianism', in *Nature* 139 (1937): 784-786.

from all directions of space with equal intensity provides the most compelling evidence for large-scale spatial uniformity.

However, the most heartening aspect of modern cosmology lies beyond its vigorous scientific character. Cosmology has been part of human thought since the beginning of history. As human attempts to understand the universe, cosmology is the oldest human intellectual endeavour where origins are lost in the mists of time. Ever since human beings first began to reflect upon their situation within the world of natural things, the need to have an acceptable picture of the universe has been pursued under a variety of practices. Within Indonesia's vast literary traditions, we find for instance the *I La Galigo*, a fourteenth century epic myth from Bugis, Sulawesi. A myth like *I La Galigo* provides not only an account of creation and the initial residence on earth of the gods and their descendants, but also a stage for human kinds daily activities and the forces of nature against which the play of fascinating mysterious powers take place.

When seen from this broad perspective of human attempts to understand the universe a whole, modern cosmology is a very peculiar science. Behind its scientifically well-structured paradigms is the longest human striving to understand the mystery of existence. At the heart of Javanese mystical speculation, this persistent interest which is to be found in virtually every culture of recorded history is presented as '*kawruh sangkan paraning dumadi*': knowledge (*kawruh*) of the origin (*sangkan*) and final destination (*paran*) of all creation (*dumadi*).

Beginning in the sixteenth century, science has begun to make its own contributions in dealing with questions of existence, of the origin of life and humankind, of our place in the world and of our knowledge. However, in the prevailing positivism of the nineteenth century astronomy was confined to our solar system, and cosmology concerned only with its geometrical aspects. At the height of logical positivism in the early twentieth century, intellectual passion guided by the goals of achieving objective knowledge led science to present a universe in which the very asking of the questions about origins was itself cognitively meaningless. The physical theories were also subjected to a reduction of status. Theories were mere tools, a set of rules devoid of any ontological implications, for guiding future observational expectations in the light of past experience. Science contented itself with establishing regularities among the phenomena and devising a mathematical system for economical representation and ordering of these regularities.

Modern human beings delegated to the specialists their irrepressible needs to understand the mystery of existence only to find that their quivers bristling with mathematical items devised by the scientists. To many people, and even many scientists, modern cosmology is satisfying because not only it provides empirically testable explanations for many observable phenomena, but also because it inspires science to ask new questions that had previously been neglected due to its metaphysical baggage. Over the past two decades, there has been a tremendous growth of interest concerning the philosophical implications of modern cosmology.

In the preface to the first English edition of *The Logic of Scientific Discovery*, Karl Popper wrote,

> Language analysts believed that . . . the problems of philosophy, if any, are problems of linguistics usage, or the meaning of the words. I, however, believe that there is at least one philosophical problem in which all thinking men are interested. It is the problem of cosmology: the problem of understanding the world—including ourselves, and our knowledge, as part of the world.[3]

The primary goal of cosmology is to make the universe intelligible, but intelligibility raises some philosophical questions such as, how shall we understand the term 'universe'?[4] To what entity does the universe refer? How is the intelligibility of the universe is achieved? What kinds of limits are there to confront human efforts to make the universe intelligible? How much confidence can we place in the results of cosmological inquiry and how great is the weight of evidence in cosmology? To most laypersons the issues of cosmology raise questions that are similar but differently stated. One looks into the world, into the sky, into self and asks, what is it all about? Why did it all begin? What is the point of it all? Why do I exist? The curiosity of

---

3.   See Karl Popper, *The Logic of Scientific Discovery* (New York/London: Basic Books).

4.   See M Munitz, *Cosmic Understanding* (Princeton: Princeton University Press).

both specialists and non-specialists is surely bridged by one single question, namely, how would the results of research in recent cosmology bear on one's search for the meaning of existence?

The image of the big bang as a cosmic fireball explosion ejecting material is useful but misleading. First, the big bang is not an explosion localised in space; it is the upsurge of compressed space, which carries along matter and energy up to this day. The big bang model describes how our universe is evolving. We have evidence that the model successfully describes the evolution back in a time when the density of the radiation greatly exceeded the density of matter, and the mean distance between conserved particles was much smaller than it is now. However, the nature of the beginning of the universe, like its end, lies beyond the power of present understanding. This takes us to the second reason why the term is unfortunate. It suggests we are identifying the event that started the expansion.

Based on the study on the global structure of space-time, Penrose and Hawking[5] showed that in the mathematical model of relativity time must have a beginning at a cosmological singularity. At a singularity, the spatial structure of the whole universe shrinks to a zero volume, the density of matter is infinite and the classical general relativity breaks down. This could be interpreted as the rise of space, time and matter out of nothing, or the beginning of the world and at the same time the beginning of time. The Penrose-Hawking model, to paraphrase Hawking, delighted religious leaders for it stood, in conjunction with the CMBR, as scientific evidence for the 'act of creation'[6] renowned in some religious doctrines. Development of ideas in cosmology during the last three decades, however, has made us learn that the path to God is not that smooth yet.

As cosmologists push the horizon of our understanding of the universe ever closer to the very beginning of our history, we eagerly ask ourselves: Does cosmology offer a plausible description of creation? How should we interpret the notion of creation? Many cosmologists believe that the state of infinite energy, density and temperature is more a sign for a conceptual boundary rather than a real description of the physical conditions of the very early universe.

---

5.   Stephen W Hawking and Roger Penrose 'The Singularities of Gravitational Collapse and Cosmology', in *Proceedings of the Royal Society of London*, Series A 314 (1970): 529-548,

6.   Stephen W Hawking, *The Universe in a Nutshell* (Bantam, 2001).

From the geometric point of view, singularity is understood as incompleteness of space-time. It is the boundary of a space-time region as described by the classical, non-quantum relativity. Singularity represents an outer limit of what we can know about the universe at this stage of inquiry. It is then of a great temptation for cosmologists to construct a theory that would transgress the boundary.

Cosmology attempts to describe the evolution of the entire universe by using the fundamental laws of physics. In addition to these laws, we need to know the rules that worked at the beginning of time that gave rise to our universe. These rules or cosmic initial conditions constitute the special circumstances to which the laws should apply. At this moment, we do not know what the initial conditions—the boundary conditions—of the universe were, or even the concepts that should be used to describe them. Until then, the question of why the universe is the way it is can be answered by merely saying that because it was the way it was. Even a 'theory of everything' is far from sufficient to give a full understanding of the observed universe if it is not complemented by an understanding of the conditions of the early universe.

In current cosmology, we can identify at least two distinctive approaches with regard to the problem of initial conditions. One is to show that the present state does not depend very sensitively on the initial state of the universe. The inflationary model of the expanding universe originally proposed by Guth[7] offers an elegant way to achieve this goal. The other is to eliminate the initial event and in consequence abolishes the problem of cosmic initial conditions. In the quantum cosmological theory of Hartle-Hawking, for instance, the universe has no beginning, although time is still finite in the past.[8] In Hawking's analysis, the boundary condition of the universe is that it has no boundary. The theory would have profound implications for theology if 'creation' were still understood according to its traditional religious interpretation. The universe would be entirely self-contained and explicable by the laws of science and by quantum random process.

---

7. Alan Guth, 'Inflamatory Universe: A Possible Solution to the Horizon and Flatness Problems', in *Physical Review* D23 (1981): 347–356.

8. J Hartle and S Hawking 'Wave Function of the Universe', in *Physical Review* D28 (1983) 2960–75.

It would not need anything outside to start its history. This means that our universe exists without explanation.

The Hartle-Hawking theory is at this stage more of an approach to the problem than a complete theory. It requires a theory of quantum gravity that is far from being complete. Our current understanding of the universe penetrates to remarkably early times, but the theoretical models that have been explored so far regarding the physical state of the earliest moments of the universe remain inconclusive. Still another interesting, highly speculative approach to quantum cosmology is the Vilenkin quantum tunnelling proposal,[9] which considers our entire universe as the result of a barrier penetration that would be totally forbidden in classical physics. The model assumes a pre-existent universe in a false vacuum as a tiny empty geometry. The birth of our universe is wholly a matter of quantum probability. It is not the idea that the universe came out of 'nothing' which is philosophically appealing (the quantum vacuum is indeed not absolute nothing), but that creation was an inevitable outcome of the laws of physics. Does this lead us to the abandonment of the idea of a Creator?

Creation is one of the most important teachings in many religions. Creation marks the relation between God and the world. God is hidden but God the Creator is at the same time apparent. The act of creation is God's self-disclosure through the signs of the creatures. One needs only to meditate upon the creation to find God's traces in the immensity and harmony of creation.

Many people believe that the big bang model stands as a physical proof of divine creation. Given the recent development in cosmology, 'creation', however, should be understood as a far broader concept than just of temporal origin, the moment of the big bang. Even more, we have learnt from the history of science that to appeal to a 'God of the gaps' in explaining scientifically unexplainable facts is unrevealing, and even precarious. It is within the structure of the universe itself and the laws that operate in it and which guide its large-scale evolution, that the most important aspect of creation should be sought, namely the intelligible finely-tuned world. Exploring the concept of creation beyond its traditional theistic interpretation would bring us to a question of ontological origin, of why everything exists at all.

---

9.   A Vilenkin, 'Creation of Universes from Nothing', in *Physical Letters* B 117 (1982): 25-28.

The success of the big bang model in describing the universe back to its very early stages is impressive. Almost all the observational evidence that we have today is not only in agreement with the picture of a universe that started off very hot and cooled as it expanded, but seems to corroborate postulates assumed on a purely theoretical basis such as the cosmological principles. Nevertheless, the model leaves a number of unanswered questions regarding the initial state of the universe.

One of the most important issues in modern cosmology is the horizon problem. It lies in the partial failure of the model to give a plausible explanation of the observed large-scale homogeneity and isotropy of the universe. The microwave background radiation was emitted at the earliest moments after the big bang when different, separated parts of the expanding universe were far enough apart for light to have enough time to travel between the regions. The regions were isolated from each other and could not possibly have thermo-dynamically equilibrated to a common state. In the standard big bang model the universe arose from a myriad of completely unrelated regions. We would expect each region to be very different from one another. How could those regions be so similar?

The second problem with the standard big bang model relates to energy density of the universe that is so close to the critical density. If the density of the universe were slightly different from the critical density within a few seconds after the big bang, the universe would have either recollapsed within a time-scale much lower than the stellar lifetimes, or expanded so much that it would be devoid of matter before there would be time for galaxies to form. Our observable universe seems to have emerged from a very peculiar set of initial conditions such that the spatial geometry is almost flat.

Within the standard big bang framework one has to assume the homogeneity and isotropy as part of the initial conditions, together with the supposition that the rate of expansion is everywhere the same throughout the universe. A satisfactory cosmology would require no assumptions or postulates to be able to explain all the observed physical facts.

In the big bang model with inflation, the universe underwent a tremendous expansion that caused the universe to inflate by a large amount. In the pre-inflationary period, the universe was small enough and different parts of the universe were so much closely together that there would be enough time for those regions to be in causal contact with each other. Irrespective of the initial conditions, the observed large-scale features of the universe resulted from this very short period of inflation. As to the flatness problem, the inflation scenario predicts that the inflationary expansion would have brought the energy density close to the critical density and the expansion rate to the critical rate. The flatness of the space curvature is a direct consequence of the enormously accelerated expansion during the inflation period. After the inflation period, the universe pursued a process of expansion and cooling similar to that described in the standard big bang model.

Despite the fact that the inflation scenario offers the only reasonable solution to the several long-standing cosmological conundrums, at this stage of inquiry it is not a complete or well-tested physical theory. Many different variants of the scenario have been presented, yet there is no generally accepted inflation model.

From the fact that the universe is unique, that it is 'given to us only in one copy', many writers in cosmology, scientific or popular, stress the peculiarity of cosmology as a science. This peculiarity goes deeply into the methodological aspect of cosmology.

A common type of explanation in the natural sciences has the structure of a deductive argument in which the explicandum is a logically necessary consequence of the explanatory premises. The deductive pattern of explanation consists of general laws of nature and a number of initial conditions, which assert that given objects or certain events have definitive properties. The uniqueness of the universe and our lack of knowledge of the initial conditions means that the deductive strategy cannot be readily employed in cosmology. At the empirical level, a series of works by Ellis clearly stated that ideal astronomical observations are not enough to uniquely reconstruct a model of space-time whose structure and evolution we could trust a way back to the past.[10] Without the help of some assumptions, many different world models can show consistency with observational data.

The situation has led some cosmologists to employ a pragmatic strategy to find the most admissible model of the universe, namely the anthropic principle. The controversial anthropic principle starts with the fact that the universe is an exceptionally hospitable place for life. Many features in the universe—long-lived stable hydrogen stars, the

---

10.   George Ellis, *Before the Beginning: Cosmology Explained* (London/New York: Boyars/Bowerdean)

strength of the fundamental forces, the masses of the elementary particles, and so forth—seem so finely tuned that a slight change in one of the fundamental constants of nature related to each of the features would mean that in the universe could not have possibly evolved.

There are two versions of the anthropic principle as proposed by Carter.[11] The anthropic principle briefly states that what we can expect to observe must be restricted to the condition necessary for our presence as observers. The weak version states that we must be prepared to take account of the fact that our location in the universe is *necessarily* privileged to the extent of being compatible with our existence as observers. The strong version states that the universe (and hence the fundamental parameters on which it depends) must be such as to admit the creation of observers within it at some stage.

The anthropic principle is easily misinterpreted when quoted out of context. The situation was worsened because Carter was insufficiently explicit in conveying the meaning of the principle. He did not interpret to how the term 'must' in the strong version should be understood, whilst the weak version, at first glance, look like a mere tautology. A thorough inspection, however, shows that the anthropic principle functions as an elementary consistency check in cosmology that we could only construct a model of the universe that allows life to exist and evolve; its disregard would lead to erroneous conclusions being drawn about the structure of the universe.

The basic idea of the anthropic principle disregards versions that the existence of life imposes a selection effect on what we could expect to observe with respect to the universe. The anthropic principle integrates the historicity of the observers into cosmological inquiry. It is a background knowledge required in order to confirm the evidential import of a set of data to a hypotheses. By referring to the fact that both the age and the physical conditions of the universe are being constrained by the requirement of the necessity for life, the optimum condition for choosing one model among several others is laid. By examining certain facts about the existence of observers (human

---

11.   Brandon Carter, 'Large Number Coincidences and the Anthropic Principle in Cosmology', in *Confrontation of Cosmological Theory with Astronomical Data*, edited by MS Longair (Dordrecht: Reidel, 1974), 291–298.

beings), the character of other facts can be deduced. The anthropic principle is a methodological principle. It is the recognition that our own existence imposes a selection effect upon the kind of universe that would be supportive for carbon-based life.

The anthropic principle is simply a statement which enables us to comprehend the strong connections between the structure of the universe as a whole and the conditions necessary for life. The anthropic principle does not explain why the universe possesses those necessary properties for the evolution of observers, but it provides the answer to the epistemic question, 'Why is the universe like this?'

It is a mistake to think that the anthropic principle provides an ontological explanation for the question. To some people, even some scientists, the anthropic principle is heartening. One of the interpretations expresses the assurance that the universe is designed to include life and uses it as a proof of God's existence. Interpretation of this kind will take us back to a naïve introduction of God into the hole of ignorance in human knowledge. We have learnt from the history of science that to flirt with the 'God of the gaps' to explain unexplainable facts that may eventually be explicable by science is unrevealing, and even precarious.

Stepping out from cosmology, the controversy between Louis Pasteur and Felix-Archimède Pouchet in the mid-nineteenth century gives us a simple illustration of how God can be brought into play as an extra-scientific factor to equally support each side in a dispute. At the height of the controversy over evolution, Pasteur and Pouchet were involved in a debate on the possibility of demonstrating the spontaneous generation of a microscopic living creature in the laboratory. While Pouchet used spontaneous generation to preserve the idea of God's continuing act of creation and to attack Darwinism, Pasteur argued for the opposite: to believe in spontaneous generation is to abandon God. He brilliantly associated his opponent's position with materialism, atheism, and Darwinism. Interestingly, both agreed that a laboratory experiment was the only judge of bringing the dispute to an end.

The conclusion is clear. The anthropic principle brings to our attention the link between the finely tuned universe and ourselves, which we would not otherwise realise existed. The more we study the universe and carefully examine the unique concatenation of the physical and cosmic conditions, the more it becomes difficult for us to accept that we are the outcome of a mere chance. The anthropic reasoning causes us to reflect upon our situation, which is probably best expressed by Freeman Dyson, 'I do not feel like an alien in this universe.' Why is the universe like this? These beings who search for a home in the universe bear themselves out in a cosmology which is bounded to the epistemic horizon. As long as cosmology is pursued as a scientific discipline, there is no way of escaping the horizon. One can push the horizon further by employing ever-progressing scientific knowledge, but one can never escape. Reason is able to grasp its horizon from within reason itself.

The horizon, however, always points to something beyond, and cosmology is not the whole Cosmology as much as the universe is not the whole Universe. Cosmology, as the hidden part of a methodologically rigorous scientific cosmology, embraces all possibilities that come out from cosmological inquiries. The problems and methods employed in cosmology are closely associated with physics and astronomy. However, to say that since cosmology deals with factual issues, then it must belong to science rather than to philosophy, is the result of an epistemological dogma (Popper, 1996).

The anthropic reasoning which represents cosmology perceiving its own 'anthropic' limitation when meticulously employing the language of science, offers a point of departure for a reflection beyond the rigidity of the scientific horizon. The issue of 'creation' related to the big bang modern cosmology certainly is an important aspect of cosmology that needs to be reflected upon. However, the search to have a universe in which we ourselves are meaningfully present is doomed to go astray unless we realise that science is an ever-shifting conjecture. Cosmology, as well as other sciences, is mainly an open-ended search for a satisfactory world picture, but also a journey into the unknown.

An intellectual is always in a painful search for a coherent and authentic position that would express her/his religious faith. Many scientists develop a kind of religious feeling which is very difficult to put in plain words, especially because—as once expressed by Einstein —there is no anthropomorphic conception of God corresponding to it. The feeling is driven by a deep conviction of the beauty and rationality of the universe, and the fact that they can be known by our rational inquiry. Copernicus did not deliberately overthrow Ptolemy's geocentric picture of the universe. His heliocentric picture of the universe was born out of dissatisfaction with what he considered as irrationality in Ptolemy's system. He believed that the truth about the heavens could be discovered by rational investigation.

The universe is a message written as a sign to be interpreted. We have interpreted part of the sign. It is a source of wonder for those who realise how such immense complexities could be made intelligible to conscious beings who are also part of those complexities. Some people believe that there is a deep-seated relationship between our rationality and the rational order of nature. Einstein believed that the strength of the emotion derived from this awareness could only be grasped by those who have experienced the immense efforts and devotion, which the struggle for an intelligible universe demands.

In face of the difficulties of transforming various religious experiences into a coherent and authentic worldview, a number of people—theo-logians and scientists as well—choose an easier path. Without carrying out enough systematic inquiry into the teaching of the Holy Scriptures they picked up and chose from some of its verses, and combine them with some scientific theses to show that they are not contradictory to each other. Without a systematic study of theHoly Scriptures and an in-depth comprehension of the scientific context in which a hypothesis is constructed, to read the Holy Scripture message in terms of a particular theory will only end up in a glorification of a superficial harmony between science and religion.

At the fiftieth commemoration of Higher Education of Astronomy in Indonesia, Magnis-Suseno stated that within astronomy, human striving for knowledge is mostly driven by his/her quest as a historical being for origin, to know where he/she comes from. Science brings us to the edge of the world of meaning but never to enter; the insights arising from our understanding about the universe, call for some thoughtful considerations. By its very nature, this attempt will go beyond what science itself can provide.

There are some scientific concepts and religious teachings which could be integrated, while at the same time there are some others which need not be in contact with each other.

In the nineteenth century, Percy Bysshe Shelley wrote that one of the noble tasks of an artist is to absorb the new science, assimilate it into human needs, paint it with human desire, and transform it into human blood and bones. Two centuries earlier, 'in the presence of the Bavarian soldiers . . . and the death of the soldiers and ordinary people', Kepler wrote, 'there is nothing I want to find out and long to know with greater urgency than this. Can I find God, whom I can almost grasp with my own hands looking at the universe, also in myself?'

What Kepler wished to know is precisely the main problem we are now confronting. Naturally a question would arise, 'What is the contribution of cosmology?'

Cosmology brings us into a reflection that the interactions that took place in the universe were complicated, yet the universe is so well tuned that the process which produced the consciousness that asks about itself is enough to make us realise that human beings are not an outcome of an accidental process in the universe. The empirical language of cosmology might not speak about this reality, yet a profound reflection will lead us to the question, 'Will science and religion be able to cooperate to help us answer the question—how meaningful is this conscious being so that its existence needed a more than ten billion years period of time on a spectacularly amazing cosmic stage?'

8

How Did the Universe Begin? Cosmology and a Metaphysics for the Twenty-first Century

Bruno Guiderdoni

According to a commonly acknowledged idea, science deals with 'facts' whereas religion deals with 'meanings'. If science attempts to answer the 'how' and religion the 'why', there should not be any conflict between the two. Unfortunately, the situation is not so simple. It is true that science deals with *efficient* causes and religion with *final* causes, to use the technical words of the Aristotelian philosophy.[1] But the general trend in the development of sciences is that the efficient causes push the final causes backwards and eventually eliminate them.

This progressive replacement of the explanation in terms of final causes by the explanation in terms of efficient causes has been happening in the West since the Renaissance. In the Middle Ages, the Jews, Christians and Muslims shared the same prospect on the world, even if there were already long-lasting controversies and hot debates on cosmological issues. The men and women of faith of the Middle Ages did not see only things and phenomena around them: they primarily contemplated symbols, and looked for spiritual unveiling through their study of the cosmos. The epoch of the medieval synthesis between the Aristotelian-Ptolemaic cosmology and the teachings of the Holy Scriptures has passed away, and the development of modern science has led to a profound spiritual crisis in the West. Humankind has lost its central place in the cosmos, and has been rejected onto a standard planet orbiting a standard star in a standard galaxy located somewhere in the dull immensity of space. Such a science is value-

---

1.　To the question 'Why does the sun shine ?', an answer in terms of final causes could be 'It shines to give light to Human beings', whereas an answer in terms of efficient causes could be 'It shines because its surface is hot'.

neutral and devoid of any meaning. To quote the words of Claude Levi-Strauss, 'The universe has meaning only with respect to the Human, and the Human has no meaning '.

The conflict between science and religion ceased in the West when religion admitted that it has nothing to say on cosmology. The fields simply do not overlap because science has colonised the whole of 'reality'. To do so, it has defined 'reality' as being only what can be studied scientifically. Theologians now have to explain why God appears to be hidden under the thick curtain of the phenomena. Ideas such as those of *kenosis* and *tsimtsum* that flourished respectively in Christian and Jewish theological thinking have undergone a fascinating revival, and are now used by these theologians to explain why God 'retires' to let the cosmos apparently be ruled by its own laws, without any sign of direct divine intervention. The emphasis is put on the (relative) independence granted by God to the laws of nature, and on the (relative) freedom granted by God to humankind.

As it is well known, the Islamic tradition has always taught that God is nearby and continuously acts in creation. 'Each day some task engages Him.'[2] So Muslim theologians are unwilling to follow the path of some of the Western theologians in the direction of a *Creator* who would let his creation behave by itself with so much independence that he finally becomes a new kind of *Deus otiosus*, either by will or by experience of human weakness. God is hidden, but he is also apparent, according to his beautiful Names *azh-Zhahir wa-l-Batin*. The Creator is so Great that his creation has no flaw. But he is also apparent in/through His creation.

The fundamental mystery that subtends physics and cos-mology is the fact that the world is intelligible. For a believer, the world is intelligible because it is created. The Koran strongly recommends us to ponder, and meditate upon the creation to find the traces of the Creator in its harmony. Hence the so—called cosmic verses which are frequently quoted as one of the intellectual miracles included in the Koranic text:

> In the creation of the heavens and the earth, and in the
> alternation of night and day, there are signs for men of
> sense; those who remember God when standing, sitting

---

2.   Koran, 55:29.

and lying down, and reflect on the creation of the heavens and the earth, saying: 'Lord, You have not created this in vain. Glory be to you! Save us from the torment of the fire'.[3]

The exploration of the world is encouraged, provided the explorer is wise enough to acknowledge that the harmony that is present in the cosmos originates in God. By looking at the cosmos, the intelligence God has put in us constantly meets the Intelligence he has used in creating the things. The Koran mentions the regularities that are present in the world: As well as 'you will find no change in God's custom'[4], 'there is no change in God's creation'.[5] Clearly, this does not mean that the creation is immutable, but that there is a 'stability' in the creation that reflects God's immutability. The reader's attention is also drawn to the 'numerical aspect' of cosmic regularities. The Koran says: 'The Sun and the Moon [are ordered] according to an exact computation (*husban*).'[6] So a Muslim cosmologist is not surprised that the laws of physics we design and use to describe cosmic regularities are based on mathematics.

We live in a very peculiar epoch for the understanding of the structure and history of the cosmos. In the last decades, there have been spectacular breakthroughs mainly due to the extra-ordinary development of observing techniques. As a consequence, we have acquired a treasury of images we are the first generation to contemplate: the image of our planet in the darkness of the sky, the wide diversity of appearances of the surfaces of other planets and satellites in the solar system, the mapping of our galaxy at all wavelengths, the discovery of very energetic phenomena such as star explosions, or the potential census of billions of distant galaxies in deep surveys. We now have access to distances, epochs and structure sizes that were simply unthinkable at the epoch of the Middle Ages when the Arab astronomer al-Farghani computed the distance to God's throne from the assumptions of the Ptolemaic cosmology, and found a value of 120

---

3.   Koran, 3:190–191.
4.   Koran, 35:43.
5.   Koran, 30:30.
6.   Koran, 55:5. See also 6:96, 10:5, 14:33.

million km.[7] The new images of astronomy have deeply changed our awareness of the cosmos.

To understand the structure of the universe, the cosmologists must track its history. This history is theoretically reconstructed from the data by means of elaborated mathematics. No doubt there are a good many of bold speculations and crazy ideas in the interpretation. But reality resists, and not all theories are in agreement with the facts. On the contrary, the standard theory now appears as a powerful tool to guide new discoveries. To cut a long story short, cosmologists now think that the universe is expanding, and that the expansion phase started from a dense, hot stage called the big bang. During the expansion, the matter/radiation content of the universe dilutes and cools, and the relative abundance of various species of elementary particles change. About 100 sec after the big bang, light nuclei begin to form. About one million years after, the universe becomes neutral and transparent, and the light emitted by the so-called last-scattering surface at that epoch is observed as the 2.725 K black body radiation of the cosmic microwave background. The story is now well documented, but there are several topics for which our incapacity to solve recurrent puzzles probably points at the metaphysical structure of reality. In the following, I would like to briefly address two of these puzzles.

The first puzzle deals with fine-tuning in structure formation. Regions that are separated by more than about one arcmin on the last-scattering surface have never been in causal connection before, and should have widely different temperatures, in contrast with the remarkable isotropy that is actually measured. This is the so-called 'isotropy problem'. Moreover, the density of the universe is close to unity, and the spatial geometry is almost flat, whereas all values for the density parameter are a priori possible. This is the so-called 'flatness problem'. As a result, our observable universe seems to have emerged for a very peculiar set of initial conditions. In parallel, it is now clear that these patterns are necessary conditions for the appearance of complexity in the universe. For instance, a very large density parameter would have produced a fast collapse in a time-scale much lower than the stellar lifetimes that are necessary for the chemical enrichment of the interstellar medium (and the subsequent formation of planets),

---

7.   Edward Grant, *Planets, Stars & Orbs, The Medieval Cosmos, 1200–1687* (Cambridge: Cambridge University Press, 1994), 433.

whereas a very low density parameter would have resulted in a very diluted universe, with low mass structures that are unable to retain their gas. Of course, a philosophical explanation in terms of final causes can be introduced to give meaning to this type of fine-tuning (and other cosmic coincidences gathered under the term of the *anthropic principle*).[8] It can be divine intervention in a religious prospect, or a natural trend of matter towards self-organisation, in a pantheistic prospect. But this is unacceptable for modern science. As a matter of fact, the elimination of explanations in terms of final causes is at the heart of the development of cosmology. The current explanation of the isotropy and flatness problems (and other related puzzles) is that the universe has undergone a stage of exponential inflation that has inflated a small, causally connected patch beyond the size of the observable universe, and has erased spatial curvature. This explanation avoids the introduction of any argument based on final causes about the set of initial conditions the universe started from.

By the same token, the origin of the inhomogeneities that will produce the large-scale structures after gravitational amplification is explained by inflation: they are simply quantum fluctuations inflated to macroscopic scales. The problem is that the current theory is not able to predict the amplitude of these fluctuations, which is measured at the relative level of one part in 100 000 ($Q=10^5$) on the last-scattering surface. When a complete theory of inflation emerges, it will have to predict this value, which now appears only as a free parameter. But it is already clear that this value is also a necessary condition for the appearance of complexity in the universe. With $Q=10^{-6}$, gas cannot cool in the potential wells of haloes and no stars can form. With $Q=10^{-4}$, galaxies are so dense that frequent stellar encounters hamper the existence of stable planetary orbits, which are a necessary condition for the existence of living ecosystems that draw their energy from stellar radiation. Again, our observable universe seems to have emerged for a very peculiar set of initial conditions.

The cosmologists have a new theory that avoids the introduction of final causes: it is called chaotic inflation. In chaotic inflation, inflation eternally takes place and makes new patches of exponentially inflating space-time that causally decouple one from each other. Subsequently,

---

8.   JD Barrow and FJ Tipler, *The Anthropic Cosmological Principle* (Oxford: Oxford University Press, 1986).

the inflationary stages turn into the normal expansion phases. In this context, the laws and constants of physics are fixed by symmetry breaking and get different values in the different patches. Consequently, with an infinite number of realisations, we must not be surprised that there is at least one patch of the universe that has the values of the laws, constants, and of Q suited to the appearance of complexity. The question of knowing whether this theory is testable is still open. But it is not our concern here.

At the current stage of explanation, the apparent fine-tuning in the universe is not due to a peculiar set of initial conditions, but to the exploration of a range of possible values in various patches of the universe. We simply live in a patch that has values suited to the existence of complexity. But this type of explanation ignores the ' power ' allotted to the principles of quantum mechanics and the fundamental field theory. When an over-arching field theory is developed (maybe some kind of super-symmetric string theory), it will turn out that it has the possibility of generating patches where complexity is possible. So we shall have to push our explanation forwards again to a broader theory. This quest appears to be endless. The irony is that when cosmologists try to evacuate final causes, they make new theories and discover new phenomena, but they always face the same type of puzzle. The existence of fine-tuning in the universe surely tells us something about reality. But what? Humankind can readily understand that it is a divine sign. If we do not, the door is open to an endless exploration of the cosmos that displaces and magnifies the puzzle, till we finally acknowledge it. 'Whichever way you turn, there is the Face of God.'[9]

The second puzzle deals with the universality of the laws. Some cosmologists use the word 'universe' for each of these causally disconnected patches, and the word 'multiverse' to name the ensemble of all these patches generated by chaotic inflation. Of course, there is some ideology in the choice of the names. According to its symbolical etymology, the universe is a sign that is directed 'towards the One' (*unum versus* in Latin). Do many worlds suggest many gods? In any case, in the mind of some of those who promote the multiverse, new cosmology seems to be more sympathetic with polytheism than with monotheism. However, all these patches of the universe are actually

---

9.   Koran, 2:115.

linked by the fact that they are ruled by the same principles of quantum physics and the same over-arching field theory. For that reason, there is actually a *single* universe. Why are the laws of quantum physics so *universal*?

Here again, modern cosmologists do not wonder enough about the continuous validity of the laws. There has been a long controversy in Islam on the existence and status of the secondary causes. It is well known that the Ash'arite theology strongly questions the very existence of causality. The position is that there are no 'secondary' causes, simply because God, as the 'primary' cause, does not cease to create again the world at each instant. In this continuous renewal of creation (*tajdid al-khalq*), the atoms and their accidents are created anew all the time. As a consequence, the regularities observed in the world are not due to causal connection, but to a constant conjunction between the phenomena, which is a custom established by God. This principle of Islamic theology should be primarily understood as an emphasis on a metaphysical mystery: the continuous validity of the laws. God's permanence makes creation behave regularly in spite of the continuous renewal: 'you will not see a flaw in the Merciful's creation. Turn up your eyes: can you detect a single crack?'[10]

The renewal of creation taught by the Islamic doctrines also means the continuous appearance of new creatures. According to the views of the Akbarian school, funded after the work of Muhyi-d-din Ibn Arabi, who died in 1240, the creation is God's self-disclosure to Himself through the veils and signs of the creatures. The things 'are' not, since only God is. They only own a given preparation to receive being and qualities from God. As a consequence, since the status of the cosmos is paradoxical, between absolute Being and absolute nothingness, we cannot expect to reach clear-cut statements about the fundamental reality of the world. The ultimate reality is hidden, and our descriptions will always be approximate.

God is infinite and 'self-disclosure never repeats itself'. So God's self-disclosure is endless. At each level of the cosmos, there are always new things continuously 'poured' into disclosure. What appears in the creation exactly corresponds to the flow of possible things. This is why, according to the great theologian and mystic al-Ghazali, who lived in the eleventh century, 'there is nothing in possibility more wondrous

---

10.   Koran, 67:3.

than what is', because what is actually reflects God's desire to show up to us. This helps us understand the prophetic saying: 'Curse not time, for God is time'. After all, the production of an infinite number of 'patches' of the physical universe described by chaotic inflation could fit in this view of God's eternal self-disclosure. The appearance of 'emerging properties' at all levels of complexity, and particularly the appearance of life and intelligence, is another aspect of this continuous self-disclosure. This is why Ibn Arabi comments: 'God does not become bored that you should become bored.' We cosmologists surely understand this, since we are continuously astonished by the beauty of the phenomena unravelled by our new observing tools.

The appearance of the human being was made possible by many anthropic 'coincidences' in the laws of physics and the values of the constants, which fix the properties of the cosmic and terrestrial structures. The extension of time behind us and of space around us is a necessary condition for our existence, as well as the vast extensions of the deserts of sand and ice are necessary for the ecological balance of the earth. But this is of little interest in the face of our spiritual call for an endless quest: the quest for knowledge that is the core of our nature and dignity.

However, there is a significant difference between the scientific pursuit and the spiritual quest, which deals with the ending point of our existence. Contrary to the scientific pursuit, the spiritual quest is not limited to the intellectual search for truth and the production of useful consequences. It primarily aims at transforming humans, so that they can be prepared to the afterlife. Let us come back to Averroes and Ibn Arabi who happened to meet in Cordoba, probably around 1180. Averroes, who then was already a renowned philosopher, defended that human reason was able to reach all the truth accessible to the humankind, and not less than what was brought by revelation under the veils of the dogmas and symbols for the benefit of those who are not experts in science. Averroes had heard that the young Ibn Arabi had been granted spiritual enlightenment and he was eager to meet him. Ibn Arabi reports on their meeting: 'When I entered in upon [Averroes], he stood up in his place out of love and respect. He embraced me and said, "Yes". I said, "Yes". His joy increased because I had understood him. Then I realised why he had rejoiced at that, so I said, "No". His joy disappeared and his color changed, and he doubted what he possessed in himself.' Then comes the explanation of these strange exchanges. Averroes asked the crucial question which we are interested in: '"How did you find the situation in unveiling and divine effusion? Is it what rational consideration gives to us?" Ibn Arabi replies, "Yes no. Between the yes and the no, spirits fly from their matter and heads from their bodies", and he reports on Averroes' reaction: 'His color turned pale and he began to tremble. He sat reciting, "There is no power and no strength but in God', since he has understood my allusion.'[11]

Ibn Arabi alluded to eschatology, by recalling that even if reason can go very far in its attempt to grasp reality, nobody has been intimately changed by one's scientific knowledge. According to the teachings of Islam, we shall have to leave this world at the moment of our death, in order to pursue our quest for knowledge, and enter another level of being which is a broader locus for God's self-disclosure. The Islamic tradition promises that the quest for knowledge will end when the elect contemplate God's face on the so-called 'Dune of Musk' (*al-kathib*) that is located on the top of the heavenly Gardens, at the last frontier of creation. Religion is providentially revealed to prepare us to face absolute reality, which is another name of God. But this end of the quest will not be the end of knowledge. On the contrary, the elect's contemplation of God will continuously be renewed, as they will know, according to the Koranic verse, 'what no eye has seen, what no ear has heard, and what has never passed into the heart of any mortal'. Our reason could estimate that this is impossible, since we do not conceive 'how' this can physically happen. But indeed, the 'Dune' is the locus of the answers to the 'why' questions, without 'how'.

Because of our spectacular progress in the scientific under-standing of the universe, we have forgotten contemplation, which is necessary to human beings. It is this kind of awareness that can help 'reconcile' science and religion, and not a low-level concordism. To conclude, we would like to mention three qualities that seem to be relevant for all those who, as scientists and believers, keep a continuous tension towards truth. These are gratefulness (*shukr*), fear (*taqwa*) and perplexity (*hayrah*). Gratefulness is for the marvels of the cosmos, fear for the sense of Transcendence it inspires, perplexity for the continuous existence of unsolved puzzles that points at more fundamental

---

11. I use the translation by William Chittick in *The Sufi Path of Knowledge*, SUNY.

mysteries. These qualities are known in religious and mystical knowledge. In the Islamic prospect, we can add that gratefulness refers to the 'names of beauty' (*asma' al-Jamal*), and fear to the 'names of majesty' (*asma' al-Jalal*) that show up in the worlds, whereas perplexity refers to the coexistence of opposite qualities that can be solved only in *Allah* who is the 'name of the synthesis' (*ism al-jami'*). The spiritual pursuit is not limited to the intellectual contemplation of truth, but it aims at salvation, which is the ultimate meaning of humankind. Gratefulness, fear and perplexity are three modes of the fundamental bewilderment that is produced by the contemplation of the cosmos. This bewilderment is a way of worshipping God. Such an attitude should lead scientists to an increasing sense of responsibility in the technological applications of modern science.

9

Big Bang Cosmology and Creation Theology: Towards a Fruitful Dialogue between Science and Religion

Justin Sudarminta SJ

1. Introduction

I would like to divide my response paper into five parts. First, I shall try to summarise the gist of the argument for the big bang theory of cosmology as a contemporary and commonly accepted scientific theory on the origin of the universe. Second, I will affirm Dr Karlina's critical remark on some simplistic ways of connecting big bang cosmology with creation theology. In particular I shall refer to the notorious statement by Pope Pius XII that big bang cosmology supports the biblical idea of creation, and Robert Jastrow's statement that the astronomical evidence leads to a biblical view of the origin of the world. Third, to avoid the mistake of falling into what Dr Guiderdoni calls 'a low-level concordism' or in Dr Karlina's term to 'choose an easier path' in reconciling science and religion, I shall point out some prerequisites that should be met in order to have a fruitful dialogue between big bang cosmology and creation theology without violating the integrity of either. In this third section I will also reinforce matters that should be kept in mind if we are to develop some partnership or to maintain a close contact between big bang cosmology and creation theology without jeopardising the distinctive characteristics of either. Fourth, I will point out some implications of big bang cosmology that are theologically relevant. Finally, I also point out some ideas derived from creation theology that have some relevance to the believing scientists in doing cosmology.

2. Big bang cosmology as a generally accepted scientific theory about the origin of the universe

As evident from the papers of both Dr Guiderdoni and Dr Karlina, in contemporary cosmology, the generally accepted scientific theory or model of explanation about the origin of the universe is the big bang theory/model. According to this theory/model of explanation, the universe is not eternal, but started with the big bang which took place approximately fifteen billion years ago. The universe is not something static either. Rather, it keeps changing. The theory about the expanding universe was initiated in 1917 when Willem de Sitter, the Dutch physicist, working with Einstein's general relativity equations, found a solution that predicted an expanding universe. If the universe were eternal and static, the various masses would bb now have collapsed gravitationally upon one another. In 1922, Alexander Friedman, a Russian mathematician, calculated that general relativity challenges the idea of an eternally unchanging universe or the steady state theory. Then, in 1929, American astronomer, Edwin Hubble, who examined the 'red-shift' of light from distant nebulae using the powerful Mount Wilson telescope, provided what seemed to be observational evidence of a dynamic universe. Extrapolating backward in time the so-called Edwin Hubble's law (the velocity of the recession of a nebula is proportional to its distance from us), scientists have concluded that the universe seems to be expanding from the common origin, called the big bang. This conclusion was further substantiated when, in 1965, Arno Penzias and Robert Wilson discovered a faint background of microwaves coming from all directions in space. The spectrum of those waves corresponded very closely to the residual radiation that had been predicted from relativity theory. The radiation itself is the cosmic fireball's afterglow, cooled by its subsequent expansion.

Doubts about the big bang theory, however, still lingered on until the early 1990s. The main reason for the doubt is the seemingly incompatibility between the theory and with the astronomical fact that our cosmos is made up of very unevenly distributed galaxies, clusters and super-clusters of galaxies, stars, planets, gasses, and other kinds of matter. If the universe really began with a smooth big bang, why there is such an irregularity and unevenness in the distribution of matter. To produce such an irregularity, the universe must have possessed the 'seeds' of such unevenness even when the universe was still in its infancy. This hypothesis seemed to be confirmed in 1992. Data carefully collected from Cosmic Background Explorer showed that as early as 300.000 after the big bang, the radiation out of which later forms of matter evolved had already shown a primordial wrinkles, which were probably the 'seeds' of our uneven universe. So, at least for the time being, the big bang theory as a scientific account of how the universe came into being remains confirmed.

3. A critique of some simplistic ways of connecting big bang cosmology and creation theology

What does the big bang cosmology mean for those who accept the theory and also believe in creation theology? Does the big bang theory of cosmic origin support the biblical idea of creation, as Pope Pius XII has maintained? Is it true that 'the astronomical evidence leads to a biblical view of the origin of the world' as the astrophysicist Robert Jastrow has argued? Many people now would say that they both have made too hasty a claim and seem too simplistic in connecting big bang cosmology and creation theology. I agree with Dr Karlina's argument that to consider the big bang as the act of God's creation of the universe in its ontological meaning is somewhat naïve. Cosmology does not make an ontological claim. It simply provides models to understand the cosmos. If the word 'support' in the Pope's statement simply means that there is no contradiction or fundamental conflict between the big bang theory and the teaching of the theological doctrine of creation, the statement would still be acceptable. However, if it means to say that the big bang theory has provided a scientific certification of the theology of creation, then the statement would be mistaken. The theology of creation does not need any scientific certification in order to be believed. Looking for a scientific certification by building a theological doctrine upon a scientific finding, albeit the latest one, as its foundation, is to put the doctrine in a very shaky ground.

Robert Jastrow's statement would also be mistaken if by the word 'leads' he means to say that whoever accepts the astronomical evidence with regard to the big bang theory would necessarily accept the biblical view of the origin of the world. Despite the available astronomical evidence, there are still many scientific sceptics around. They will need much more than big bang astronomical evidence to lead them to religious faith in God's creation of the world. It is by no means self-evident that just because the universe had a beginning, it also had to have a God as its creator. There are still some cosmologists who maintain that the universe might have created itself by chance. A physicist named Alan Guth, for instance, has stated: 'People often say that there is no such thing as a free lunch. But the universe might be called a free lunch.'[1] What he means to say is that based on the principle of quantum fluctuation which is also applicable to the universe as a whole, the universe seems to have popped up by itself without any external cause. There may have been many universes with differing parameters, and we just happen by chance to live in one of those in which the conditions proved favourable for intelligent life. This theory denies the anthropic principle, according to which there is a fine-tuning of the universe so as to make it habitable for intelligent life, namely human beings. According to the anthropic principle, what we can expect to observe must be restricted by the conditions necessary for our presence as observers. Reflection on the way the universe seems to be fine-tuned for human life as intelligent being has led some cosmologists to formulate the anthropic principle. To simply take this principle as an argument for God's design in the world, or as a theological affirmation for the fine-tuning of the universe is, as Dr Karlina has pointed out, certainly unac-ceptable. In this case, her criticism is well put.

4. Prerequisites for a fruitful dialogue between big bang cosmology and creation theology

To have a fruitful dialogue between science and religion regarding the origin of the universe, we should not conflate the two. There is indeed a great temptation to read theological

---

1.   As quoted by Paul Davies on his book *God and the New Physics* (New York: Simon & Schuster, Inc. 1983), p. 216.

implications directly out of favourable new cosmological discoveries. And yet, being a temptation, it should always be resisted. Cosmology and theology are two different disciplines of knowledge, each with its own subject matter, purpose and methodology. For the right rendering of both disciplines, one should always be differentiated from the other.

The subject matter of cosmology as an empirical science is dealing with natural phenomena. Cosmology lies in the realm of the natural world. Its purpose is to provide models to explain and understand how the whole material cosmos works. Its method is a scientific one, using mathematical models and computation, empirical observation, and experimental testing. Whereas the subject-matter of theology deals with the realm of faith and divine revelation. The purpose of theology as a reflection of human faith experience is to understand better the religious doctrines or articles of faith in each religion and to make religious life, in this world and in the world to come, more meaningful and worth pursuing. Theology does not limit itself to the realm of the empirical, because it deals with the ultimate questions of life and existence, from the perspective of certain religious faith. Theological argument is indeed rational, but religious rationality gives room to what is supra-rational, to the data of divine revelation. The method of theology is not a scientific method in the strict sense of the term. Rather, it is an interpretive or hermeneutical method, applied by the community of believers in their attempts to understand their life experiences in the light of their faith in their search for their ultimate meaning of life and existence.

Understood properly, big bang cosmology actually tells us nothing about what creation means in its religious meaning. On the other hand, creation theology, as a religious account, has nothing to teach about the physical origin of the universe either. This does not mean that cosmology and theology are two totally separate domains. They are not two totally independent aspects of human life. Borrowing Ian G Barbour's term,[2] they are not 'strangers' to each other. As science and religion can be partners,

---

2.   Ian G Barbour, *When Science Meets Religion, Enemies, Strangers, or Partners?* (New York: Harper San Francisco, 2000).

so can cosmology and theology. But how can this partnership, especially in the case of big bang cosmology and creation theology, be developed without jeopardising the distinctive characteristics of each?

First, we should keep in mind that the scriptural doctrine of creation, such as is presented in the Bible, for instance, should be understood religiously and not scientifically. The text in that book should indeed be taken seriously by its believers, but not literally. From the Christian perspective, for instance, the ideas in the pre-scientific cosmology as presented in the book of Genesis, which were taken from the pre-scientific cosmology of the day when the book was written, certainly are no longer consistent with modern scientific cosmology. But this should not bother Christian believers, because the book of Genesis was, and still is, not meant to be a scientific book on cosmology. The religious ideas conveyed in that book are still valid up to now. Religiously understood, the book of Genesis makes at least five theological affirmations, and they still hold now. Those five theological affirmations are: (1) the world is ontologically dependent on God; (2) the world is essentially good, orderly, and coherent; (3) God is sovereign, free, trans-cendent, purposive and powerful; (4) humankind has a high dignity; (5) the evil and sufferings in the world are not caused by God but by human sinfulness. These articles of faith are generally accepted by many religions and not dependent on a certain scientific cosmology.

Second, we should also keep in mind that creation stories, as depicted in the sacred stories, serve a different function in human life than scientific theories about the origin of the universe. The function of creation stories is to provide a larger framework of meaning and significance for human life within a cosmic order. Whereas the function of scientific theories about the origin of the universe is to give a rational account, based upon the lawful relations among natural phenomena, on how the universe came into existence. As already noted by Barbour,

> the idea of creation can also be seen as an expression of enduring human experiences, such as: (1) a sense of dependence, finitude, and contingency; (2) a response of wonder, trust,

gratitude for life, and affirmation of the world; and (3) a recognition of interdependence, order, and beauty in the world. The religious idea of creation starts from wonder and gratitude for life as a gift. Theological doctrines are an attempt to interpret such experiences within the context of a particular historical tradition. The theological meaning of creation can be combined with a variety of physical cosmologies, ancient or modern, and does not require any one cosmology.[3]

Even though big bang cosmology and creation theology each serve a different function in human life, and thus should be differentiated from each other, this does not mean that there are no points of contact, or even some possible integration, between the two. Linguistically speaking, they are not two *entirely* different language games in which all possible roads to meaningful communication are blocked. We do need to be cautious in drawing the theological implication from any cosmology, including big bang cosmology. However, in talking about the relation of God to the world, theology cannot help thinking about God in terms of some cosmology. And today, the big bang theory, along with all the other things that relativity and quantum physics are implying about our world, should be taken into consideration.

5. Implications of big bang cosmology that are theologically relevant

Which implications of the big bang theory of cosmology are theologically relevant? The first implication derived from big bang cosmology that is theologically relevant is the contingency of the universe. The universe implied by big bang cosmology is neither eternal nor necessary, but radically finite. If the universe is radically finite, then it is contingent. The contingency of the universe implies that there is no necessity for its having come into

---

3.   *Ibid*, 51.

existence, for being the way it is. The existence of the universe or of the cosmos as a whole is, therefore, not self-explanatory. One question that is of greatest interest to theologians corresponding to the religious meaning of creation and has some connection with cosmology is: 'Why is there anything at all, instead of nothing?' By asking the question 'Why does the universe exist anyway?' After considering how the universe in fact came into existence, as described by the science of cosmology, we have already brought cosmology in close contact with theology, science with religion. Indeed, the question as to why the whole cosmos exists arises quite independently of big bang cosmology. Nonetheless, the fact that today the question arises spontaneously out of a scientific cosmology certainly places science in a context where a close contact with religion seems appropriate. Science has thus brought us to some limit questions that cannot be answered by science itself. Our sense of wonder at the fact that the universe exists at all has been given a powerful boost by current cosmology. Since the religious faith in God's act of creation is inseparable from this same sense of wonder at the mystery of being, theologians cannot be indifferent to the new scientific developments. To that limit question regarding why the universe ever exists at all, creation theology gives a straightforward and uncomplicated answer. It is due to God's free act of love that the universe exists. God has created it out of nothing.

Another implication derived from big bang cosmology that is theologically relevant is the idea that our cosmos is still in the making. As Dr Guiderdoni points out in his paper, 'the Islamic tradition has always taught that God is nearby and continuously acts in creation'. This is actually also in the Christian tradition. Only those theologians who embrace deism would consider 'a creator who would let his creation behave by itself with so much independence that he finally becomes a new kind of *Deus Otiosus*, either by will or by experience of human weakness'. Christian belief in God's incarnation in Jesus Christ, who, as the divine Logos patterning the whole act of God's creation and work of salvation, also has a cosmological implication. God is not simply transcendent but is also immanent in the evolution of the universe.

According to the big bang cosmology, there is a cosmic expansion and evolution beginning with the big bang. Combined with the theory of evolution in biology, the big bang theory of cosmology can help us understand the theological idea of continuing creation. God's act of creation is not confined to the originating moment in the remote past. Rather, it is still going on, and it has never stopped. The idea that God has created the world in the past, once for all, and then let the world mechanically function for itself, is the idea put forward by deism. This idea seems to be inconsistent with big bang cosmology. The creation theology, as taught by monotheistic religions, is not deistic, because it contains the idea of continuing creation. This idea, which is consistent with the big bang cosmology, makes room for the idea of God's continuing presence in, and conservation of, the world. Creation is far from being a finished product once for all.

The idea that our cosmos is still in the making is also theologically relevant to seeing the inadequacy, and possibly the need for modification, of our traditional images of God as Creator. For instance, God as Creator is often traditionally depicted through the images of the potter and craftsman. These images seem to be inconsistent with the whole idea that our cosmos is still in the making. They give the wrong impression about creation as a static and finished or completed product. Theologians who talk about creation without forgetting the relevance of the idea—derived from big bang cosmology—that our cosmos is dynamic and unfinished, would certainly be sensitive toward the need to provide more appropriate symbols and images of God as Creator. The images of God as Creator we found in the text of the Scriptures should not be understood apart from the sociohistorical and cultural contexts from which they were taken. The new development in cosmology might make us aware of the need to revise our images of God as Creator. Our openness to the new developments in science and our willingness to revise our images of God and our religious symbols in line with the new developments will help us to keep alive our religious faith.

6. Ideas derived from creation theology, relevant for doing cosmology

Aside from paying attention to some possible theological implications of the big bang cosmology, we also need to find some ideas or concepts derived from creation theology that have some relevance for the scientists who do scientific research in cosmology. First, the ideas that God is rational and that there is a rational or intelligible order in the universe are central ideas in creation theology. These ideas are not only consistent with, but also inherently supportive of, scientific research in cosmology. The goal of science is basically looking for lawful connections between natural phenomena. Based on those lawful connections we make certain predictions and have certain control over nature. We can use scientific knowledge to solve puzzles that arise from, and in our interactions with, nature. The scientists would never find the lawful connections between natural phenomena unless nature itself is lawful. So scientific activity itself presupposes that there is an intelligible order in the universe. In Dr Guiderdoni words: 'The fundamental mystery that subtends physics and cosmology is the fact that the world is intelligible'.

Second, as John Haught has pointed out:

> the theological notion that the world was [and still is] created—and is therefore neither necessary nor eternal—gives a stature to empirical science that other ways of looking at the world do not. Had the world existed necessarily and eternally, then the empirical science would have been irrelevant, for every feature of the universe could in theory be deduced from necessary first principles . . . Science would finally be superfluous.[4]

As we have noted before, creation theology, however, implies that the actually existing universe is not necessary, but

4.   John F Haught, *Science & Religion, From Conflict to Conversation* (New York: Paulist Press, 1995), 119.

contingent. The universe need not have existed at all, and it need not have turned out the way it has. Since the universe and its nature came into existence due to the free decision of God the Creator, we can only know the universe inductively through empirical observation. Religious faith in creation, therefore, in Haught's words, implicitly propels us on a journey of discovery to find out *by observation* what the world is like. Since it expels rigid necessity from our view of the universe, creation theology opens us up to the possibility of being surprised by the actual facts. It is especially in an intellectual and cultural milieu molded by the creation theology of the God-religions that the empirical imperative of science, the injunction to attend to what we actually experience, is explicitly confirmed.[5]

Bibliography

Barbour, Ian G. *When Science Meets Religion, Enemies, Strangers, or Partners?* (New York: Harper San Francisco, 2000).

--------------. *Religion in an Age of Science* (London: SCM Press, 1990).

Davies, Paul. *The Mind of God* (New York: Simon & Schuster, 1992).

------------. *God and The New Physics* (New York: Simon & Schuster, Inc, 1983).

Greene, Brian. *The Elegant Universe* (New York: Vintage Books, 1999).

Haught, John F. *Science & Religion, From Conflict to Conversation* (New York: Paulist Press, 1995).

Hawking, Stephen W. *A Brief History of Time* (New York: Bantam Books, 1988).

Jastrow, Robert. *God and the Astronomers* (New York: Norton, 1978).

Polkinghorne, John. *Science and Creation* (London: SPCK, 1988).

Pope Pius XII. 'Modern Science and the Existence of God', in *The Catholic Mind* (Mar 1952): 182–192.

Sudarminta, J. '*Sains dan Masalah Ketuhanan*', *Diskursus* (April 2002): 35–46.

5.　*Ibid*, 119.

10
Towards a Constructive Theology of Evolution

William Grassie

1. Introduction

The purpose of this essay is to give a brief introduction to the theories of evolution, the variety of religious response to evolution and, in conclusion, a survey of some constructive theologies of evolution prominent among Christian thinkers today. In this paper, I draw heavily upon the works of two authors. Holmes Rolston III is a professor of philosophy at Colorado State University and author of numerous texts, including *Philosophy Gone Wild, Environmental Ethics, Science and Religion,* and *Genes, Genesis, and God: Values and Their Origins in Human and Natural History*. John F Haught is a professor of systematic theology at Georgetown University and the author of a number of texts, including *God after Darwin: A Theology of Evolution, Science and Religion,* and *The Cosmic Adventure.*

2. Before evolution

In today's urban technological civilisation, we are disconnected from the natural processes necessary for the sustenance of human life. Most today could not name a dozen indigenous plant or animal species, let alone a dozen invasive non-indigenous species. Most today cannot see the stars at night and do not know the phases of the moon. Most today have little understanding of agriculture and what it means to work in the soil and muck with domesticated plants and animals. If we think back a mere fifty or one hundred years ago, such concerns were of primary importance to the vast majority of humans on the planet. Understanding the natural world was necessary to humanity's physical survival. Interpreting the natural world was of primary importance to constructing human culture. It turns out that these concerns are no less important today, but we shall return to this radically different contemporary context of understanding nature in the twenty-first century at the end of the talk.

When we look attentively upon the natural kinds, we notice that plants and animals appear to be elegantly designed to inhabit different niches, different modes of being in the world. The nature of an owl, for instance, is vastly different than the nature of a tiger or a mouse, or for that matter of a reptile, fish, or plant. Aristotle saw this diversity of species in their independent 'natures' or 'natural kinds'. Aristotle saw these natural kinds as eternal and unchanging. The theistic religions of the Judaism, Christianity, and Islam interpreted Aristotle in the Middle Ages with the doctrine of separate creation, which is to say that God created each species as a separate entity. In many ways, the theories of natural kinds and separate creation are much more intuitively self-apparent than the theory of evolution that would replace them in the nineteenth century. In this matter, evolution is no different than the uncommon vision of other sciences. For instance, it is not self-apparent that the earth rotates on its axis and revolves around the sun as in the new seventeenth century heliocentric model of the solar system. We still talk of the Sun rising and setting, even though we know this not to be the case.

The world of nature was significant also in the construct of human culture. In the Middle Ages, nature was understood to be hierarchically organised with plants and animals at the bottom, followed by humans in the middle, angels and archangels above the humans, and God at the top. The hierarchy of nature was then also mapped out onto political and ecclesiastical hierarchies in human culture. People knew where they stood in the orders of culture and who their natural superiors and inferiors were. All of this was rationalised through an understanding of natural orders and cosmic purpose. Our revealed texts were placed alongside the book of nature, which nature could be read for its theological and moral significance, as well as its scientific and practical significance.

3. The rise of evolution

Why then would people abandon this intuitively pleasing and culturally sanctified worldview? In the eighteenth and nineteenth centuries, European naturalists began to travel the world on scientific expeditions. In trying to classify the great variety of natural kinds discovered in far-off places, they paid closer attention to morphological similarities between species. For instance, Alfred Russell Wallace, credited with co-publishing the theory of natural selection with Charles Darwin in 1858, did extensive fieldwork in the Indonesian archipelago. Biologists wondered about why the same bone structure repeats itself in the arms of mammals as different as dolphins, bats, chimpanzees, and humans. Why did the embryos of different species go through similar patterns of development (ie ontogeny recapitulates phylogeny)? Why are the internal structures of organs in animals similar (eg hearts, lungs, digestive tracts, nervous systems, and brains)? Geologists discovered the fossil remains of extinct species like dinosaurs. Fossils of sea creatures were found high on the tops of mountains. A new geological time-scale was postulated dating the history of the earth in millions and later billions of years. Today we would add radiographic dating and shared genetic structures to the mounting evidence for some kind of evolution from common descent over a vast time-scale. Biologists have come to accept that the earth is approximately four billion years old, that life began as single cellular bacteria, which complexified approximately two billion years ago into eukaryotic cells, which then gave rise to plants, fish, amphibians, reptiles, birds, mammals, and also humans.

What troubled our eighteenth and nineteenth century forebears was not evolution per se but a mechanism that could describe how evolution occurred. The French biologist Jean Baptiste Lamarck (1744–1829) proposed a theory of evolution prior to Darwin's theory of natural selection. Lamarck argued that acquired characteristics could be passed on to future generations. A giraffe, for instance, that acquired its food by browsing leaves and twigs from trees would always be stretching its neck to reach higher into the trees. The offspring of the giraffe would then be born with longer necks. Unfortunately, such evolutionary patterns cannot be observed in nature, though it did not prevent some, like Charles Darwin's father, from being attracted to this theory, largely on political grounds. Today, the term 'Lamarckism' is used in Anglo-American biological circles as a term of derision, though as we shall see later, the process of passing on acquired characteristics to future generations is precisely the pattern that we observe in human cultural evolution.

Charles Darwin (1809–1882) is widely credited with discovering the mechanism by which evolution from common origins occurs. Darwin was trained in theology at Cambridge University. He was most interested in what was then still called natural theology or natural philosophy. One of Darwin's favorite books as a student at Cambridge was William Paley's *Natural Theology*. Paley employed the metaphor of a watch discovered on a beach. One would not know who made the watch, but one could infer that there was certainly a watch-maker. One might even come to understand the design and function of the watch. In such a way, humans studying nature could also come to understand God as the creator and designer of nature. Darwin would come to reject this design metaphor and question the existence of God.

Darwin circumnavigated the world as the naturalist on the HMS *Beagle* from 1831 to 1836. He published *The Origin of Species* in 1859. The impact of his new theory of natural selection was immediate and widespread. Darwin's long argument is based on a few simple premises. First, there are among offspring not only similar hereditary characteristics resulting from having the same parents, but there are also variations among offspring from the same parents. Second, every species exhibits an exponential ratio of increase resulting from the number of offspring they are able to produce. Third, this exponential rate of increase results in a universal struggle for survival as individual members of a species compete for food, water, habitat, and mates. Fourth, those variations among offspring that increase the likelihood of survival and reproduction for individual members of a species will tend to persist over time, while those variations that do not increase the likelihood of survival and reproduction will tend to die off. Fifth, the accumulation of all of these 'selections' over long periods of time, involving also changes in the environment and geographic isolation, will result in the transmutation of one species into others; hence the title of Darwin's revolutionary book, *The Origin of Species*.

Darwin wrote:

> Owing to this struggle for life, any variation, however slight and from whatever cause proceeding, if it be in any degree profitable to an individual of any species, in its infinitely complex relations to other organic beings and to external nature, will tend to the preservation of that individual, and will generally be inherited by its offspring. The offspring, also, will thus have a better chance of surviving, for, of the many individuals of any species which are periodically born, but a small

number can survive. I have called this principle, by which each slight variation, if useful, is preserved, by the term of Natural Selection, in order to mark its relation to man's power of selection (i.e., in the breeding of domesticated plants and animals in agriculture). We have seen that man by selection can certainly produce great results, and can adapt organic beings to his own uses, through the accumulation of slight but useful variations, given to him by the hand of Nature. But Natural Selection, as we shall hereafter see, is a power incessantly ready for action, and is as immeasurably superior to man's feeble efforts, as the works of Nature are to those of Art (*The Origins of Species*).

4. The challenges of evolution to religious worldviews

In the *Origins*, Darwin did not discuss the place of humans in this evolutionary story, but others latched on to the theory and applied it to human affairs. In 1871, Darwin published *The Descent of Man*, in which he explicitly laid forth the argument that humans evolved from ancestors common to today's primates. Indeed, if we go back far enough in the genetic, evolutionary muck, we share a common ancestry with all life on the planet. This is perhaps the most significant insight gained from the recent mapping of the human genome—that we carry inside of us lengthy strings of base pairs in our DNA which we have in common with bacteria, chickens, dinosaurs and just about any other species to be found on the planet. On the genetic level, we are kissing cousins with chimpanzees with a ninety-eight per cent overlap in our genetic structure.

Humans, as noted above, always seem to use nature as a metaphor and context for interpreting cosmic purpose and moral order. This is no less true of Darwinism than the earlier Aristotelian view of natural kinds and separate creation. Darwinism seemed to support the view that the universe is governed not by a powerful and benevolent God, but by random genetic drift and natural selection. The process necessitated an inordinate amount of suffering, death and waste. If God exists, then natural selection rendered God an incompetent or malevolent Creator. Of course, the challenge of theodicy existed prior to Darwinism, but this theory of evolution multiplied the doubts of

God's goodness with the magnitude of the ages and the multitude of struggling species. So Darwin's theory of evolution contributed to undermining the earlier cosmological hierarchy and sense of moral purpose.

Some latched on to the new theory of evolution to argue for the natural superiority of the European races over other races of the world; so late nineteenth and twentieth century racism shares an ugly legacy which often used Social Darwinism to lend it 'scientific' legitimacy. Others latched on to the theory to promote predatory capitalism. Herbert Spencer coined the phrase 'survival of the fittest', which Darwin incorporated into later editions of *The Origins*. The term 'survival of the fittest' would quickly become the short-hand for natural selection cited by the baron-robber capitalists of the early twentieth century to rationalise their extreme wealth. Karl Marx, however, also saw Darwin's theory as a validation of his theory of dialectical materialism and wanted to dedicate *Das Kapital* to Charles Darwin, though Darwin declined the offer.

Early twentieth century eugenics also drew on Darwin's theory, though the controlled breeding of humans was sometimes cast as a moral response to the immoral implications of Social Darwinism and sometimes involved mixing races rather than preserving racial purity. Of course, both eugenics and Social Darwinism would provide ideological fuel to Stalinism and Nazism, which on sheer scale were perhaps the greatest tragedies in human history. Historians suggest that the real impetus for the conservative religious reaction against Darwinism arose not from concern about the origins of species, but from the perception that the theory of natural selection as applied to humans was inherently immoral.

The challenge of Darwinism was also that it undermined our early sense of cosmic purpose and made atheism intellectually plausible and contributed to scientism as the dominant ideology of the modern university. Richard Dawkins, the contemporary biologist, notorious atheist, and prolific writer, notes that 'The [Darwinian] universe we observe has precisely the properties we should expect if there is, at bottom, no design, no purpose, no evil and no good, nothing but blind, pitiless indifference'.

Dawkins represents one of the theological responses to evolution, which is to say that evolution by natural selection proves that God does not exist or at least need not exist in order to account for the origins of life. This should be understood as a theological response because, like many atheists, Dawkins has very definite ideas about the kind of God that he believes does not exist.

Dawkins sees Darwinism as a revolutionary break from the past. All of the old attempts of theology and philosophy to answer the questions of how humans ought to live and act are no longer valid. 'The point I want to make now', writes Dawkins, 'is that all attempts to answer that question before 1859 are worthless and that we will be better off if we ignore them completely' (1989).

Now there are many others we might quote here who would support this contention that Darwinism proves atheism, notably EO Wilson, Daniel Dennett, Michael Ruse, and Stephen Jay Gould. Suffice it to say that if such thinkers did not exist, many religious thinkers would have had to invent them in order to carry on their feud with Darwinism. In the context of the warfare between evolution and creationism in the United States, the problem is less with believers who read the Bible as a literal account of creation and more with believers who read Dawkins *et al* as a literal account of evolution.

5. Anti-evolutionary responses

There is an array of religious positions in opposition to Darwinism. Christian fundamentalism originally saw evolution as evidence of God's greatness at the turn of the twentieth century, but later adopted anti-evolution as a central tenet of their belief and began interpreting the Bible as a scientific text, seeking evidence to undermine evolution and support specific biblical interpretations. The most extreme version of this is called alternately scientific creationism, young earth creationism, or simply creationism. The term 'creationism' might better apply more broadly to any religious believer, including those that affirm evolution, but in popular usage today it refers specifically to those who deny evolution.

On both sides of this polarised conflict, there is a tendency to conflate the *observed pattern* with the *theorised process*. The long natural history of this planet with the gradual complexification of life forms and periodic mass extinctions of species is now well established. The process by which this happens and the significance of this process are open to debate and interpretation, as we will soon see. Evolution is not the same as Darwinism, though the terms are often conflated.

Evolution is the observed natural history of the planet. Darwinism, or more precisely natural selection, is a theory of how this evolution occurred.

This demarcation between *what* and *how* is critical in distinguishing competing religious responses to evolution. Always clarify what is the timeline account of natural history. It is one thing to debate the meaning and significance of the Cambrian explosion, or for that matter the French Revolution; it is another thing completely to deny that they ever happened. Young earth creationism is a misreading of science and, I would argue, also a misunderstanding of Scripture. Scientific creationism has a bad case of science envy trying to flatten a richly complicated and challenging scriptural tradition into a one-dimensional 'literal' interpretation.

Unfortunately, the Christian fundamentalist rejection of evolution has found followers in the Muslim world and apparently these Christians also offer financial support to such efforts. Of particular significance in the Muslim world is the work of Harun Yahya (Adnan Oktar) in Turkey <www. harunyahya.com>, who has latched on to this unfortunate logic—evolution equals Darwinism equals materialism equals atheism equals everything-that-is-wrong-in-the-world.

Other religious intellectuals have tried to latch scriptural apologetics onto scientific prestige by arguing that the Bible or the Koran anticipated specific scientific discoveries, for instance dinosaurs, quantum mechanics, or big bang cosmology. Contemporary science is then offered as evidence for the validity of the sacred Scripture. Here we might wonder again about the hermeneutics of the 'precursor-itis' that turns science into a proof-text for our holy Scriptures. We might also wonder about what happens ten or a hundred years hence when the science turns out to be radically different.

In the last few years, the intelligent design movement has gotten a lot of press in the United States. While vague about which version of natural history they support, the young or old earth variety, the intelligent design advocates argue that random genetic drift and natural selection alone cannot account for 'irreducibly complexity' in certain natural phenomena. The classic example of this is the human eye, to which Darwin himself called attention. How could such a complex mechanism with so many independent parts have arisen by incremental changes, when the mechanism would not function without all of the parts working together? Intelligent design advocates argue that some outside agency would be needed to specify such complexity. This can be seen as a new version of the God-of-the-gaps argument and suffers from all of the earlier attempts to insert God as an explanatory fix in science's progressive history of accounting for the unknown. God is either everywhere present in creation in all processes at all times or God is nowhere.

6. Beyond Darwinism

The theory of evolution has itself evolved in the last 150 years. Darwin, of course, knew nothing about modern genetics. He knew that there is a pattern of inheritance with variation among offspring, but not how this happens. It is not until the work of the Austrian monk Gregor Mendel (1822–1884) was rediscovered at the turn of the twentieth century and synthesised with Darwin's theory that we get neo-Darwinism, also known as the Modern Synthesis. Mendel discovered laws of inheritance based on dominant and recessive 'genes'. Today scientists have extended these insights to understanding the complex macromolecules of life and the biochemical reactions that structure protein synthesis, reproduction, and development. Genetics adds a structure of inheritable traits and rates of mutation or drift within species upon which natural selection operates through the necessities of survival and reproduction.

As paleontologists collected more evidence of the fossil record of the evolution of species, it was noted that the actual history of evolution is often abrupt with long periods of stasis and relatively short periods of rapid change. When first presented by Stephen Jay Gould and Niles Eldridge, this theory of 'punctuated equilibrium' was touted as a serious blow to the gradualism implied in Darwin's theory, but such concerns have largely evaporated.

At this point we start moving into serious debates in biology about what might be called post-Darwinism. For instance, biologists do not agree about the level upon which natural selection operates. Some have argued that selection operates only at the level of the gene, that genes are 'selfish', noting for instance the capacity of outlaw genes to survive independently of the wellbeing of the host individual. Others argue that selection occurs at the level of groups of genes or with the individual as a whole, or how else would any gene be able to reproduce? Others argue that selection also occurs with groups, for instance in social species. Group selection theory provides a tentative answer to the riddle of altruism within a theory that would otherwise predict reproductively selfish maximising behavior. Still others note that a kind of selection exists within and between ecosystems and between groups of species in symbiotic relations. Far from nature being at war, many species exhibit complex symbiosis. Sometimes life appears to be the proverbial Darwinian jungle in which survival and repro-duction is paramount, while in other instance life seems more like a 'white elephant sale' with a hodge-podge of eclectic knick-knacks thrown together by happenstance in the bazaar. Multi-level selection theory presents a serious challenges the reductionistic, explanatory simplicity that makes Darwinism so appealing to some.

In the case of bacteria, which have the largest biomass on the planet and are still in some sense also the most foundational kind of biological entity, it may not even be appropriate to talk of clear lines of descent required by Darwin's theory. Among bacteria, genetic information is shared not only by cell division, but also via viral vectors and direct membrane transfers throughout the gene pool of like and unlike bacteria. So it would seem that in addition to making room for symbiosis and multi-level selection in our post-Darwinist view of evolution, we are going to allow for some context-specific confusion within life itself about the genetic boundaries between what were previously thought to be distinct breeding populations.

Other post-Darwinian theories deal with saltation or non-gradual jumps between forms observed in the fossil records, but poorly understood. One clue might lie in the bureaucratic nature of the genome itself, which far from being a linear system of causation is interlinked in complex mutually determinative relations and feedback loops. We might better think of the genome as a molecular bureaucracy that has its own emergent, collectivist agenda. Another post-Darwinian frontier deals with indirect Lamarckism, whereby rates of adaptation, for instance in the stress breeding of *ecoli* bacteria, exceed what would be expected from the background rate of genetic mutations. Again, contrary to the so-called central dogma of biology, we should actually expect to discover some kinds of indirect feedback loops from the phenotype to the genotype, which will probably emerge in the field of developmental genetics and embryology.

Nor does natural selection per se illuminate anything about the mathematical patterns often manifested by natural entities. The field of mathematical biology lies wholly outside of the orthodox neo-

Darwinism, like a platonist idea among radical materialists. This leads to the related fields of systems theory and complexity theory as applied to life. Biologists have made a lot of progress on some levels by abstracting individuals from the webs of their relationships, even though the individual never really exists apart of these relational matrices. So whether we're talking about a single gene or a single individual or even an entire species separate from its ecosystem, these are abstrac-tions from reality, and we risk committing what AN Whitehead referred to in science as 'the fallacy of misplaced concreteness'. Systemic analyses of natural phenomena will reveal different patterns, complex patterns, often not easily accounted for by the reigning neo-Darwinian orthodoxy. Here we see the productive application of mathematical complexity theory to illuminating the workings of nature in nonlinear systems and fractal-like elegance.

Speaking of neo-Darwinism, biologist Lynn Margulis says, 'It is totally wrong. It's wrong like infectious medicine was wrong before Pasteur. It's wrong like phrenology is wrong. Every major tenet of it is wrong'. Those are fighting words for most biologists, but Margulis has in mind the symbiosis she observes in bacteria and other species and the vectors of genetic information sharing which cross-lines of descent. A more carefully argued case for rejecting neo-Darwinism in favour of some kind of post-Darwinism is made by David Depew and Bruce Weber in their book *Darwinism Evolving: Systems Dynamics and the Geneaology of Natural Selection* (1997). They conclude:

> Whatever else may happen, we are reasonably certain that evolutionary theory will remain incomplete as long as self-organizational and dissipative phenomena are kept at a distance. This still leaves open, of course, whether complex dynamical models and non-equilibrium thermo-dynamics will testify in favor of the developmentist or of the Darwinian tradition . . . Can self-organization and dissipative structures be brought into the present evolutionary synthesis or some expanded version of it? Alternately, will assimilation be so challenging that it will require a change of background assumptions in the Darwinian tradition com-parable to that which produced the modern synthesis itself? Or, finally, are self-

organization and dissipative structuring so foreign to Darwinism's core concept, natural selection, that giving them an important place in evolutionary theory will put an end to the Darwinian tradition itself?

By framing the history of the Darwinian tradition in the way we have, we have in effect been arguing for the second alternative. We concede that it is far too early to be entirely confident about this. Nonetheless . . . (Depew and Weber, 1997, 479–480).

Now in arguing for post-Darwinism, we need only quote Darwin in our defence, who wrote in the introduction to *The Origin of Species*: 'I am fully convinced that species are not immutable; but that those belonging to what are called the same genera are lineal descendants of some other and generally extinct species . . . ' Which is to say that the fact of evolution from common descent seemed to him to be incontrovertible, and has become even more so in the ensuing years of scientific advance. Darwin continues, however, to note that the process by which evolution occurs is open to debate. 'Furthermore', writes Darwin, 'I am convinced that Natural Selection has been the most important, but not the exclusive, means of modification'. As an outsider and non-expert, I need only note that there are serious and heated debates within contemporary biology about the qualifiers 'most important' and 'exclusive'. Perhaps we might formulate the problem as such: natural selection is necessary but not sufficient explanation for the evolution of the diversity of life forms. It does not help matters that evolutionists and their critics regularly equate evolution and Darwinism, the former being an observed pattern and the latter being a theory to account for the process which animates this pattern.

These debates in biology have important implications for religious thought, though the battles are more appropriately waged in the professional journals of biology. Certainly these post-Darwinian accounts undermine a thorough-going reduc-tionism and leave much more room for divine participation in the evolutionary epic than the standard model, but we should not pretend that it solves all of the religious questions. For instance, the challenge of theodicy remains before, during, and after the question of how evolution occurs.

7. Evolutionary psychology

There is a new academic fad that seeks to apply evolutionary theory to understanding human nature, though with much greater sophistication and nuance than the early Social Darwinists. The term sociobiology has become stigmatised, so the scholars refer to this new paradigm as evolutionary psychology. The project seeks to apply evolutionary concepts to understanding human psychological and social phenomena. For instance, Richard Dawkins coined the term 'memes' to refer an imagined mental equivalent of a gene, which replicates in human culture. The metaphor has inspired some to chase after mathematical models and empirical studies for the spread of memes in culture, whether they be an advertising jingle or a religious movement.

Evolutionary psychology tends to analyse human nature always with a view to questions of survival and reproduction. Many books and articles have been penned and processed in this endeavour, which try to explain religion away as an elaborate fiction which promotes group cohesion and increased fitness for individual and group survival and reproduction. For instance, Moses' ten commandments become a recipe for enhancing the group fitness of the Hebrews in competition with their neighbors, the Canaanites.

While the claims of evolutionary psychology often lack humility and make far too much of very limited data, religionists need in principle not fear the attempts of the social scientists to account for the functionality of religion in promoting human wellbeing. Authentic religion should also certainly welcome any help in trying to understand and reform the dysfunctionalities that manifest themselves in the name of religion. Nevertheless, by reducing all human thought and behaviour to merely an expression of survival and reproduction, this new sociobiology misses the truly big story of human history as a rupture with previous biological processes.

Human culture evolves in a Lamarckian pattern in which the acquired, learnt characteristics of one generation are passed on more or less directly to the next generation. Our children do not need to reinvent the wheel or the microprocessor; they do not need to recreate Shakespeare or the Bhagavad-Gita; nor need they be directly related to those who did so, as they benefit by virtue of their education and common humanity. Through our abilities to learn, humans have dramatically changed every bioregion in the world and the atmosphere as a whole, thus changing the selective environment for all future evolution. Humans are about to embark upon large-scale genetic engineering of other species and ourselves. So the human phenotype now directly edits the selective environment and the genotype through intentional processes. Humans are now the motive force for future evolution, for better or ill. This innovation in the 'how' of evolution is as profound and potentially catastrophic as the invention of photosynthesis some two billion years ago. Humans are a Lamarckian wildcard in the epic of evolution. In this respect it will not be science and technology so much as our religiously derived moral and aesthetic sensibilities which determine the future of our planet and our humanity.

8. Constructive theologies of evolution

Let us turn now to a number of constructive theologies of evolution, in which Christian thinkers and others have sought to understand their traditions anew within an evolutionary framework. I draw here in broad brushstrokes on the works of Alfred North Whitehead and Pierre Teilhard de Charden and their contemporary interpreters.

First, we must contextualise the evolutionary account of life on earth within the larger cosmic adventure. Scientists now believe that the universe is approximately twelve to fifteen billion years old, that it began in a singularity of infinite heat and infinite density, that the specific laws of physics coalesced in the early stages of the universe, and that there are a number of extremely specific values that needed to be just so in order for more complex entities like stars, galaxies, and heavy elements to evolve. Push a hard-nose physicist and you're likely to find a soft-hearted neo-platonist. In the beginning, it seems, God created mathematics. The material domain of the universe is generated from an immaterial informational domain. In the words of physicist John Archibald Wheeler, 'It comes from Bit'. Of course, religionists have long intuited the significance of this pre-existent immaterial domain. The Gospel of John reads, 'In the beginning was the Word'.

On the other hand, the universe is so big and so old that we should all feel rather puny on this little planet with our rather parochial images of God and our own self-importance. Catholic theologian John Haught uses the following mnemonic to make the point. Imagine that the history of the universe is told in thirty volumes, each volume consisting of five hundred pages, each page lasting one million years.

The first twenty volumes is 'lifeless, mindless matter'. The earth story begins in volume twenty-two. Life begins as simple bacteria in volume twenty-three and continues as mostly microbial life up until volume twenty-nine, when we witness the Cambrian explosion. Dinosaurs go extinct on page 435 of volume thirty. All of human history is a brief footnote at the end of volume thirty. In the words of the philosopher Bertrand Russell, if the purpose of the universe is to create human intelligence, then why did it take so long to create so little?

One could imagine a God who would be more like a Chairman Mao or a Comrade Stalin. This God would have designed a universe with photographs of himself hung everywhere in nature. We would be compelled to believe in the existence of this God, because everywhere we turned with our microscopes and telescopes there would be both the evidence for his existence and the secret police to enforce our acquiescence. Everything in the universe would occur by divine order, micromanaged in five-year plans and designed in a command economy. Some people today actually choose to believe in such a vision of God and appoint themselves to be the secret police, though we might wonder whether such a dictator God would be worthy of our admiration and love.

The God whom we encounter through the contemporary science of evolution and the God whom we encounter through our revealed Scriptures is not such a dictator. The philosopher-theologian Holmes Rolston notes in his book *Genes, Genesis, and God: Values and Their Origins in Natural and Human History* that:

> The word 'design' nowhere occurs in *Genesis*, though the concept of creativity pervades the opening chapters. There is divine fiat, divine doing, but the mode is an empowering permission that places productive autonomy in the creation. It is not that there is no 'watchmaker'; there is no 'watch.' Looking for one frames the problem the wrong way. There are species well adapted for problem solving, ever more informed in their self-actualizing. The watchmaker metaphor seems blind to the problem that here needs to be solved: that informationless matter-energy is a splendid information maker. Biologists cannot deny this creativity; indeed, better than anyone else

biologists know that Earth has brought forth the
natural kinds, prolifically, exuberantly over the
millennia, and that enormous amounts of information
are required to do this.

So while the God of creation chooses to be or at least seems to be
concealed from our direct perception, yet we can discern in the
universe as understood today by science a kind of directionality. If not
the telos of traditional Aristotelian cosmology, there is still an
observable teleonomy in which the universe gives rise to greater
complexity of form. With the increasing differentiation of form, there is
also a greater integration of entities in a marvellous communion of
beings. Take for instance our very bodies, a condominium for micro-
organisms. We have now come to recognise that our bodies are
continually circulating material with the outside world. Every two
weeks you practically become a brand-new person as you exchange
air, water, food, and excretions with the outside environment. Only the
calcium in our bones stays with us for any duration. We are a complex
manifestation of ocean water contained in a sack of epidermis talking
about ourselves. Every atom in our bodies is literally recycled stardust
and has been on a fifteen billion year journey towards our particular
consciousness. The universe can appreciate its pathos and beauty
through us, because we are part of the universe. The very energy with
which we conduct these deliberations is brought to us courtesy of our
sun through photosynthesis and the food chain. And the languages
that we use to express these insights are themselves the accumulated
wisdom of generations of human civilisation, which language humans
originally acquired in the semiotically and semantically rich schools of
nature. Rather than seeing our minds and personalities as incidental to
the universe, we may begin to see them as signs of a greater mind and
greater personality that animates the universe. The beginning and end
of our thirty-volume history of the universe, and everything in
between, may be an expression not of materiality, but of a universal
mind that we only dimly perceive.

Our religious traditions can now be seen as profound intuitions
about the deep structure of the universe. This new view of the cosmos
and ourselves allows us to recover some of the insights of our
traditions that have been lost in the early Enlightenment synthesis of
science and religion, when we turned God into a mechanical engineer

of nature reduced to a wind-up watch. The creator-sustainer-redeemer God of this universe could not be an authoritarian control freak, but a God of mercy and compassion, as the Koran so oft repeats. This is a God who manifests divine providence in humble, self-giving love and promise, as emphasised in the Christian tradition. This universe as we now understand it through science requires a God who values adventure, beauty, the interplay of order and open possibilities. God must surely value freedom, the self-creative autopoeisis of other creatures and ourselves. God, understood in light of this evolutionary epic, can lure the universe towards the future, the good, and the beautiful, through divine inspiration. Our trials, tribulations, failures, and deaths are resolved not through the dogmatic certainties of our beliefs, but through a warranted faith in an eschatological promise of redemption. Such a faith is fully consistent with the best of science, which can only intimate at this transcendence, and the best of our religions, which reveal to us this future promise.

9. Conclusions

I have attempted to give a brief overview of evolutionary theories, the challenges that these theories have presented to earlier religious worldviews, and a variety of religious responses to the challenges of evolution. Our intellectual task today is not unlike that of our forebears—Ibn Rushd, Maimonides, and Aquinas—who took the best science of their time and advanced a grand synthesis with their religious traditions. Today the best science is vastly different, but the intellectual and spiritual challenge is the same. The stakes today are also vastly different, for it is not just about achieving a pleasing unification of faith and reason. We live at a unique moment in the natural history of this planet and the cultural evolution of our species. The dialogue between science and religion stands at the crossroads of the twenty-first century and of our hopes for a healthier and safer future. We have a lot of work to do, but may take some comfort in knowing that God and the universe have previously erred on the side of improbability. So too might we achieve the improbable in our self-creative responsibilities to feed the hungry, heal the sick, educate the young, preserve the environment, wage peace, and celebrate the blessings of this day and the marvellous universe which we inhabit.

Bibliography

Abram, David. *The Spell of the Sensuous: Perception and Language in a More-Than-Human World* (New York: Pantheon Books, 1996).

Aviezer, Nathan. *Fossils & Faith: Understanding Torah and Science* (Hoboken: KTAV, 2001).

Ayala, Francisco J, Robert John Russell, and William R Stoeger SJ, editors. *Evolution and Molecular Biology: Scientific Perspectives on Divine Action* (Berkley CA: CTNS, 1998).

Barlow, Connie, editor. *Evolution Extended: Biological Debates on the Meaning of Life* (Cambridge, MA: MIT Press, 1994).

Berry, Thomas and Brian Swimme. *The Universe Story* (San Francisco: Harper, 1992).

Berry, Wendell. *Life Is a Miracle: An Essay against Modern Superstition* (Washington, DC: Counterpoint, 2000).

Boyer, Pascal. *Religion Explained: The Evolutionary Origins of Religious Thought* (New York: Basic Books, 2001).

Darwin, Charles. *The Origin of Species* (online). 1859.

Darwin, Charles. *The Descent of Man* (online). 1871.

Dawkins, Richard. *River Out of Eden: A Darwinian View of Life* (New York: Basic Books, 1995).

Dawkins, Richard. *The Blind Watchmaker: Why the Evidence of Evolution Reveals a Universe without Design* (New York: Norton, 1986).

Dawkins, Richard. *The Selfish Gene* (New York: Oxford University Press, 1976).

Dembski, William A. *No Free Lunch: Why Specified Complexity Cannot Be Purchased without Intelligence* (Oxford: Rowman & Littlefield, 2002).

Dembski, William A. *The Design Inference: Eliminating Chance through Small Probabilities* (New York: Cambridge University Press, 1998).

Dennett, Daniel C. *Darwin's Dangerous Idea: Evolution and the Meanings of Life* (New York: Simon & Schuster, 1995).

Depew, David and Bruce Weber. *Darwinism Evolving: Systems Dynamics and the Geneaology of Natural Selection.* 1997.

Ellis, George FR and Nancey Murphy. *On the Moral Nature of the Universe: Theology, Cosmology, and Ethics* (Minneapolis: Fortress Press, 1996).

Haught, John F. *God after Darwin: A Theology of Evolution* (Oxford: Westview, 2000).

Huchingson, James E. *Pandemonium Tremendum: Chaos and Mystery in the Life of God* (Cleveland: Pilgrim Press, 2001).

Johnson, Philip E. *Reason in the Balance: The Case against Naturalism in Science, Law, and Education* (Downer Grove: Inter-Varsity Press, 1995).

Katz, Leonard D, editor. *Evolutionary Origins of Morality: Cross-Disciplinary Perspectives* (Bowling Green: Imprint Academic, 2000).

Kelly, Kevin. *Out of Control: The New Biology of Machines, Social Systems, and the Economic World* (New York: Addison Wesley, 1994).

Krieger, David J. *The New Universalism: Foundations for a Global Theology* (Maryknoll, NY: Orbis, 1991).

Larson, Edward J. *Summer for the Gods: The Scopes Trial and America's Continuing Debate over Science and Religion* (Cambridge, MA: Harvard University Press, 1997).

Pennock, Robert T. *Tower of Babel: The Evidence against the New Creationism* (Cambridge, MA: MIT Press 1999).

Rolston, Holmes. *Genes, Genesis, and God: Values and Their Origins in Natural and Human History* (New York: Cambridge University Press, 1998).

Ruse, Michael. *Can a Darwinian Be a Christian?* (New York: Cambridge University Press, 2001).

Ruse, Michael. *Monad to Man: The Concept of Progress in Evolutionary Biology* (Cambridge MA: Harvard University Press, 1996).

Wesson, Robert. *Beyond Natural Selection* (Cambridge, MA: MIT Press, 1991).

Wilson, Edward O. *Consilience: The Unity of Knowledge* (New York: Knopf, 1998).

Wright, Robert. *Non-Zero: The Logic of Human Destiny* (New York: Pantheon, 2000).

11

Creation or Evolution? The Reception of Darwinism in Modern Arab Thought

Mahmoud M Ayoub

1. Introduction

The question of the creation of the world, and particularly of humankind, has occupied the imagination of men and women since the dawn of human civilisation. Answers to this question have varied greatly, depending on the nature and development of various cultures. These include myths of theogony, the birth or emergence of the universe from a divine primordial being, cosmogony, the birth of the cosmos out of a primordial cosmic egg, and the creation of order or cosmos out of primordial watery chaos. Some of these myths came to be expressed in religious beliefs and philosophical views, such as the belief that God created all things by his divine command 'be', and the philosophical view of the eternity of the universe, or at least of the primal matter out of which it evolved. In most accounts of creation the universe comes into being in stages, or as in the Jewish, Christian and Islamic traditions, the 'six days of creation'.[1]

The idea of creation as a process, or what may be termed the cycles of creation, naturally implies some form of change or evolution. This process of creation or coming into existence of the universe may be regarded as due to an inherent force in primordial matter or the conscious and teleological will of an omnipotent and omniscient creator. The first view has generally characterised philosophy, beginning with the ancient Greek sages, as well as much of modern science. The second view has been identified with religion, and more specifically with the monotheistic traditions of Judaism, Christianity and Islam. The idea of natural evolution, which since the mid-nineteenth century has been identified with Charles Darwin, goes back to the aeonian philosophers of ancient Greece, who asserted that the

---

1.   See Genesis 1:3 ff. and Q 10:3.

universe evolved out of atoms randomly moving in a void, or through a dynamic process of constant change in matter. These ancient ideas challenged the theologians of medieval Christendom and Islam, who countered them with the doctrine of the origination of the universe by God out of nothing. Scientists and philosophers have since the Middle Ages made them the subject of an ongoing debate. Nor was this debate limited to scientists and philosophers; rather, it has occupied the intellectual circles of both communities to the present. Examples of this debate in nineteenth and twentieth century Arab thought will occupy us in this essay.

We shall first present a brief historical account of the impact of Darwinism on Christian, Muslim and secular Arab thinkers in the nineteenth and early twentieth century. Our primary interest, however, will be in modernist thinkers who played a significant role in the Arab intellectual renaissance which began in the second half of the nineteenth century and continued well into the twentieth.[2] With this background, we shall focus in some details on a few contemporary Muslim thinkers.

Two significant and interrelated conclusions may be anticipated. The first is that while religious and secular Christian Arab thinkers lost interest in Darwinism since World War II, this issue continues to occupy many Muslim thinkers to the present day. The second is that while Darwinian evolution did not create a religious crisis in the Muslim world as it did in the West, Muslim intellectuals have continued the debate, but have generally tried to harmonise the Qur'anic ideas of creation with modern science, including some form of modified Darwinism. It is worth noting that the few contemporary Muslim thinkers who continue to oppose Darwinism do so as part of their political opposition to the West in general, and particularly to what they regard as Western materialism and atheism, and not for the alleged danger Darwinism may pose to their faith or the veracity of their sacred Scriptures. It may be further argued that this opposition has in large measure been inspired by contemporary Western religious and scientific critiques of Darwinism.

---

2.   For a good and lucid discussion of Arab thought in this period, see Albert Hourani, *Arab Thought in the Liberal Age* (London: Oxford University Press, 1962).

2. Darwinism and the intellectual Arab renaissance

To appreciate the impact of Darwinism on modern Arab thought, at least three important cultural, theological, and philosophical factors must be taken into consideration. These will provide the necessary contextual framework for our subsequent discussion. The first and obvious factor is that modern Arab thought has largely been shaped by Western science and technology, literature, philosophy and the social sciences. We shall return to this crucial factor presently. Theologically, the Qur'an presents not one but several scenarios of creation. We shall discuss in some details the use of these scenarios by a few modernist Arab Muslim thinkers later. It must, however, be observed here that some form of evo-lutionary process of creation can be easily argued for on the basis of some Qur'anic accounts of creation.

The impact of Greek philosophy on Muslim thought began in the second half of the first Islamic century, that is before the end of the seventh century.[3] In the ninth century, a group of philosophically oriented thinkers called *Ikhwan al-Safa'* (the Brethren of Purity) presented a quasi-evolutionary view of creation based on the Qur'an and Islamic tradition and Greek philosophy.

The clearest assertion of a natural evolutionary creation was made by the Andalusian philosopher Ibn Tufayl (d 1185) in his famous philosophical romance *Hayy bin Yaqzan* (Alive, son of the Awake). *Hayy*, a human infant, is said to have evolved out of the interaction of natural elements on a lonely island. The child also evolved rationally, so that he was able on his own, and without the use of language, to discover the sublime truths of religion and philosophy.

Ibn Tufayl's pupil Ibn Rushd [d 1198], who was the chief Muslim proponent of Aristotle's philosophy, attempted to harmonise what he regarded as the 'truths of philosophy' with the truths of religion. Ibn Rushd presented a view of the coming into being of all things as an eternal process of divine production within an eternal universe. He thus tried to harmonise the Qur'anic view of the creation of the universe by God with Aristotle's view of the eternity of primal matter,

---

3.   According to some accounts, it began with Khalid b Yazid (d 704) commissioning the translation of some ancient scientific treatises from Greek to Arabic. See Majid Fakhry, *History of Islamic Philosophy* (New York: Columbia University Press, 1983), 5.

and hence of the universe.[4] These and other views of both ancient Greek and Muslim philosophers were invoked by some Arab thinkers in their defence of evolution.

The most important factor, which was alluded to above, is the great impact of post-Enlightenment Western thought and culture on the development of Middle Eastern and particularly Arab thought and general culture. When Napoleon landed on Egyptian shores in 1798) he took with him not only an invading army, but a group of scholars and a printing press. Egypt continued to seek acquisition of European science and technology under Muhammad 'Ali (r 1805–1848) and his successors. This process, moreover, was greatly aided by the establishment of schools and colleges in the nineteenth century by European and American Christian missionaries in most countries of the Middle East. It was largely through such missionary institutions of higher learning that Western sciences, including Darwinism, reached the Arab world.[5]

Arab intellectuals took from the West not only scientific but also social Darwinism. Scientific Darwinism was used to explain the origin of the universe, as well as the origin and evolution of plant and animal life, particularly human evolution, while social Darwinism was used to explain and justify racial or ethnic superiority theories. In both cases, Darwinism in the Arab world as in the West clashed with traditional religious myths, ideas and worldviews.

Darwinism divided both Christian and Muslim Arab intellectuals into two camps: religionists and evolutionists. Yet in each of the two camps there were dogmatic and liberal individuals. The most vocal representative of the conservative Christian wing was Louis Cheikho (d 1928), who was a Catholic priest and a noted scholar of Eastern Christianity and Islam. His attitude towards Darwinism, however, reflected the official Catholic position at that time, rather than the tenure of Arab thought. An important representative of the moderate

---

4.   See Fakhri, *op cit*, 276–284.

5.   The best and only study in English, to my knowledge, of the impact of Darwinism and Western science in general on Arab thought during this period is Adel A Ziadat, *Western Science in the Arab World: The Impact of Darwinism, 1860–1930* (London: Macmillan, 1986). I have drawn heavily on this work for this section of the present study.

wing was Ya'qub Sarruf who was a scientifically inclined liberal thinker and a well-known writer.

Most of the Muslim thinkers of the Arab renaissance were religious leaders, or at least religiously oriented reformists. They included traditionalists, or religious conservatives such as Husayn al-Jisr (d 1909) and Muhammad Rashid Rida (d 1935) and reformists such as Jamal al-Din al-Afghani (d 1897) and his famous Egyptian disciple Muhammad 'Abduh (d 1905). There were also some liberal thinkers, as well as a small, but noteworthy group of secularists. A few representative examples of both trends will be briefly discussed below.

Secular Christian responses to Darwinism exhibited ideological and even religious characteristics. Thinkers such as Shibli Shumayyil (d 1917), Salama Musa (d 1958), and Ya'qub Sarruf (d 1927) accepted Darwinism not only as a scientific theory, but also as the framework of a natural religion. Salama Musa, for instance, wanted to westernise Egypt, in order for it to participate in the rise of the superman of the German philosopher Nietzsche and the British littérateur George Bernard Shaw.[6] This and similar ideas of the special place of Egypt in world history arose out of a nationalistic vision of a Pharoanic and Hellenistic rather than Islamic Egypt. They are imitations of European romantic and fascist nationalistic ideologies.

In contrast with such radical ideas and nationalistic visions, Ya'qub Sarruf, who was a Syro-Lebanese intellectual, represented a much more moderate and questioning approach. Perhaps his approach was in part inspired by the serious doubts in the primacy of reason, materialism and science which came as reactions to the collapse of nineteenth century romantic optimism under the symbolic weight of the sinking *Titanic* and the human carnage of the First World War. The resulting disillusionment with nineteenth century romantic and materialistic values gave way to interest in spirituality, and even in some forms of bizarre spiritualism and magic. The war was seen not as a means of preserving the fittest but the unfit, as many of the so-called fittest of Europe were killed in the war. However, interest in the Darwinian theory of natural selection as the framework of racist ideas of social Darwinism was revived in Europe between the two world wars, especially in the Nazi ideology of the 'master race'. Some Arab thinkers voiced such in interest in eugenics and thus held that

6.   *Ibid*, 29; see also 29–62.

handicapped and weak people should be eliminated or at least sterilised, so as not to impede the process of natural selection.

3. Muslim responses to Darwinism

While Christian scholars, critics and supporters of Darwinism were able to draw on the rich resources of Western science and philosophy in their scholarly and intellectual endeavours, Muslim thinkers, for the most part, did not have direct access to such resources. Their knowledge was largely based on partial translations or summaries of Darwin's works and the views of his admirers and detractors.

The great reformist, religious and political activist Jamal al-Din al-Afghani, for instance, knew no European languages, and thus could not have read Darwin's writings or those of his critics in their original languages. Yet in his single work, *al-Radd 'ala al-dahriyyin* (Refutation of materialist philosophers), which he wrote in Persian in India,[7] he provided later critics of Darwinism not with the substance of scientific or religious criticism of Darwin's theories, but with the form of logical arguments against evolution and particularly natural selection.

Afghani rejected both pure Islamic traditionalism and the blind imitation of Western science. As an intellectual, he was influenced by his Iranian Shi'ite philosophical tradition and modernist Indian thought. He therefore served as a bridge between Indo-Iranian thought and culture and the Arab world.

As a traditionalist Muslim, Afghani at first vehemently rejected Darwinian evolution. But as a modernist reformer, towards the end of his life he tempered his criticism and attempted to distinguish Darwin from the Darwinian materialists of his own time. He even came to accept some form of evolution, but continued to defend the traditional Islamic belief of the creation of humankind by god.

Afghani's contemporary, the Syro-Lebanese religious leader and intellectual Shaykh Husayn al-Jisr, was a prolific writer. His most important work was a large treatise defending Islam and the sacred

---

7.   An Arabic translation of this work by 'Uthman Amin, edited by Muhammad 'Abduh was published in Egypt (np) in 1947.

law vouchsafed to the prophet Muhammad by God.[8] Husayn al-Jisr was willing to accept most scientific theories, including that of evolution, and to interpret the Qur'an to accommodate them. This attitude was born out of his strong conviction that the Qur'an does not contradict modern science.

Jisr's faith in the truth of modern science was itself based on the scientific principle of the empirical verification of any theory before its truth can be accepted. He therefore provisionally rejected the Darwinian theory of natural selection until it could be empirically proven. If it is proven to be true, then support for it will be found in the Qur'an through proper interpretation. Thus Jisr set the stage for later committed Muslim thinkers to read all scientific theories, including evolution, into the Qur'an. In fact, there are today numerous individuals and institutions throughout the Muslim world engaged in this venture, which for them constitutes the incontrovertible proof of the inimitable miracle (*I'jaz*) of the Qur'an.

One of the most interesting and original thinkers of the period under discussion was Muhammad Rida al-Isfahani. Isfahani was a well-known Shi'ite religious thinker as well as a scientifically well-informed humanist from Karbala', an important centre of Shi'ite learning in Iraq. While Isfahani shared most of the arguments and ideas of his time, his open-mindedness, breadth of vision and originality of thought are uniquely his own.

Isfahani produced a substantial work on science and religion, which he divided into two parts.[9] In the first he presents a good background and critique of Darwinism and in the second he sets forth the reasons and arguments for his critique. His honesty and critical approach are demonstrated in urging the readers of his own book to approach it critically and objectively.

Isfahani's view was that the truths of religion and science should not oppose or contradict but compliment and uphold each other. In his critique of evolution he attempted not to defend Islam but religion as such. He accepted the scientific ideas of evolutionists, including those of Darwin, so long as they did not deny God's primary role in the

---

8.   The work was dedicated to the last Ottoman Sultan 'Abd al-Hamid II [r 1876-1909] and entitled *al-Risalah al-hamidiyyah fi haqiqat al-diyanah al-islamiyyah wa-haqiqat al-shari'ah al-muhammadiyyah*. See Ziadat *op cit*, 91–5.

9.   *Naqd Falsafat Darwin*, published in 1914.

creation and evolution of the universe. To him there was nothing inherently wrong with the idea that the ancestor of the camel may have been a bird or a frog, since in all cases it was God who originated and directed the evolutionary progress of his creation.[10]

As for the evolution of humankind from a lower animal species, Isfahani argued that there no conclusive scientific proofs of this fact. Furthermore, similar views have been held even by primitive tribes which believed that they had descended from animals, including the ape. His Shi'ite tradition of esoteric interpretation (*ta'wil*) of sacred texts allowed him to interpret both the Qur'anic and biblical accounts of the creation of Adam, and hence the origins of humankind, in the light of modern science. On the basis of the Qur'anic account of a group of Jews who were transformed into apes for having violated Sabbath laws,[11] Isfahani argued that it is possible for man to evolve into a higher form, but also to devolve into an ape or any other lower animal. Perhaps the purpose of these speculations was to undermine the theory of evolution by depriving it of its novelty, and hence of its special significance.

Isfahani did not oppose science, but sought to harmonise the truths of science with the universal truths of revelation. He wished to attribute the processes of nature not to a blind force in matter, but to the will and wisdom of God. He thus argued that 'all knowledge and scientific discoveries could be explained through one medium, the word of God'.[12]

An Egyptian contemporary of Isfahani, Mustafa Hasanayn al-Mansuri, was a secular socialist thinker. He wrote a large work on socialist doctrines entitled *Tarikh al-madhahib al-ishtirakiyyah* (1914), in which he devoted a chapter to Darwin's life and thought. He defended Darwin's ideas against the charge of atheism, arguing that the notion that all animal species evolved from a single species does not necessarily imply denial of God's existence. For him, as for many Muslim intellectuals of his time, Darwin was a great scientist who

---

10. See Ziadat, 97–98.
11. They were so punished for fishing on the Sabbath. This is called in the Qur'an *maskh*, that is the deformation of a human being into a lower and uglier animal form. See Q 2:65.
12. Ziadat, 106.

brought the light of reason to dispel the darkness of conservative religious fanaticism.

Like Isfahani, Mansuri tried to narrow the chasm between science and religion. In his defence of science, he was obliged to contradict one of the basic doctrines of socialism, namely the principle of guided social cooperation and non-competitive cohesion as the necessary means for establishing social equality. He defended Darwin's theory of natural selection, which demands social, economic as well as physical competition to ensure the 'survival of the fittest'.[13] Yet it is a known fact that modern capitalism necessarily implies competition, and there-fore essentially contradicts the basic tenets of socialism.

One final important example that should be included in this brief survey is another Egyptian scholar Isma'il Mazhar (d 1962). Mazhar was perhaps the most scientifically minded Muslim scholar of the first half of the twentieth century. He was contemporary with Salama Musa, Ya'qub Sarruf and Shibli Shumayyil, among others. Shumayyil's writings in particular influenced him greatly. He was also influenced by the positivist thought of the French sociological philosopher August Comte, and particularly Comte's idea of the three stages of the development of human thought and civilisation. These were: the theological, metaphysical and positivist stages. In Mazhar's view, Arab and Islamic civilisation did not progress beyond the second stage.[14]

Mazhar published a partial Arabic translation of Darwin's *Origin of Species*, consisting of the first ten chapters of the book. It must be observed that a complete Arabic translation of this work did not appear until 1964.

Under the direct influence of Western philosophy and science, which was no doubt enhanced by his knowledge of at least one European language, Mazhar became a thorough-going secularist. He had no patience with traditional religion and thus called on all Arabs and Muslims to adopt what he called the Western scientific mentality. He was a great admirer of the Turkish revolution, under the leadership of Mustafa Kamal Ata-Turk, which limited religion to a personal relationship between individual believers and their Lord. His secular orientation, and particularly his view of Arab culture, was severely condem-ned by a number of important Muslim intellectuals of the

---

13. See *ibid*, 108–10.
14. See *ibid*, 115.

time. Unfortunately, Mazhar's significant contribution to the literature on modern Western science in Arabic was over-shadowed by his antipathy to religion and his uncritical espousal of Western secularism.

As has already been observed, in the Arab world as in the West, the debate on Darwinism was largely between religious and material-istically oriented Christian and Muslim thinkers. In this regard, Isma'il Mazhar was closer to Christian secular scholars than to the Muslim intellectuals of his time. While Christian thinkers generally used Darwinism to refute the biblical doctrine of creation, many educated Muslims still regard Darwin's theory of evolution as a useful tool to understand the Qur'an.

4. The Qur'an and modern science: apologetic responses

It is clear from our discussion so far that the impact of Western science on modern Arab thought was not limited to lay scholars and intellectuals. Rather, modernist religious leaders were equally affected by it. Their reactions were largely positive and apologetic, as we saw in our discussion of men like Afghani, Jisr and Isfahani. In this final part of our study we shall concentrate on the views of a few religious leaders and intellectuals of the relationship of the Qur'an to modern science. We shall conclude with a brief discussion of some non-Arab Muslim voices in this ongoing debate.

The only modernist Arab religious leader who attempted to write an entire scientific commentary on the Qur'an was Shaykh Tantawi Jawhari. He describes his commentary as: 'Jewels of the interpretation of the noble Qur'an, containing marvels of the beauties of the creation and wonderfully luminous divine signs'.[15] The author even includes pictures of animals and plants to illustrate his quasi-scientific views.

Tantawi accepted the truth of evolution and sought to read it into the Qur'an. On the basis of Qur'anic verses which speak of the stages of the growth of a human being from a sperm and an ovum into a foetus and finally a well-shaped person,[16] he presents what he calls a

---

15.   The title of this commentary is *al-Jawahir fi tafsir al-qur'an al-karim al-mushtamil 'ala 'aj'ib bada'I' mukawwinat wa-ghara'ib al-ayat al-bahirat*, ed. Muhammad Amin 'Imran, 25 parts in 13 vols: [Cairo], Mustafa al-Babi al-Halibi (1350), vol 4, 2 ff.

16.   See, for examples, Q 15:22, 23:12 and 25:54.

'*jadwal* (a schedule or timetable) of the evolution of life on earth'.[17] The highest animal on this evolutionary scale is the monkey, which is just below man. Thus man, who is the crown of creation, must pass through all the animal evolutionary stages on his way to humanisation. The human fetus therefore begins as a single and simple cell, like unicellular sea creatures. It then evolves into a worm, then a snail, then a fish and then into a simple land animal. It then becomes an ape before it loses its tail and reaches the human stage.

Tantawi then attempts to discern the categories of human beings as to their different races and temperaments and the role of each in life. He, however, goes far beyond the phenomenon of physical and psychological evolution. Human beings, he observes, then progress into the realms of divine light, 'For to your Lord shall be the ultimate destination' (Q 53:42).[18]

Tantawi belongs to the rationalist school of Afghani, 'Abduh and 'Abduh's disciple and successor Sayyid Muhammad Rashid Rida. After the untimely death of his teacher, Rida embarked on a voluminous rationalistic Qur'an commentary based on the thought and direct contributions of his mentor. The Qur'an asserts that when God announced his intention to 'place a steward in the earth', the angels protested that such a creature will 'shed blood and spread corruption on earth' (Q 2:30). Rida agrees with classical Qur'an commentators who asserted that there must have existed earlier human-like creatures who in fact shed blood and spread corruption in the earth. He argues that there was a bygone species of rational creatures who shed blood, which led the angels to analogically conclude that humankind would do the same, and thus they protested at the creation of such a creature. Rida continues:

> If this view is correct, then Adam was not the first rational animal on this planet. Rather he represents a new species of speaking animals, resembling earlier such species in essence and substance, but differing

---

17.   Tantawi, vol 4, 19.
18.   *Ibid*, 19.

from them in some moral characteristics and natural dispositions.[19]

While Rida agrees with the general consensus of Muslim scholars that Adam was not the first rational creature to live on this earth, he rejects the myths regarding the names and identities of the creatures who populated the earth before Adam and how they were destroyed by God. He was able to accept modern scientific theories of the ascent of man. He, however, bases his view not on Western science, but on Jisr's view of humankind, which he accepts unreservedly. Rida states Jisr's interesting idea as follows:

> The real man is an atom [or essence] (*dharrah*) which dwells in the heart. In this atom dwells the spirit which bestows life on it. Life then runs through the body. The body is in fact only an instrument through which this atom fulfills its functions in this world and acquires the proper branches of knowledge appertaining to it. It is this atom and the spirit dwelling in it that is addressed by God with moral and religious obligations, and will therefore be brought forth by God for the last judgment.[20]

Rida then concludes that this does not negate the theory of the ascent of man, 'so long as it is formulated within the Islamic purview of the soul, which is this atom'.[21]

Rida and Tantawi approached the relationship of the Qur'an to modern science as religious leaders and Qur'an commentators. They, moreover, were products of the Arab renaissance and its rationalist school. Our two final examples are living men whose two small volumes appeared at the close of the last century and the start of this one. They wrote not as religious leaders, but as contemporary thinkers

---

19. Muhammad Rashid Rida, *Tafsir al-qur'an al-hakim* [known as *Tafsir al-manar*] fourth edition (Cairo: Dar al-Manar, 1373) ah vol 1, 258. This important modern commentary unfortunately stops at the end of part 12 of the Qur'an, that is the middle of s. 12. Thus the work consists of 12 parts in 6 large volumes.
20. *Ibid*, 8. 477.
21. *Ibid*.

who are concerned with demonstrating the universality of the Qur'an as a source of all scientific ideas and discoveries. In this regard they are typical modernist Muslim intellectuals whose aim is to defend Islam against Western secularism by demonstrating the uniqueness of its Scripture, on the one hand, and affirming its concord with secular rationalism and modern science on the other.

While our first author Talal Ghazal is not a well-known thinker, he is a systematic and well-informed writer, perhaps of Lebanese or Syrian background. His aim is to recount the story of the world from its early genesis (*takwin*) to its final collapse (*takwir*). He describes this long process in scientific terms, but uses the Qur'an to argue for their veracity.

Ghazal's main purpose is to harmonise the Qur'anic accounts of creation with modern scientific theories. The process of an ordered creation, he argues, began, as the Qur'an states, with the initial division or separation of the planet earth from the undivided mass of the universe. This is expressed in the Qur'an as follows, 'The heavens and earth were one mass (*ratqan*) and We unstuck them' (Q 21:30). Then the waters of the earth retreated, so as to allow dry land to appear as one single continent. Then slowly, over a period of hundreds of millions of years, the earth acquired its present typography, which allowed for the appearance of plant and animal life.

Ghazal then argues that both the Qur'an and modern science assert that the source of all life on earth is water. The Qur'an states: 'God created every animal from water. Some crawl on their belly, some walk on two feet and others walk on four' (Q 24:45).[22] The long process of evolutionary divine creation, first of the primal matter out of which the universe evolved, then of the planets and finally of life on earth, has so far culminated in the appearance of Homo sapiens, which is the pinnacle of creation.

The evolutionary stages of the creation of humankind began, Ghazal continues, with God creating man of 'hot and putrefying potter's clay' (Q 15: 26.) This means, our author concludes, that man was created from hot clay mixed with water. He further argues that 'The first humans were closer to animal characteristics than to human attributes'. Then they evolved and multiplied within their natural environment like all other creatures. Those creatures who failed to

---

22.   Ghazal, 77.

adapt themselves to their environment and the changing climate of the earth vanished, as did the dinosaurs. But the human creatures that were able to evolve towards better states attained to the best stature. Our own humanity begins with Adam and his descent with his spouse into the world. Adam was the first prophet and messenger of God to the earth and with him begins the process of divine obligation and of rewards and punishments.[23]

Ghazal unquestioningly accepts the theory of evolution and natural selection. Like most modernising Arab Muslim intellectuals, he attempts to find some Qur'anic basis for it. He argues that life here on earth rests on dualities, such as life and death, good and evil, male and female, and so forth. The principle of generation and corruption, or life and death, is in a continuous evolution towards the best, in accordance with the demands and characteristics of the environment in which different species of creatures live. He avers that

> There were humans in bygone epochs who differed from us in certain characteristics, but the stage which today's humankind has reached made humans better in all respects. Future generations, moreover, will possess more advanced characteristics, which are better suited to the environment of the man of the future.[24]

Thus Ghazal concludes that there is no proof of sudden creation; rather, God established natural laws of evolution and growth and of life and death for all living things, including human beings.

Our second author 'Abd al-Sabur Shahin is an Egyptian writer who vacillates between the garb of an Azharite shaykh and a modernising religious thinker. In his small book *Abi adam* (My father Adam)[25] Shahin seeks to establish an evolutionary theory within the Qur'an itself. This he does by chronologically examining the verses dealing

23. *Ibid*, 79.
24. *Ibid*, 81.
25. The full title of this controversial book is *Abi adam: al-khaliqah bayn al-usturah wal-haqiqah* (My father Adam: the created universe between myth and reality), Cairo: Maktabat al-shabab, 1998. The book is still banned by the Egyptian government, but it circulates illegally outside Egypt.

with the creation of humankind, arguing that the stages of evolution are clearly depicted in the Makkan and Madinan *surahs* (chapters) of the Qur'an. In other words, the chronology of revelation of the Qur'anic verses itself relates the story of evolutionary creation.

Shahin starts from the assumption that 'real contradiction between the Qur'anic accounts of creation and the ultimate truths discovered by modern science is impossible'. Rather, he argues, apparent contradiction is due to the fact that 'science has not yet come to rest on the firm ground of the perfect truth. It still moves within the framework of theories that are based on conjectural proofs.'[26] As a solution to this problem, the author proposes that classical modes of Qur'anic interpretation be abandoned and that the Qur'an be re-interpreted in the light of modern science. It must be observed that this is the dominant view in both the Arab and Muslim world today.

Shahin rejects the theory of evolution from one animal species to another. Instead, he argues that both religion and modern science agree on the reality of the independent creation of every species. Evolution occurs within the species from a lower to a higher form. He says: 'Ever since man (*insan*) was brought into existence, he was nothing else but a mortal human being (*bashar*), and an ape has never been anything but an ape . . .It all happened', he concludes, 'in accordance with the absolute Divine will, and in fulfillment of a cosmic Divine purpose'.[27]

Like many contemporary Muslim thinkers, Shahin erroneously uses Qur'anic verses which describe the stages of the growth of a human foetus from a sperm and an ovum into a human being of good stature to argue for the evolutionary stages of the creation of man. On the basis of such verses and others that specifically describe the creation of Adam as a mortal being (*bashar*) from clay, he builds an elaborate theory of pre-Adamic quasi-human creatures, which he calls *bashar*, out of which Adam and his descendants evolved. The Qur'anic stages of the Divine 'project' of human creation are: 1) the blood clot ('*alaq*, as in Q 96:2); 2) Fashioning or shaping (*taswiyah*, Q 87:2); 3) 'the best of stature' (*ahsan taqwim*, Q 95:4). These stages are preceded by the creation of a pre-human creature [*bashar*] from clay, as reported in Q 38:71–72, where we read: 'Remember when your Lord said to the

---

26.   *Ibid*, 42.
27.   *Ibid*, 39.

angels, I am about to fashion a mortal man (*bashar*) from clay. When I shape him and breathe into him of my spirit, then fall prostrate before him'.[28]

It should be noted that the Qur'an uses the terms *insan* (human being) and *bashar* (mortal man) interchangeably. Yet our author states: 'The *bashar* proceeds out of clay and the *insan* proceeds out of the *bashar*. This process', he continues, 'begins with the form of an undefined *bashar* as the exemplar upon which the act of shaping (*taswiyah*), fashioning (*taswir*) and the inbreathing of the spirit of God took place.' Shahin interprets these divine actions to mean, endowing this primitive creature with high potencies, such as reason, language and religion. It is these potencies which transformed this *bashar* creature into humankind.[29]

This ingenious theory of human evolution appears to be erroneously imposed on the Qur'an. Generally speaking, all references in the Qur'an to a *bashar* of clay are not to a pre-Adamic being, but to Adam and his progeny. Thus Shahin's theory is itself conjectural and is Qur'anically without foundation. It is, nonetheless, quite imaginative and intriguing.

5. Conclusion

The foregoing discussion has, we hope, amply demonstrated the keen interest Arab, and particularly Muslim, intellectuals and religious scholars have shown in Darwin's theory of evolution. For secular thinkers, Darwin's theory presents an enlightened scientific alternative to what they take to be the superstitious scriptural myths of creation. Muslim religious thinkers in contrast continue to use Darwinism not to oppose the Qur'anic view of creation, but to corroborate what they regard as the scientific and rationalistic nature of the Qur'an.

This ostensibly positive attitude is not limited to Darwinian evolution, but it includes all scientific theories. It is actually based on arguments which affirm that all scientific discoveries have, in some way or another, been anticipated in the Qur'an. Such apologetic notions have often resulted in uncritical approaches to scientific theories and their bearing on religious truths. These apologetic, and in our view unprofitable approaches to religion and science, can be easily

---

28. *Ibid*, chapter 4, 51–64.
29. *Ibid*, 88.

discerned in the thought of both the religious leaders and lay intellectuals discussed above in this essay. Nor is it limited to Arab thinkers. In fact many Muslim scholars have tried to find ideas of evolution in the thought of classical mystical poets, such as Jalalud-din Rumi,[30] men of letters, historians and philosophers, such as al-Jahiz,[31] the well-known historian and heresiographer al-Biruni[32] and Muhammad Iqbal,[33] the last classical Indo-Muslim poet-philosopher, who died in 1938.

Among the most vocal non-Arab Muslim critics of Darwin are Shaikh Abdul Mabud, a Pakistani religious leader, and a Turkish scholar who writes under the pen-name of Harun Yahya. Abdul Mabud examines Darwin's theory from an Islamic point of view. His critique is largely a polemical rejection of evolution in favor of the Qur'anic view of creation.[34]

Harun Yahya appears to be a well-informed and solid critic of Darwin's thought and of the idea of evolution in general. In itself, his critique of evolution and particularly of Darwin's theory is convincing. However, he obscures the real value of his scientific approach behind virulent attacks on Western materialism, which he sees as the evil basis of all evolutionary theories. Harun Yahya presents himself as a militant Islamic fighter against evolutionism, which is to him a call to atheism and materialism.[35]

With all its pitfalls, the apologetic modernist Islamic approach to science and the Qur'an can itself evolve into a creative dialogue between modern Islamic thought and science. Science means knowledge, which is neither Western nor Eastern. The truths of both

---

30. See KM Jamil, 'Jalalud Din Rumi's Theory of Evolution', in *Bulletin of the College of Arts*, Baghdad, 7, 1964: 63–80.

31. See Mehmet Bayrakdar, 'al-Jahiz and The Rise of Biological Evolutionism', *Islamic Quarterly* 27, 1983: 149-155.

32. JZ Wilczynski, 'On the Presumed Darwinism of al-Beruni Eight Hundred Years before Darwin', *Isis*, 50, 1959: 459–466.

33. See LS May, 'A Unique Aspect of Iqbal's Evolution Theory', in *Iqbal Review*, 16, III, 1975: 26–31.

34. Shaikh Abdul Mabud, *Theory of Evolution: An Assessment from the Islamic Point of View*, Cambridge, Islamic Academy and Kula Lumpur, Islamic Academy of Science (1991).

35. See his web site: harunyahya.com and specially the article *A Reply to Andya Primanda*; and his book, *The Evolution Deceit*.

religion and science are universal truths which point to the marvels of this great universe and its all-knowing and all-wise creator.

The scientific theories of evolution should not be used to affirm or deny the truth of religion. Nor do they in themselves necessarily lead to the denial of God's existence or his role in the coming into being of the universe. These, as all scientific theories, should not be confused with religious truths, nor should religious truths be viewed as scientific theories. Science is in essence the human quest for knowledge of the universe, and religion is the human quest for knowledge of God. To know the universe is, the Qur'an declares, to discover the signs of God in his creation: 'We shall show them Our signs in the horizons and in their selves, in order that it becomes manifest to them that it is the truth' (Q 41:53).

12

Creation and Evolution: Islamic Perspectives

Teuku Jacob

The papers of Dr Grassie and Dr Ayoub contain some very interesting and challenging accounts on evolution and religion. I would like here to present some notes on ideas which occurred to me during my time spent in paleoanthropology and human origins.

Discussions about biological evolution among some religious thinkers not infrequently concentrate on Charles Darwin and Darwinism and the rejection of evolutionary theories. Interpretation of natural phenomena is posited against interpretation of the Holy Scriptures regarded as unfalsifiable facts. Disregarded are the facts that Darwin brought forth his ideas in the second hall of the nineteenth century before genetics and human paleontology were widely known, and that many new verifications and theories are expounded based on discoveries of the hardwares (fossils) and the softwares of evolution (hypotheses and theories) supported by the sythesis of so many biological and related disciplines. Darwin and Darwinism have become the focus of criticisms, while facts derived form morphological sciences (comparative anatomy, embryology), geneties, geosciences including geochronology, biogeography and paleogeography, anthropology and archeology are conspicuously ignored.

Weaknesses in theories and hiatuses in the fossil records are exaggerated, disregarding the dynamics of science, educated extrapolation, the 'softness' and insecurities (low predictability) of historical sciences, the tentativeness of scientific truths, the continual fossil discoveries (hypodigms) which throw impact on the software (paradigms), and the multiple hypotheses due to incomplete information. But hard facts cannot be ignored forever, and the fragmentary, scattered evidences have to be utilised to gain some understanding of the human past. Human evolution is primarily opposed, much more than geological, botanical and non-human animal evolution. The creation of man from dust or clay is preferred to evolutionary creation through primate evolution. Unwittingly the holy books are considered textbooks of ail knowledge by making literal and non-contextual interpretation.

It would be more fruitful if the attack on biological evolution converges not to the original Darwinian naturalist thoughts, but on the current facts and synthetic theories which still evolve concurrent with new findings in all field of natural sciences. The main problems of disagreement between creationism and the synthetic theory are presented below.

1. Both science and religion cover the universe, but both concentrate up till recently on the planet earth, which is only a miniscule part of the universe.

2. Science and religion are not opposing systems of explanation of life and nature. The discrepancies between the two are mainly due to the different paradigms used. To be a scientist does not necessarily lead to being an atheist, and on the other hand, to be religious does not mean to be anti-science. Consequently, to accept evolutionary theories is not the same as being a religious and an atheist may not be an evolutionist.

3. Disagreements between the synthetic theory of evolution and doctrinal creationism particularly concern:

    a. short earth history and late date anthropogenesis vs long earth history and early date anthropogenesis (ca 6000 years vs 4.5 billion and ca 3 million years respectively) ;

    b. direct separate creation and fixity of species vs evolutionary creation and evolving taxa of organisms;

    c. micromonitoring of the course and mode of life vs megaprograming of evolving living creatures (each species is created and monitored individually vs creation of life by megaprograms which evolves according to principal rules);

    d. everything begins and ends with *causa priina* which is also the ultimate concern vs human autonomy and freedom of choice, and man as problem creator and solver;

    e. the universal flood influenced the varieties of species vs periodic catastrophes but not accompanied by total extinction (the ubiquitous mythical flood vs cosmic catastrophes) ;

    f. literal straight-line interpretation of metaphoric scriptural account of creation vs multifactorial and reticular evolutionary pathways at different levels of the living systems;

g. fixture and statism of exegesis of the holy scriptures vs. dynamic and evolving understanding of nature;

h. direct individual creation from dust or clay of a pair of ancestors vs. population concept of evolution, mostly gradual but interrupted by occasional explosive or saltatory mode of evolutionary processes; in other words, God acts as a watchmaker or pottery maker vs. God as grand designer and mega-programer;

i. unfalsifiable and deductive interpretation of creation vs. tentative and inductively-derived theories of evolution, progressing from Aristotelian via Cuvierian and Lamarckian, Darwinian, neo-Darwinian to synthetic theory of evolution, based on facts and theories presented by various scientific disciplines, from comparative anatomy, embryology, physiology and biochemistry, physics and chemistry, geo-sciences, pareo-sciences, biogeography, geochronology, archeology and genetics ;

j. recognition of the distinction between phylogenetic and ontogenetic development in science;

k. the sequence of creation differs (eg in vertebrate evolution);

l. interpretation of the hardware of evolution is also different;

m. the concept of creation of the universe and the Creator diverges.

4. Current weaknesses in human evolutionary theory are still present:

a. gaps in the fossil series, both vertically and horizontally, due to minimal fossilisation frequency and incomplete world-wide exploration;

b. scarcity of finds of complete individual skeletons and inadequate numbers of synchronic and sympatric remains;

c. personal bias in interpretation and classification with continual arguments on definitions and criteria;

d. competing theories based on uni-disciplinary analyses and, conclusions ;

e. the problem of integrator in random opportunistic; evolution in relation to coordination, direction and purpose;

f. no perfect and accurate or convincing method of absolute, especially A1 dating (of the fossil *per se*) at present ;

g. arguments on replacement and/or *in situ* evolution, interbreeding and migration routes: most likely both take place at one or different times.

5. Current problems:

a. No serious primary rejection of evolution (*an-nushu*) by Islam until recently as consequence of influence of other religions.

b. Special mention should be made here of the provocative work by Adnan Oktar (*nom de plume*: Harun Yahya), which strongly resembles a campaign pamflet, and seems to be intruded by Protestant fundamentalist ideas of creationism. It is alleged that the Islamist creationist movement is ideationally and financially instigated and supported by the aforementioned group.

   The fact that the author used a pen name indicates that it does not deserve serious consideration by biological and religious thinkers. Many incorrect and outdated facts and conclusions are presented in the luxury publication. It is most unfortunate that the editor accused adherents of evolutionary theories as commit-ting a grave sin. This work, both in book and videocassette form, seems to be very popular among biology students in certain cities and universities who lack a balanced curriculum of science and religion at pre-university levels.

c. Darwin's theories have historic significance, but present-day criticisms, if any, should be directed against the synthetic or total biological theory of evolution.

Bibliography

Ali, Maulana Muhammad (translation). *The Holy Qur'an* (Lahore: Ahmadiyyah Anjuman Isha'at Islam, 1973).

Couperus, Molleurus. 'Tensions Between Religion and Science'. In *Spectrum*, 10, 1980:74-88.

Draper, John–William. *History of the Conflict Between Religion and Science* (London: Henry S King & Co, 1875).

Dundes, Alan, editor. *The Flood Myth* (Berkley, CA: University of California Press, 1988).

Eliade, Mircea 1994, *Geschichte der religiosen Ideen*. Bd. 3/1,2. (Freiburg: Aufl. Herder, 1994).

Gauvin, Marshall J. *The Struggle Between Religion and Science* (New York: Peter Eckler Publishing Co, 1923).

Gillespie, Neal C. *Charles Darwin and the Problem of Creation* (Chicago: University of Chicago Press, 1979).

Jacob, Francois. *The Possible and the Actual* (New York: Pantheon Books, 1982).

Jacob, Teuku. *Perkembangan Makhluk Hidup dalam Prespektif Islam (The Evolution of Living Beings In the Islamic Perspective)* (Jogyakarta: Kursus Universitas Islam Indonesia, 1998).

————. 2001 Biologi evolusi *(Evolutionary Biolog')* Seminar Evolusi Universitas Negeri Yogyakarta, 2001.

———— 2002 *Antropologi Ragawi dan Islam (Physical Anthropology and Islam)* Sem Agama dan Antropologi.Semarang.

Jassin, HB (terj.) 1982 *Bacaan Mulla (The Glorious Book)* Yayasan 23 Januari 1942, Jakarta, 1982.

Khoury, Adel Theoder, Hegemann, Ludwig, & Heine, Peter 1991 *Islam-Lexikon: Geschichte, Ideen, Gestalten Bd 1* (Freiburg: Herder, 1991).

Kornfield, William J. 1974 'The Early Date Genesis Man'. In *Spectrum*, 3/4 1974:37–43.

Oldroyd, DR. *Darwinian Impacts: An Introduction to the Darwinian Revolution* (Milton Keynes, UK: Open University Press, 1980).

Panati, Charles. *Sacred Origins of Profound Things* (New York: Penguin Group, 1986).

Pickthall, Mohammed Marmaduke (translation) *The Meaning of the Glorious Koran* (New York: New American Library, 1953).

Ruse, Michael. *Darwinism Defended: A Guide to the Evolution Controversies* (Reading, Mass: Addison-Wesley Publishing Company, 1982).

Siddiq, Ahsanullah. 'Evolution in Islam'. In *JIMA* 14 1982:37–44.

Werner, Max (translation). *Der Koran* (Wiebaden: VMA-Verlag).

White, AD. *A History of the Warfare of Science with Theology in Christendom*, vol 1. (New York: Dover Publications Inc, 1960).

Yayasan Penyelenggara Penterjemah Al-Qur'an 1982 *Al-Qur'an dan Terjemahnya. (Al-Qur'an and Its Translation)* Dept Agama RI Jakarta.

Yucelen, Yuksel 1988 *Was sagk der Koran dazu? 2. Aufl.* dtv, Munchen.

Ziadat, Adel A. 1986 *Western Science in the Arab World: The Impact of Darwinism, 1860-1930* (London: Macmillan, 1986).

Part Four

The Care of the Earth: The Future of Science

and Religion

13

The Care of The Earth: The Future of Science and Religion

Larry Rasmussen

In 1968, the year he was assassinated, Martin Luther King, Jr published *Where Do We Go from Here: Chaos or Community?* One of the essays, 'The World House', includes the following.

> Some years ago a famous novelist died. Among his papers was found a list of suggested plots for future stories, the most prominently underscored being this one: 'A widely separated family inherits a house in which they have to live together.' This is the great new problem of mankind. We have inherited a large house, a great 'world house' in which we have to live together—black and white, Easterner and Westerner, Moslem and Hindu—a family unduly separated in ideas, culture and interest, who, because we can never again live apart, must learn somehow to live with each other in peace.[1]

The events of September 11, 2001, have underscored the nature of our life together in a world house, and especially the vulnerabilities of a tightly coupled world. The target of attack in New York City—for the second time, not the first—was the World Trade Center, next to the World Financial Center, in lower Manhattan near Wall Street, the capital of global as well as US capitalism. At 8: 46 am, American Airlines Flight 11 struck the North Tower, known as One World Trade Center between the 94th and 98th floors. At 9:02 am, United Flight 175,

---

1. Martin Luther King, Jr, *Where Do We Go from Here: Chaos or Community?* (Boston: Beacon Press, 1968), 167. A copy of this book, together with *Strength to Love*, was found in Dr King's briefcase at the Lorraine Motel in Memphis, Tennessee, the day of his assassination.

struck the South Tower, Two World Trade Center between the 78th and 84th floors. People from thirty-eight nations and at least forty states of the USA died in the twin towers' collapse. All those mentioned by King were among the victims—black and white, Easterner and Westerner, Gentile and Jew, Catholic and Protestant, Moslem and Hindu—and more. Those few city blocks, only sixteen acres, were one of the rooms in the present world house.

The rise of systems that created a vulnerable 'world house' is complex and centuries deep. I mention only two causes. The first is Western-led globalisation that reaches back at least to Christopher Columbus and the Age of Exploration. This is sometimes referred to as 'the first wave of globalization'.[2] It is commerce and colonisation, conquest and Christianity, sliding out from Europe to establish neo-European settlements and systems on every continent save Antarctica. The result, in Alfred Crosby's words, was 'a self-replicating and world-altering avalanche'[3] that upended culture and nature together on every continent and put every region in contact with every other region, thus establishing a genuinely global web of traffic and transformation. The result was also to establish patterns of power and privilege that, in dynamic and modified forms, continue to this day, and are sometimes described as neo-colonialism and/or post-colonialism. The second cause of global systems and vulnerability is this: quantum leaps in human power that erase distance and increase impact. Some, like Hans Jonas, have even argued that these quantum and cumulative leaps in human power, enabling humans to affect all of life in fundamental and unprecedented ways, is *the* distinctive mark of our epoch.[4] Human power affects all of life, whether in sky, land, or sea. Ours is a humanly-dominated biosphere, for better and worse.

Reinhold Niebuhr, writing in the 1940s and viewing the global march of science and technological developments as a major cause of

---

2.   See the discussion of Vandana Shiva in *Biopiracy: The Plunder of Nature and Knowledge* (Toronto: Between the Lines Press, 1997).

3.   Alfred W Crosby, *Ecological Imperialism: The Biological Expansion of Europe, 900–1900* (Cambridge: Cambridge University Press, 1986), 194.

4.   See the argument of Hans Jonas in *The Imperative of Responsibility* (Chicago: University of Chicago Press, 1984).

these enhanced human powers, refers to this as 'the age of technics'.[5] Like King, Niebuhr pondered chaos and community as alternative fates in this epoch. 'The task of creating community and avoiding anarchy is constantly pitched on broader and broader levels',[6] Niebuhr contended. More sophisticated technologies have entered 'the fields of production and communications,' he wrote in 1945, after citing the atomic bomb as an example of 'the progressive development of technics' for, in this case, an ominous development; namely, the onset of new weapons of mass destruction. Overall, the 'ever increasing introduction of technics,' Niebuhr went on,

> constantly enlarges the intensity and extent of social cohesion in modern man's common life; and also tends constantly to centralize effective economic power. The effect of technics upon communications is to create a potential world community, which we have not been able to actualize morally and politically. The effect of technics upon production is to create greater and greater disproportions of economic power and thus to make the achievement of justice difficult.[7]

Niebuhr warns that greater concentrations of economic power tend 'to destroy the more organic and traditional forms of community" within nations, producing 'atomic individuals' and 'dynamic [rather than static] inequalities and injustices'[8] Since for him it was axiomatic that 'disproportions of power increase the hazard to justice',[9] this bodes ill for community and any good held in common. 'To be armed with power means that the temptation to do what one wants increases' and what one wants in the moment is 'usually not the common welfare'.[10] His summary conclusion was that 'the total effect of the rise

---

5. Reinhold Niebuhr, *The Nature and Destiny of Man,* vol II (New York: Charles Scribner's Sons, 1943), 245.
6. Niebuhr, *The Nature and Destiny of Man,* vol II, 245.
7. Reinhold Niebuhr, in an article in *Commentary,* no 12, 1945: 2–3.
8. Reinhold Niebuhr, in *The Church and the Disorder of Civilization* (Geneva: World Council of Churches Publications, 1948), 17.
9. Niebuhr, in *Commentary,* no 12, 1945: 4.
10. Niebuhr, in *Commentary,* no 12, 1945: 4.

of a technical civilisation and an industrial society has been the destruction of community on the national level and the extension of conflict on the international level'.[11]

In other writings of the mid 1940s, Niebuhr spoke of 'the world community, toward which all historical forces seem to be driving us', as both a possibility and an impossibility.[12] One era is clearly gone. 'The age of absolute national sovereignty is over', Niebuhr says, but 'the age of international order under political instruments, powerful enough to regulate the relations of nations and to compose their competing desires, is not yet born'.[13] We thus find ourselves as a generation living in a tragic era between two ages. While 'the fact that world-wide economic and technical interdependence between the nations makes a world-wide system of justice necessary',[14] and while historical forces seem to be driving us toward world community as a genuine possibility, world community remains out of reach, an impossibility bordered by chaos.

The subject of this essay is 'Care for the Earth: Religion, Science and Sustainable Community'. King and Niebuhr themselves have both joined the ancestors by now, yet their discussions of forty and sixty years ago lead directly to our question: In the presence of vulnerabilities that will not wane in a 'world house' in an 'age of technics', and against the historically unprecedented transformations of nature and culture together, what ways of living make for greater security? What ways of living tend to foster flourishing and sustainable communities?

Before I turn to lessons from three Earth Summits (Stockholm, 1972; Rio de Janeiro, 1992; Johannesburg, 2002) to address this question, I insert a gloss on community itself for Christianity and for Islam.

'Community' on various levels is a notion that rests somewhere near the center of both Islam and Christianity. Indeed, the interconnectedness of all existence in what is claimed as no less than a *cosmic* community has been taught by virtually all religions for hundreds, even thousands of years. Islam, Christianity, and Judaism

---

11. Niebuhr, *The Church and the Disorder of Civilization*, 18.
12. Niebuhr, *The Children of Light and the Children of Darkness* (New York: Charles Scribner's Sons, 1944), 190.
13. Niebuhr, *Discerning the Signs of the Times*, 39–40.
14. Niebuhr, *Discerning the Signs of the Times*, 42.

certainly conceive creation in such terms. All creation has standing before Allah (God); and creation, in its awesome diversity, is one. It is the cosmic manifestation of divine ordering. Moreover, creation as cosmic community is sacred. It is no less than the habitat of the Divine Life. Seyyed Hossein Nasr, in his *Religion and the Order of Nature*, opens his very first chapter, on 'Religion and Religions', with this text:

> The One cannot in the many but appear,
> In creation as in these sacred forms,
> Which, diverse in their outwardness,
> Manifest a single inner Light, eternal.
> I gazed upon Thy countenance in singleness,
> How bewildered I am to behold Thy many Faces now.[15]

Secondly, 'community' in the Abrahamic traditions carries equally pregnant meaning as a term for the called people of God. Divine power is experienced not only as cosmic power displayed in the powers of nature, but as a power for peoplehood itself. Community as the life of the faith community on a scale that runs from the local gathering to a world-spanning fellowship of the faithful is central to Muslim, Jewish and Christian faiths. These faiths cannot be conceived apart from community in this strong sense. What is more compelling and more binding for Muslims than the worldwide *umma* (community)? What metaphor is more common to the notion of church than the body of Christ?

Lastly, these faiths picture earth itself, all of it together, in a manner that, more and more, takes on the tone and texture of community. That at least seems the testimony as we face the 'eco-crisis' squarely and respond to 'earthrise' in those stunning pictures of the marbled planet taken from space. I choose but one example of this from Christian literature. It has now become common in Christian theology and ethics to picture the planet with a Greek image common in Christian origins—*oikos*, the literal meaning of which is 'house' (King's 'world house'). *Oikos* can also be properly rendered the 'whole inhabited

---

15. Nasr cites this in both Arabic and English but does not identify the source. See Seyyed Hossein Nasr, *Religion and the Order of Nature* (New York and Oxford: Oxford University Press, 1996), 9.

world,' or 'ecumenical earth', or simply 'habitat earth'. It is the root for the English words economics (*oikonomia*), ecumenics (*oikumene*), and ecology (*oikologia*). The intercon-nectedness and commonality is apparent here, even linguistically. Earth itself is a 'community' in a profound empirical and material sense, a dynamic, but closed, system, a one-time endowment of enormous, but interdependent, diversity, a world house and a bestowed trust.

With this kind of affinity for 'community' and its treasures on several levels in Islam, Judaism, and Christianity, from the created order as a whole to the planet in this moment to the weekly gathering of the faithful themselves, we turn to the specific subject of care for the earth and the flourishing of sustainable communities in our 'world house'.

My preoccupation, as indicated at the outset, is our shared vulnerability in a world that is small, round, and beautiful, but without an exit ramp. My preoccupation is also the search for alternatives to the world of present economic globalisation and the imperial reach of US and Western power. With all this in mind, I ask how the earth summits and the backlash against globalisation in a post-colonial world might instruct Christians and Muslims invested in sustainable community inclusive of the whole Community of Life.

Let me invite you into a real-world thought experiment. Step back for a moment from the frenzy of the present and ask how, as collective citizens of the world house, we might create security and sufficient well-being to address what human communities together with the rest of nature require for their flourishing. Start your thought experiment with what you would *not* do. If you wanted security as care for the earth, you wouldn't, for example, create societies reliant on distant sources of food and energy that have to be secured by intimidation, costly incentives, great webs of regulation, or plain, brute force. And you wouldn't overhear yourself, as US or Japanese or Chinese citizens, for example, talking about *our* critical oil supplies in the Asian republics or the Middle East, and about American or Japanese or Chinese petroleum security abroad. Neither would you would demand inexpensive, long-distant transport when that can only be granted by 'cheap fuel, international peace, control of terrorism, prevention of sabotage, and the solvency of the international economy'[16] Nor would

---

16.   Berry, 'The Idea of a Local Economy', in *The Presence of Fear*, 29.

you create highly complex technologies that require knowledge and skills possessed by a limited priesthood of scientists, engineers, and technicians, technologies that have to be secured indefinitely not only against terrorists but against plain, old-fashioned common human error in a world not overly burdened with perfection. And you would not want to see basic human needs of food, shelter, clear air, water, and sustainable livelihoods go unmet. The think-tanks may be right that there isn't a *simple* one-to-one relationship between poverty, desperation, degraded environments, and back-breaking, Sisyphean toil, on the one hand, and uprootedness, violence, rage and terrorism, on the other. But a *complex* relationship among these will often yield much the same results, especially if powerlessness, mass humiliation and frustration are added. 'The poverty of dignity' [17] wedded to plain poverty creates great resentment toward wasteful, arrogant affluence, whether between nations or within them. And if you wanted security—another earth summit point—you wouldn't do the good and vital and needed work of attending to the health of democratic institutions, using police and military power in the interests of all, and fairly distributing wealth while neglecting the requisites of life upon which all these utterly depend—the protection and replenishment of soils, air, water, and biological diversity. Society's health is always a part of the rest of nature's. Real security has always been profoundly 'socio-ecological'. Expanded human security at the expense of earth's requirements for its own regeneration is a guaranteed downward slope and eventual dead end. A 'secured' clear-cut forest is not secure at all.

Nor, if you wanted security, would you design high-tech interdependencies for most all your basic systems, including security systems. In a high-tech world, low-tech means in the hands of martyrs, nihilists, or rebels with a cause are far more dangerous than high-tech means in a low-tech world, in anybody's hands. Box-cutters combine with commercial jets to become molotov cocktails from hell as human-guided missiles replace computer-guided ones. A few spores in a few small envelopes in a high-tech postal system evacuate the US Senate Office building and the American Media building for months. Used pickups with fertiliser nitrates and diesel oil, dirty nuclear weapons you could stuff in a backpack or ship in a carved trunk from an

---

17. The phrase is Thomas L Friedman's, from 'Iraq, Upside Down', in *The New York Times*, 18 September 2002: A31.

Istanbul bazaar, soda can-size bioterror, programmed disabling of communications networks, traffic systems, and industrial infrastructure traveling the speed of sound or light—all these are means available to the enraged, the disciplined, the few, the deranged, and the devout. And at a cost-effectiveness rate that should capture the cold respect of any business leader or banker. A sum less than the price of a single tank, to say nothing of the annual skim of even one good Corporate Executive Officer, has already been enough 'to cause hundreds of billions of dollars of damage and seize control of western media for months'.[18] The Congressional Budget Office of the US government has, to cite one example, spent $37 billion over the last year and may spend $443 billion over the next ten.[19] Protection pursued *as* high-tech means in a tightly-wired world may in fact be the prescription for bank-busting *in*security. History has enjoyed ironies less delicious than this.

Differently said, if you actually *wanted* to create a system vulnerable to terrorism, sabotage, and war, or a system friendly to fear and free-floating anxiety, you would design one that is global in extent, technologically complex, economically and demographically centered in dense metropolitan areas, and crucially dependent on a relatively few kinds of limited and concentrated resources. Then you would organise protection on a national military basis[20] and be willing to go it alone when the allies did not rally. Yet this is the kind of security/insecurity we have.

What about the environmental sustainability, and not only the security of communities in the world house? There is much you would *not* do, if sustainability as nature's health is the goal. You would not, for example, design a way of life that:

- put billions of pounds of toxic material into the air, water, and soil every year;
- measured prosperity by activity rather than legacy;

18. David Orr, 'The Events of 9–11: A View from the Margin', in *The Declaration*: 1.
19. 'New Study on Antiterror Spending Is Fodder for Rival Camps', in *The New York Times*, 6 September 2002.
20. This point is indebted to Wendell Berry's tenth point in his essay, 'Thoughts in the Presence of Fear', in *The Presence of Fear*, 4.

- required thousands of complex regulations to keep people and nature systems from being poisoned too quickly;
- resulted in gigantic amounts of waste;
- put valuable materials in holes all over the planet, where they can never be retrieved;
- eroded the diversity of biological species, cultural practices, and ways of life intricately fine-tuned to place;[21]
- considered fossil fuel a fundamental right and consuming an act of patriotism.[22]

But the modern era has done just this, and the hard message of three earth summits is that the industrial paradigm in either capitalist or socialist forms is, from the point of view of earth's well being, fundamentally flawed. The downsides to an immensely successful generation of wealth and well being for millions and millions have given rise to unsustainable development as the present course. Simply put, we cannot live in ways that deny earth's well being as primary and ours as always and utterly derivative. 'Sustainable development' must replace unsustainable. We must live with, not against, the grain of nature.

But what is the alternative to these global systems, their costs and vulnerabilities, and what role might science and religion play in a different direction for policies and structures? How might care for the earth, as the comprehensive community encompassing human and more-than-human together, proceed? The earth summits and the backlash against globalisation have given us a certain direction and an agenda, albeit an unfinished one. So consider a second real world thought experiment, this time the creation of sustainable communities.

I will sketch what I think have been overlapping concerns of thousands of socio-ecologically oriented non-governmental organisations (NGOs) in recent years. Collectively, they express an ecological vision of sustainable community already in view on the part

---

21. This is a slight modification of the list of William McDonough and Michael Braungart, 'The Next Industrial Revolution', in *The Atlantic Monthly*, October, 1998: 85. [inclusive pages of article: 82–92].
22. The sight of veritable fleets of SUVs (Sport Utility Vehicles) flying US flags from their antennae in the wake of 9/11, as the public display of patriotism, is only one example. See the later discussion of insecurity born of US American addiction to fossil fuels.

of some at the Earth Summit in Rio in 1992 and in Johannesburg in 2002. This vision and the on-the-ground efforts contrast with the global systems we described earlier. As you consider the following, remember an insight from Wendell Berry. In our kind of world of interlocking interdependencies, we can only solve for *a pattern*, not a symptom, an interest, or a supposedly isolated problem.[23] Things belong together and must of needs be treated as relevant wholes.

Most discussions of 'sustainable development' at Rio and Johannesburg assumed the globalising economy of corporate capitalism and sought ways to 'green' that. Sustainable development is seen as the necessary effort to wrap the global environment around the integrating global economy in such a way that both economy and environment are sustained. The ecological vision by contrast is 'sustainable community'. It asks, in *oikos* fashion, how you wrap economy and environment together around local communities and regions. It does not start with the question, what makes for a healthy global economy, but with the question, what makes for healthy local and regional communities? In doing so, and in contrast to the ways of globalisation as current corporate capitalism, even 'greened', sustainable community tries to preserve or create the following: greater economic self-sufficiency locally and regionally, with a view to the bio-regions themselves as basic to human organisation; agriculture appropriate to regions and in the hands of local owners and workers using local knowledge and crop varieties, with ability to save their own seeds and treat their own plants and soils with their own products; the preservation of local and regional traditions, language, and cultures and a resistance to global homogenisation of culture and values; a revival of a sense of the sacred, *vis a vis* a present way of life that leeches the sacred from the everyday and has no sense of mystery because it reduces life to the utilitarian; the repair of the moral fiber of society on some terms other than consumerism; resistance to the commodification and patenting of all things in nature, including knowledge; the internalisation of costs to the local, regional, and global environment in the price of goods; and the protection of ecosystems and Earth's 'vitality, diversity, and

---

23.   Orr, 'The Events of 9-11', in *The Declaration*, vol 5, no 1: 1.

beauty' as 'a sacred trust'.[24] All this is local *and* 'global' democratic community, not nativist localism. That is, it does not ask *whether* to 'globalis' as citizens of 'the world house', but *how*. And its answer–democratic communities democratically arrived at–is *global* community by virtue of its planetary consciousness and the impressive networking of citizens around the world made possible by electronic globalisation. Sustainable community is attentive to questions that global capitalism, even as sustainable development, rarely asks: namely, what are the essential bonds of human community and culture, as well as the bonds of the human with the more-than-human world; and what is the meaning of such primal bonds for the rendering of a healthy concrete way of life? What is cultural wealth and biological wealth and how are they sustained in the places people live with the rest of the community of life? And what is security as the protection of all that is required for the community of life, security as patterns of production, consumption, reproduction and protection from harm that safeguard earth's regenerative capacities, human rights, and local well-being? A society with many nuclear reactors, for example, or other power grids that stream electricity from big installations, some of them far away, some too close, is more vulnerable than one using decentralised solar, wind, biomass, or other regionally appropriate and regionally-sustainable energy technologies. Urban communities like mine in New York City would, for example, be less vulnerable if we were far less dependent on foreign oil, and all other fossil fuels, and more dependent on the technologies of a solar-hydrogen economy for the longer rides—and bicycles and wheelchairs for the short ones! A society fed by megafarms in the hands of industrialised, high-tech, high fertiliser and pesticide input agriculture tended by farmers who do not own them and who never see the people they feed, is much more vulnerable to food insecurity than many relatively smaller and more dispersed, indigenously-oriented and locally owned and operated farms such as those of the Community Supported Agriculture movement. And in general, communities are healthier when their community prosperity is an expression of community assets and the circulation of finance and

---

24.   This is a phrase from the Preamble of an extraordinarily important document soon coming before the United Nations General Assembly, the Earth Charter, itself a spin-off of the Earth Summit.

skills in a vibrant local and regional economy of interlocking neighborhoods. This is not anti-free trade at all. It is anti-rigged trade, with the rigging done by others, often far away. Free trade is, in any case, not about free trade at all. It is about maximum investment access for corporate capitalism, which is an entirely different matter. It contrasts with trade centered in local choice and decisions, rather than the trade of an export-dependent economy or an import-dependent one. As the World Bank and the International Monetary Fund and millions, yes, billions, of people have painfully learned, free trade always brings freedom and prosperity, except when it doesn't; and it works best of all for the richest fifth of the world's peoples. We should have been a little suspicious when the accord creating the World Trade Organization ran to 22,500 pages—not likely a free trade agreement![25] In a word, communities are healthier when they are democratic in the genuine sense: namely, affirming people's capacity to be largely self-organising, self-provisioning, and self-governing in ways that are clear to them as citizens and demanding of their responsibilities as members of the larger Community of Life. This includes their policing efforts, since human nature is not suddenly rendered peaceful by more intimate, face-to-face relationships.

To put it in one sentence: as a rule of thumb, local and regional self-sufficiency resting in high levels of local participation is the surest, safest and least expensive way to live when equity, economy, and environment needs are all respected. Such shared sufficiency is not presently possible is some great leap forward, given that our present habits are deeply institutionalised in ways that oppose collective self-sufficiency. So the steps are incremental. But this de-centralised sufficiency, focused on local democracy and stable local communities with their own political economy and indigenous wisdom, is both the starting point and the goal. And as we have learned at the Earth summits in circles of NGO networking, it is already struggling to be born in a million small ways in a million different places. It is a practical antidote to real fear and to real degradation of land and peoples in a world far too vulnerable in its present constellation.[26]

---

25.   Tina Rosenberg, 'The Free-Trade Fix', in *The New York Times Magazine*, 18 August 2002, Section 6: 30.

26.   The discussion of security and the lessons of the Earth summits above has, since the conference in Indonesia, been published in the essay, 'The

We are all aware of the obstacles. We in fact know them better than we know how much is already being done to overcome them. We know more despair than hope, even as hope blooms in so many places. Nor dare we regard the ecological vision and sustainable community as a panacea. There are no panaceas, chiefly because human nature hasn't changed notably since Homer, Moses, Mohammed, Prince Siddartha, Jesus, and any reading of sacred scriptures will testify. Life, as Martin Luther and Martin Luther King and religious sages of all manner have known, has always been a dicey, uncontrolled experiment. Sin has always been the effort to organise a security that cannot be had in life as we know it. It is certainly not less so in an age of vastly expanded cumulative human powers that fail to carry equally expanded virtue or wisdom. Peace and comprehensive care of Habitat Earth as our world house will thus remain the great venture, not of the hunkered down and over-armed, but of those who risk in faith that a different world house can come to be in which the welfare of enemies, who are real and who are dangerous, is placed in the same framework as our own welfare. Religious faith in many traditions offers precisely the unguarded security that allows, even invites, this kind of risk and venture. To be free in this way, as Muslims and Christians, as scientists, teachers, or laborers, as citizens and family members, is good news as we work for sustainable Earth communities in the presence of fear and do what we must and can to re-negotiate a globalising way of life that for so many is a way of death.

I close by pointing to a document that is trying to make its way to the United Nations for debate in the General Assembly. It has been generated with the aid of communities around the world and it has been written from careful listening to religious leaders, scientists, community leaders, business leaders, and professionals of all kinds. I refer to the Earth Charter and draw your attention to the fact that it provides a common basis for an alliance of science and religion in the direction I have tried to outline. It says what I have and far more. My specific question is this: Is not the Earth Charter itself the basis of a common endeavor that Muslims and Christians might support together?

American Way in the Presence of Fear', in the *Union Seminary Quarterly Review*, vol 56, nos 1–2, 2002: 1–20.

I will not quote any of the text of the Charter, as it appears in Appendix 1 in full. The Earth Charter embraces the whole of earthly life in a remarkable way and without remainder. After the Preamble about our critical moment, its character and requirements, the Charter in Part I on 'Respect and Care for the Community of Life' sets out four lead principles: 'Respect Earth and life in all its diversity;' 'Care for the community of life with understanding, compassion, and love;' 'Build democratic societies that are just, participatory, sustainable, and peaceful;' and 'Secure Earth's bounty and beauty for present and future generations' These are concretised in gratifying detail in sub-sections that, together with these principles, serve to ground and govern the interlocking sections that follow, on Ecological Integrity, Social and Economic Justice, (and) Democracy, Nonviolence, and Peace. Not least impressive is how the complex metabolism of the whole of earthly life is treated in ways that draws deeply from the spirit of religious wisdom and at the same time combat destructive dualisms of humanity/-nature, society/environment, wealth/poverty, and spirit/-matter, as well as gender inequalities and a present that always seems to trump the future. In any event, the Earth Charter is a concrete, timely opportunity for Muslims and Christians to make common cause in a critical partnership of science and religion. I commend it to you.[27]

---

27. The text of the Earth Charter is available in many places. Contact the Earth Council via the web site or via e-mail. www.earthcharter.org. info@earthcharter.org.

Appendix
The Earth Charter

Preamble

We stand at a critical moment in Earth's history, a time when humanity must choose its future. As the world becomes increasingly interdependent and fragile, the future at once holds great peril and great promise. To move forward we must recognise that in the midst of a magnificent diversity of cultures and life forms we are one human family and one Earth community with a common destiny. We must join together to bring forth a sustainable global society founded on respect for nature, universal human rights, economic justice, and a culture of peace. Towards this end, it is imperative that we, the peoples of Earth, declare our responsibility to one another, to the greater community of life, and to future generations.

Earth, Our Home

Humanity is part of a vast evolving universe. Earth, our home, is alive with a unique community of life. The forces of nature make existence a demanding and uncertain adventure, but Earth has provided the conditions essential to life's evolution. The resilience of the community of life and the well-being of humanity depend upon preserving a healthy biosphere with all its ecological systems, a rich variety of plants and animals, fertile soils, pure waters, and clean air. The global environment with its finite resources is a common concern of all peoples. The protection of Earth's vitality, diversity, and beauty is a sacred trust.

The Global Situation

The dominant patterns of production and consumption are causing environmental devastation, the depletion of resources, and a massive extinction of species. Communities are being undermined. The benefits of development are not shared equitably and the gap between rich and poor is widening. Injustice, poverty, ignorance, and violent conflict are wide-spread and the cause of great suffering. An unprecedented rise in human population has overburdened ecological and social systems.

The foundations of global security are threatened. These trends are perilous—but not inevitable.

The Challenges Ahead

The choice is ours: form a global partnership to care for Earth and one another or risk the destruction of ourselves and the diversity of life. Fundamental changes are needed in our values, institutions, and ways of living. We must realise that when basic needs have been met, human development is primarily about being more, not having more. We have the knowledge and technology to provide for all and to reduce our impacts on the environment. The emergence of a global civil society is creating new opportunities to build a democratic and humane world. Our environmental, economic, political, social, and spiritual challenges are interconnected, and together we can forge inclusive solutions.

Universal Responsibility

To realise these aspirations, we must decide to live with a sense of universal responsibility, identifying ourselves with the whole Earth community as well as our local communities. We are at once citizens of different nations and of one world in which the local and global are linked. Everyone shares responsibility for the present and future well-being of the human family and the larger living world. The spirit of human solidarity and kinship with all life is strengthened when we live with reverence for the mystery of being, gratitude for the gift of life, and humility regarding the human place in nature.

We urgently need a shared vision of basic values to provide an ethical foundation for the emerging world community. Therefore, together in hope we affirm the following interdependent principles for a sustainable way of life as a common standard by which the conduct of all individuals, organisations, businesses, governments, and transnational institutions is to be guided and assessed.

Principles

I. Respect and Care for the Community of Life
1. *Respect Earth and life in all its diversity.*

    a. Recognise that all beings are interdependent and every form of life has value regardless of its worth to human beings.

b. *Affirm faith in the inherent dignity of all human beings and in the intellectual, artistic, ethical, and spiritual potential of humanity.*

2. Care for the community of life with understanding, compassion, and love.

a. *Accept that with the right to own, manage, and use natural resources comes the duty to prevent environmental harm and to protect the rights of people.*

b. *Affirm that with increased freedom, knowledge, and power comes increased responsibility to promote the common good.*

3. Build democratic societies that are just, participatory, sustainable, and peaceful.

a. *Ensure that communities at all levels guarantee human rights and fundamental freedoms and provide everyone an opportunity to realise his or her full potential.*

b. *Promote social and economic justice, enabling all to achieve a secure and meaningful livelihood that is ecologically responsible.*

4. Secure Earth's bounty and beauty for present and future generations.

a. *Recognise that the freedom of action of each generation is qualified by the needs of future generations.*

b. *Transmit to future generations values, traditions, and institutions that support the long-term flourishing of Earth's human and ecological communities.*

In order to fulfill these four broad commitments, it is necessary to:

II. Ecological Integrity

5. Protect and restore the integrity of Earth's ecological systems, with special concern for biological diversity and the natural processes that sustain life.

a. *Adopt at all levels sustainable development plans and regulations that make environmental conservation and rehabilitation integral to all development initiatives.*

> *b. Establish and safeguard viable nature and biosphere reserves, including wild lands and marine areas, to protect Earth's life support systems, maintain biodiversity, and preserve our natural heritage.*
>
> *c. Promote the recovery of endangered species and ecosystems.*
>
> *d. Control and eradicate non-native or genetically modified organisms harmful to native species and the environment, and prevent introduction of such harmful organisms.*
>
> *e. Manage the use of renewable resources such as water, soil, forest products, and marine life in ways that do not exceed rates of regeneration and that protect the health of ecosystems.*
>
> *f. Manage the extraction and use of non-renewable resources such as minerals and fossil fuels in ways that minimise depletion and cause no serious environmental damage.*

6. Prevent harm as the best method of environmental protection and, when knowledge is limited, apply a precautionary approach.

> *a. Take action to avoid the possibility of serious or irreversible environmental harm even when scientific knowledge is incomplete or inconclusive.*
>
> *b. Place the burden of proof on those who argue that a proposed activity will not cause significant harm, and make the responsible parties liable for environmental harm.*
>
> *c. Ensure that decision making addresses the cumulative, long-term, indirect, long distance, and global consequences of human activities.*
>
> *d. Prevent pollution of any part of the environment and allow no build-up of radioactive, toxic, or other hazardous substances.*
>
> *e. Avoid military activities damaging to the environment.*

7. Adopt patterns of production, consumption, and reproduction that safeguard Earth's regenerative capacities, human rights, and community well-being.

> *a. Reduce, reuse, and recycle the materials used in production and consumption systems, and ensure that residual waste can be assimilated by ecological systems.*
>
> *b. Act with restraint and efficiency when using energy, and rely increasingly on renewable energy sources such as solar and wind.*
>
> *c. Promote the development, adoption, and equitable transfer of environmentally sound technologies.*

d. *Internalise the full environmental and social costs of goods and services in the selling price, and enable consumers to identify products that meet the highest social and environmental standards.*

e. *Ensure universal access to health care that fosters reproductive health and responsible reproduction.*

f. *Adopt lifestyles that emphasise the quality of life and material sufficiency in a finite world.*

8. Advance the study of ecological sustainability and promote the open exchange and wide application of the knowledge acquired.

a. *Support international scientific and technical cooperation on sustainability, with special attention to the needs of developing nations.*

b. *Recognise and preserve the traditional knowledge and spiritual wisdom in all cultures that contribute to environmental protection and human well-being.*

c. *Ensure that information of vital importance to human health and environmental protection, including genetic information, remains available in the public domain.*

III. Social and Economic Justice

9. Eradicate poverty as an ethical, social, and environmental imperative.

a. *Guarantee the right to potable water, clean air, food security, uncontaminated soil, shelter, and safe sanitation, allocating the national and international resources required.*

b. *Empower every human being with the education and resources to secure a sustainable livelihood, and provide social security and safety nets for those who are unable to support themselves.*

c. *Recognise the ignored, protect the vulnerable, serve those who suffer, and enable them to develop their capacities and to pursue their aspirations.*

10. Ensure that economic activities and institutions at all levels promote human development in an equitable and sustainable manner.

a. *Promote the equitable distribution of wealth within nations and among nations.*

b. *Enhance the intellectual, financial, technical, and social resources of developing nations, and relieve them of onerous international debt.*

c. *Ensure that all trade supports sustainable resource use, environmental protection, and progressive labor standards.*

d. *Require multinational corporations and international financial organisations to act transparently in the public good, and hold them accountable for the consequences of their activities.*

11. *Affirm gender equality and equity as prerequisites to sustainable development and ensure universal access to education, health care, and economic opportunity.*

a. *Secure the human rights of women and girls and end all violence against them.*

b. *Promote the active participation of women in all aspects of economic, political, civil, social, and cultural life as full and equal partners, decision makers, leaders, and beneficiaries.*

c. *Strengthen families and ensure the safety and loving nurture of all family members.*

12. *Uphold the right of all, without discrimination, to a natural and social environment supportive of human dignity, bodily health, and spiritual well-being, with special attention to the rights of indigenous peoples and minorities.*

a. *Eliminate discrimination in all its forms, such as that based on race, color, sex, sexual orientation, religion, language, and national, ethnic or social origin.*

b. *Affirm the right of indigenous peoples to their spirituality, knowledge, lands and resources and to their related practice of sustainable livelihoods.*

c. *Honor and support the young people of our communities, enabling them to fulfill their essential role in creating sustainable societies.*

d. *Protect and restore outstanding places of cultural and spiritual significance.*

IV. Democracy, Nonviolence, and Peace

13. *Strengthen democratic institutions at all levels, and provide transparency and accountability in governance, inclusive*

participation in decision making, and access to justice.

    a. Uphold the right of everyone to receive clear and timely information on environmental matters and all development plans and activities which are likely to affect them or in which they have an interest.

    b. Support local, regional and global civil society, and promote the meaningful participation of all interested individuals and organisations in decision making.

    c. Protect the rights to freedom of opinion, expression, peaceful assembly, association, and dissent.

    d. Institute effective and efficient access to administrative and independent judicial procedures, including remedies and redress for environmental harm and the threat of such harm.

    e. Eliminate corruption in all public and private institutions.

    f. Strengthen local communities, enabling them to care for their environments, and assign environmental responsibilities to the levels of government where they can be carried out most effectively.

14. *Integrate into formal education and life-long learning the knowledge, values, and skills needed for a sustainable way of life.*

    a. Provide all, especially children and youth, with educational opportunities that empower them to contribute actively to sustainable development.

    b. Promote the contribution of the arts and humanities as well as the sciences in sustainability education.

    c. Enhance the role of the mass media in raising awareness of ecological and social challenges.

    d. Recognise the importance of moral and spiritual education for sustainable living.

15. *Treat all living beings with respect and consideration.*

    a. Prevent cruelty to animals kept in human societies and protect them from suffering.

    b. Protect wild animals from methods of hunting, trapping, and fishing that cause extreme, prolonged, or avoidable suffering.

    c. Avoid or eliminate to the full extent possible the taking or destruction of non-targeted species.

16. *Promote a culture of tolerance, nonviolence, and peace.*

   a. Encourage and support mutual understanding, solidarity, and cooperation among all peoples and within and among nations.
   b. Implement comprehensive strategies to prevent violent conflict and use collaborative problem solving to manage and resolve environmental conflicts and other disputes.
   c. Demilitarise national security systems to the level of a non-provocative defense posture, and convert military resources to peaceful purposes, including ecological restoration.
   d. Eliminate nuclear, biological, and toxic weapons and other weapons of mass destruction.
   e. Ensure that the use of orbital and outer space supports environmental protection and peace.
   f. Recognise that peace is the wholeness created by right relationships with oneself, other persons, other cultures, other life, Earth, and the larger whole of which all are a part.

The Way Forward

As never before in history, common destiny beckons us to seek a new beginning. Such renewal is the promise of these Earth Charter principles. To fulfill this promise, we must commit ourselves to adopt and promote the values and objectives of the Charter.

   This requires a change of mind and heart. It requires a new sense of global interdependence and universal responsibility. We must imaginatively develop and apply the vision of a sustainable way of life locally, nationally, regionally, and globally. Our cultural diversity is a precious heritage and different cultures will find their own distinctive ways to realise the vision. We must deepen and expand the global dialogue that generated the Earth Charter, for we have much to learn from the ongoing collaborative search for truth and wisdom.

   Life often involves tensions between important values. This can mean difficult choices. However, we must find ways to harmonise diversity with unity, the exercise of freedom with the common good, short-term objectives with long-term goals. Every individual, family, organisation, and community has a vital role to play. The arts, sciences, religions, educational institutions, media, businesses, nongovernmental organisations, and governments are all called to offer creative leadership. The partnership of government, civil society, and business is essential for effective governance.

In order to build a sustainable global community, the nations of the world must renew their commitment to the United Nations, fulfill their obligations under existing international agreements, and support the implementation of Earth Charter principles with an international legally binding instrument on environment and development.

Let ours be a time remembered for the awakening of a new reverence for life, the firm resolve to achieve sustainability, the quickening of the struggle for justice and peace, and the joyful celebration of life.

Contributors

Mahmoud Ayoub

Professor of Islamic Studies/Comparative Religion, Temple University, USA

Mahmoud M Ayoub is Professor of Islamic Studies/ Comparative Religion at Temple University, USA. He is also a regular visiting professor in the Center for Religious and Cross-cultural Studies, Gadjah Mada University (Yogyakarta, Indonesia), as well as in many other universities in the US, Lebanon, and Canada. He was educated at the American University of Beirut (BA Philosophy, 1964), University of Pennsylvania (MA 1965, Religious Thought), and Harvard University (PhD History of Religion, 1975). He has been an editorial consultant of the *Oxford Dictionary of Islam*, and *The Muslim World* journal. His publications include *Redemptive Suffering in Islam: A Study of Devotional Aspects of Ashura in Twelver Shi'ism* (1978, revised PhD thesis, written with Annemarie Schimmel as his advisor), and the two volumes of *The Qur'an and Its Interpreters* (1984 and 1992, the third volume is in progress). A significant number of research articles he published are on the comparison and relations of Judaism, Christianity, and Islam—a concern which has brought him to be invited speakers at events organised by institutions such as Arab Working Group on Christian-Muslim Dialogue, Middle East Council of Chruches, World Council of Churches, National Federation of Temple Brotherhood and Jewish Chautauqua Society. Some of his books have been translated to other languages, including Bahasa Indonesia.

Osman Bakar

Osman Bakar is the Malaysia Chair of Islam in Southeast Asia, Center for Muslim-Christian Understanding, Georgetown University. He completed his undergraduate degree with Honors and an MSc in Mathematics at London University. In 1981, an MA in Comparative Religion and a PhD in Philosophy of Science/Islamic Philosophy at Temple University. He served as the Deputy Vice Chancellor/Vice President of Academics and was the first (1992) holder of the Chair of the Professor of Philosophy of Science at the University of Malaya

(Kuala Lumpur). His books, *Classification of Knowledge in Islam; Tawid and Science;* and *Civilizational Dialogue,* among others, have been translated into Albanian, Arabic, Chinese, English, French, Indonesian, Persian, Spanish, Turkish, and Urdu. In 1994, he was awarded the Dato'ship by the Sultan of Pahang and has received additional recognition for his work to include the Fulbright Visiting Scholar at Harvard University. In addition, he has served as a consultant to various agencies, including the United Nations and UNESCO. Currently, Dr Osman Bakar is the Malaysia Chair of Islam in Southeast Asia, Center for Muslim-Christian Understanding, Georgetown University, and is a member of the Center's Academic Council.

Zainal Abidin Bagir

Center for Religious and Cross-cultural Studies, Gadjah Mada University, Yogyakarta

Zainal Abidin Bagir has a PhD from the Department of History and Philosophy of Science, Indiana University. His previous education includes undergraduate in mathemathics (Bandung Institute of Technology, Indonesia) and Master's program in Islamic philosophy and science (International Institute of Islamic Thought and Civilization, Kuala Lumpur). His Master's thesis on *The Problem of Definition in Islamic Logic (al-Faridi's and Ibn Taimiyyah's Criticisms)* was published by ISTAC (1998). Since 2002 he has been a staff at the Center for Religious and Cross-cultural Studies, Gadjah Mada University, Indonesia, where he organised the program on religion and science, which includes organizing seminars and workshops, and editing several books. He is the chairpeson of Yogyakarta Society for Science and Religion. His academic interests are mainly science and religion (especially in the context of Islam), contemporary philosophy of science, and Islamic philosophy. Prior to his study at IU he was a managing editor for a weekly news magazine in Indonesia (1994–1997), and is now a contributor of essays to several Indonesian magazines and newspapers.

Philip Clayton

Professor and Chair of the Philosophy Department, California State University, Sonoma; Principle Investigator, Science and the Spiritual Quest Project

Philip Clayton holds a PhD in both philosophy and religious studies from Yale University. He has taught at Haverford College, Williams College, and the California State University, and has just been named to the Ingraham Chair at the Claremont School of Theology. Clayton has been guest professor at the Divinity School, Harvard University, Humboldt Professor at the University of Munich, and Senior Fulbright Professor, also at the University of Munich. He is a past winner of the Templeton Book Prize for best monograph in the field of science and religion and a winner of the first annual Templeton Research Prize.

Clayton is the author of *The Problem of God in Modern Thought* (Eerdmans, 2000), *God and Contemporary Science* (Edinburgh University Press, 1997); *Explanation from Physics to Theology: An Essay in Rationality and Religion* (Yale University Press, 1989; German edition, *Rationalität und Religion*, 1992); and *Das Gottesproblem*, vol 1: *Gott und Unendlichkeit in der neuzeitlichen Philosophie* (Schöningh Verlag, 1996). He has edited and translated several other volumes and published some forty articles in the philosophy of science, ethics, and the world's religious traditions. His current research interest lies in developing a theology of emergence, to be published next year as *The Emergence of Spirit*.

Clayton is currently Principal Investigator of the 'Science and the Spiritual Quest' project (SSQ) at the Center for Theology and the Natural Sciences in Berkeley, California. SSQ has brought together over 100 top scientists from around the world to explore the connections between science, ethics, religion and spirituality. The SSQ Berkeley conference in 1998 received close to 100 million media impressions and was featured on the cover of *Newsweek*. Other major public events (past or future) sponsored by SSQ include: Silicon Valley, Harvard University, the UNESCO World Headquarters in Paris, Jerusalem, Bangalore, and Tokyo.

Steve Fuller

Professor of Sociology at the University of Warwick, UK

Steve Fuller (born 1959, New York City) is Professor of Sociology at the University of Warwick, UK. He is most closely associated with the research program of social epistemology. His latest book is *Knowledge Management Foundations* (Butter-worth-Heinemann, 2002). The issues raised in this article are being expanded into a book, *Re-Imagining Sociology: Or, Why We Have Yet to Be Human* (Sage, 2003). Originally trained in the history and philosophy of science (PhD, 1985, University of Pittsburgh), he is the founder of the research program of social epistemology. It is the name of a quarterly journal he founded with Taylor & Francis in 1987, as well as the first of his books: *Social Epistemology* (Indiana University Press, 1988), *Philosophy of Science and Its Discontents*, 2nd edition (Guilford Press, 1993), *Philosophy, Rhetoric and the End of Knowledge* (University of Wisconsin Press, 1993), *Science* (Open University Press and University of Minnesota Press, 1997; translated into Japanese, 2000), *The Governance of Science: Ideology and the Future of the Open Society* (Open University Press, 2000), *Thomas Kuhn: A Philosophical History for Our Times* (University of Chicago Press, 2000). Fuller has organised two global cyberconferences for the UK's Economic and Social Research Council: one on public understanding of science (1998), and another on peer review in the social sciences (1999). He has spoken in over twenty-five countries, often keynoting professional academic conferences, and has been a Fellow of the Royal Society of Arts since 1995. He sits on the advisory board of the Knowledge Management Consortium International and has sat on the Council of the Society for Social Studies of Science.

Mehdi Golshani

Director of the Institute for Humanities and Culltural Studies, Tehran, Iran

Mehdi Golshani was born in Isfahan, Iran in 1939. He received his BS in Physics from Tehran University and his PhD in Physics from the University of California at Berkeley in 1969, with specialization in particle physics. In 1970, he joined Sharif University of Technology in Tehran and served as the chairman of the Physics Department during 1973–1975 and 1987–1989 and as the vice chancellor of that university during 1979–1981. Since 1991, he has been a Distinguished Professor of Physics there. He founded the Faculty of the Philosophy of Science at Sharif University of Technology in 1995, and was the head of the

Department of Basic Sciences at the Iranian Academy of Sciences during 1990–2000. Currently, he is the Director of the Institute for Humanities and Cultural Studies in Tehran, Iran; and also the Chairman of the Philosophy of Science Department at Sharif University of Technology, Tehran, Iran. Golshani received the John Templeton Award for Science and Religion Course Program in 1995, and served as a Judge for the John Templeton Award for Progress in Religion during 2000–2002. Golshani's present research activity is concentrated on Foundational Problems in Quantum Mechanics and Cosmology (especially implications of Bell's Theorem and generalisations of Bohmian Mechanics), Philosophical Aspects of Physics, and Philosophy of Science and Theology. Among his recent books are *The Holy Qur'an and the Sciences of Nature* (1997, which is translated into several languages, including Indonesian), *From Physics to Metaphysics* (1997) and *Can Science Dispense with Religion?* (2002, editor).

Bruno Guiderdoni

Director of Research, Paris Institute of Astrophysics; Director, Islamic Institute for Advanced Studies

Bruno Guiderdoni is a Director of Research at the French National Center for Scientific Research (CNRS). He works on galaxy formation and evolution at the Paris Institute of Astrophysics. He has published more than 100 papers and contributions on these topics, and he has organised several international conferences on these issues. His spiritual pursuit led him to embrace Islam in 1987, with the Islamic name of Abd-al-Haqq. He is now one of the referent experts on Islam in France, and one of the founders of the Islamic Institute for Advanced Studies (IHEI) that aims at helping European Muslims recover the intellectual dimension of Islam. From 1993 to 1999, he was in charge of the TV program 'Knowing Islam' which is broadcast by the State Channel France 2 on Sunday mornings. He has given many lectures on spirituality, the interfaith dialog, and the relationship between science and religion, and he has published about 50 papers on Islamic theology and mystics. Bruno Guiderdoni is a member of the Board of Advisors of the John Templeton Foundation, and of the Scientific Advisory Board of the 'Science and Spiritual Quest' program of the Center for Theology and the Natural Sciences. He is also a founding member of the International Society for Science and Religion, and is serving in the Executive Committee.

Teuku Jakob
Faculty of Medicine, Gadjah Mada University, Indonesia

Prof Dr Teuku Jacob is known world-wide for his important discoveries of human fossil (Homo erectus erectus, Homo erectus palaeo-javanicus, Homo erectus soloensis, and Homo sapiens) in Central Java area, Indonesia. He received many international prizes for his discoveries, not only of human fossils but also in other fields, including in micropaleontology. Finishing his medical doctor education in UGM, he then pursued a Master's degree in anthropology (University of Arizona, Tucson, 1958) and PhD in physical anthropology (Howard University, Washington, DC, 1960). He is a prolific writer, writing in academic journals as well as mass media. Among his book publications are *The Racial History of the Indonesian Region* (1967), *Community Medicine* (textbook, 1972), *Miscellania on Early Man* (reader for elementary school, 1981), *Man, Science, and Technology* (1988), *Raciology and Racism in the 20th Century* (1990), *Towards a Humane Technology* (1996), *Anthropology of Healing and Holistic Medicine* (1999), and *Biological Anthropology* (textbook, 2000). Besides teaching topics in biology and anthropology, he has also taught 'Natural Science in Philosophy' at the Department of Philosophy, UGM. Recently (2002) he received the Mahaputra Medal, the honor conferred by the President of the Republic of Indonesia for his dedication to scientific development in Indonesia.

Karlina Supelli
Driyarkara School of Philosophy, Jakarta

Karlina Leksono completed her undergraduate study in astronomy (Bandung Institute of Technology, 1981) and an M.Sc. in space science (University College of London, England, 1989). Her second Master's degree and her PhD is from the Philosophy Department, University of Indonesia, Jakarta (1997). Her dissertation is a study of the cosmological anthropic principle from the perspective of philosophy of science. She has since taught various courses on introductory astronomy, philo-sophy and history of science, and women studies. Her many articles are published in academic journals as well as more popular ones. In 1998 she founded an influential non-governmental organization called Suara Ibu Peduli (Voice of Concerned Mothers) to respond to the effects of the economic, social and political crisis on women and children in Indonesia. She has also been active in several other humanitarian efforts until now, including organizing a network of supports for the families of the victims of human rights abuses.

Meera Nanda

Visiting Scholar, Philosophy Department, Columbia University

Meera Nanda is the author of two recent books. Her *Prophets Facing Backward: Postmodern Critiques of Science and the Making of Hindu Nationalism* will appear in 2003 from Rutgers University Press (with an Indian edition by Permanent Black, New Delhi). An anthology of her essays *Breaking the Spell of Dharma: A Case for Indian Enlightenment* is being brought out by Three Essays Press, New Delhi. Nanda was trained as a biochemist (PhD, Indian Insitute of Technology, New Delhi). After many years of working with People's Science Movements and as a science journalist (with *Indian Express*, New Delhi), she got another Ph.D in Science Studies in 2000 from Rensselaer Polytechnic Insitute, Troy, New York. She was awarded a research fellowship from the American Council of Learned Societies (2000-2001) and during that time was a Visiting Scholar at Philosophy Department at Columbia University.

Justin Sudarminta, SJ

Rector, Driyarkara Academy of Philosophy, Jakarta

Justin Sudarminta SJ graduated from the Graduate School of Arts & Sciences, Fordham University, New York (MA and PhD Philosophy, 1986 and 1988) with his dissertation tiled *Toward An Integrative View of Science and Value: A Study of Whitehead's Philosophy of Organism as An Integral Worldview*. He has been teaching ethics, social philosophy, history of philosophy, philosophy of education, and philosophy of science in the Theology Faculty of Wedabhakti and Universitas Sanata Dharma, both in Yogyakarta. Since 1992 he has taught in the Sekolah Tinggi Filsafat (Academy of Philosophy) Driyarkara, and now is its Rector (Signatore). His publications in Bahasa Indonesia include *Process Philosophy: A Systematic Introduction Whitehead's Philosophy*

(1991), *Introduction to Epistemology* (2002), as well as translations of Sean Kealy's *Science and the Scripture* and Michael Polanyi's *A Study of Man*.

William Grassie,

Founder and Executive Editor, Metanexus Institute on Religion and Science

William Grassie is founder and executive director, Metanexus Institute on Religion and Science <www.metanexus.net>. Grassie also serves as executive editor of the Institute's online magazine and discussion forum with over 40,000 monthly page views and over 6000 regular subscribers in fifty-seven different countries. He has taught in a variety of positions at Temple University, Swarthmore College, and the University of Pennsylvania. Grassie received his doctorate in religion from Temple University in 1994 and his BA from Middlebury College in 1979. Prior to graduate school, Grassie worked for ten years in religiously-based social service and advocacy organisations in Washington, DC; Jerusalem, Israel; Berlin, Germany; and Philadelphia, PA. He is the recipient of a number of academic awards and grants from the American Friends Service Committee, the Roothbert Fellowship, and the John Templeton Foundation. He is a member of the Religious Society of Friends (Quakers).

Larry L Rasmussen

Reinhold Niebuhr Professor of Social Ethics, Union Theological Seminary, New York City.

Larry L Rasmussen has been the Reinhold Niebuhr Professor of Social Ethics at Union Theological Seminary, New York City, since 1986. His volume, *Earth Community, Earth Ethics*, won the prestigious Grawemeyer Award in Religion in 1997. He was given a Henry Luce Fellowship in Theology, 1998–99, for the research project, 'Song of Songs: Ecumenical Christianities as Earth Faiths'.He is a member of the Science, Ethics, and Religion Advisory Commitee of the AAAS (American Association for the Advancement of Science).

Index